WOVEN BY THE
GRANDMOTHERS

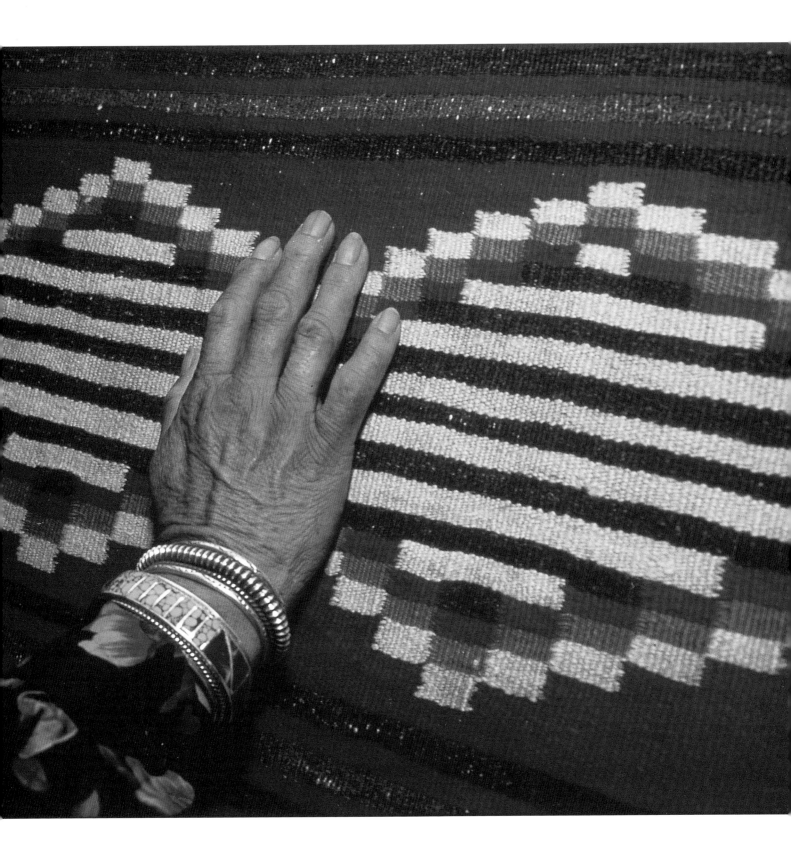

Nihimásání Deiztł'ó:
Náhást'eíts'áadahdi, Neeznádiin Nináháhááhą̨ądą̨ą̨' Adaalyaaigíí.
Bitsi' Yishtłizhii Be'i'ool'įįł Dani'l'į Bá Hooghandóó

Navajo translations by Ellavina Perkins and Esther Yazzie

Published by the
Smithsonian Institution Press
in association with the
National Museum of the American Indian,
Smithsonian Institution

WASHINGTON AND LONDON

WOVEN BY THE GRANDMOTHERS

Nineteenth-Century Navajo Textiles from the National Museum of the American Indian

Edited by Eulalie H. Bonar

Publication of *Woven by the Grandmothers* is made possible in part by a grant from John and Margot Ernst.

The exhibition *Woven by the Grandmothers: Nineteenth-Century Navajo Textiles from the National Museum of the American Indian* was sponsored in part by Philip Morris Companies Inc., with additional support from America West Airlines. Public and educational programs for the exhibition were supported by a grant from The New York Times Company Foundation.

Published in conjunction with the exhibition *Woven by the Grandmothers: Nineteenth-Century Navajo Textiles from the National Museum of the American Indian*, on view at the National Museum of the American Indian, George Gustav Heye Center, Alexander Hamilton U.S. Custom House, New York City, Oct. 6, 1996 to Jan. 8, 1997.

Library of Congress Cataloging-in-Publication Data
Woven by the grandmothers: nineteenth-century Navajo textiles from the National Museum of the American Indian / edited by Eulalie H. Bonar.
   p.   cm.
Published in conjunction with an exhibition held at the National Museum of the American Indian, New York City, Oct. 1996 to Jan. 1997.
   Includes bibliographical references and index.
   ISBN 1-56098-728-6 (alk. paper)
   1. Navajo textile fabrics--Exhibitions. 2. Navajo Indians--Social life and customs--Exhibitions. 3. Navajo philosophy--Exhibitions. 4. National Museum of the American Indian (U.S.)--Exhibitions. I. Bonar, Eulalie H. II. National Museum of the American Indian (U.S.)

   E99.N3W79   1996

   746'.089'972--DC20   96-33411

British Library Cataloguing-in-Publication Data are available

Manufactured in the United States of America

01 00 99 98 97 96 95 94 — 5 4 3 2 1

♾ The paper used in this publication meets the minimum requirements of the American National Standard for Permanence of Paper for Printed Library Materials Z39.48-1984.

For permission to reproduce illustrations appearing in this book, please correspond directly with the National Museum of the American Indian. The Smithsonian Institution Press does not retain reproduction rights for these illustrations individually.

National Museum of the American Indian
Head of Publications: Terence Winch
Project Editor: Cheryl Wilson

Smithsonian Institution Press
Designer: Kathleen M. Sims
Production Editor: Jenelle Walthour
Typeset in Bembo and Papyrus and printed on Mead Signature Dull.
Printed and bound by Walsworth Publishing Company.
Cover printed by Walsworth Publishing Company.

The National Museum of the American Indian, Smithsonian Institution, is dedicated to working in collaboration with the indigenous peoples of the Americas to foster and protect Native cultures throughout the Western Hemisphere. The museum's publishing program seeks to augment awareness of Native American beliefs and lifeways, and to educate the public about the history and significance of Native cultures.

COVER: *Beeldléí* (blanket; detail). See plate 9.
PHOTO ESSAY (*clockwise from left*): Sheep near St. Michaels, Arizona. Photo by George H. Pepper. (N3846); Hands of Ruth Roessel, July 1995. Ned A. Hatathli Museum, Navajo Community College, Tsaile, Arizona. Photo by Monty Roessel; Navajo woman weaving, ca. 1890. Photo by E. H. Maude (?). Courtesy National Anthropological Archives, Smithsonian Institution (#2438).
TITLE PAGE: *Beeldléí* (blanket; detail). See fig. 10.
PAGE VIII (fig. 1): *Biil* (two-piece dress [one panel]), ca. 1870. Handspun wool and raveled yarn, 121.9 × 87.6 cm. (23.2212)
PAGE XVI (fig. 2): *Beeldléí* (blanket), ca. 1875. Handspun wool, raveled and respun yarn, and commercial yarn, 133.7 × 86.3 cm. (23.3105)
PAGE 12 (fig. 7): D.Y. Begay (b. 1953), *Midnight in February*, 1995. Handspun wool, natural grays and indigo blue; imported Swedish wool, aniline red, 81.8 × 59.4 cm. Artist's collection.
PAGE 32 (fig. 11): *Beeldléí* (blanket), 1875–85. Handspun wool and raveled yarn, 125.8 × 79.4 cm. (22.7956)
PAGE 43 (fig. 15): *Beeldléí* (blanket), ca. 1870. Handspun wool, raveled and commercial yarn, 119.4 × 82.6 cm. (21.3286)
PAGE 46 (fig. 16): *Beeldléí* (blanket), 1875–85. Handspun wool, 202 × 134.6 cm. (23.1277)
PAGE 68 (fig. 19): *Beeldléí* (blanket), 1870–80. Handspun wool and raveled yarn, 141 × 83.8 cm. (4.8802)

For the Navajo people, especially Navajo weavers.

We take great pride in our rugs. We still weave as our great-great-grandmothers, and perhaps our great-great-grandfathers, did more than one hundred years ago. The tradition of Navajo weaving lies in the process of weaving. That has not changed much from the time the first blankets were made. The materials may change, the designs may change, the colors may change, but our techniques, values, and weaving customs remain the same.

    Our mothers and fathers encourage us to continue to weave as they have and as our great-great-grandmothers have; they say it is a way of survival. It's the Navajo way. Navajo weaving is part of our religion, oral history, language, and *k'é* (family structure).

    The weavers who had the opportunity to work on the Woven by the Grandmothers project had the privilege of touching rugs made by our great-great-grandmothers. We take great pride in what we have discussed and shared with you. Our stories represent our feelings, our ideas, and our respect for our people.

D. Y. Begay, Kalley Keams, and Wesley Thomas

Díí naaltsoos éí Diné bá ályaa. Sáanii dóó hastói da'atł'óhígíí íiyisíí bá ályaa.

Nihidiyogí ayóo át'éego nihił da'ilį. T'ahdii éí nihimásání nihichóoni' danilínéęk'ehgo da'iitł'ó. Áádóó ałdó' nihicheii dóó nihinálí danilínéę, éíshįį ałdó' da'atł'óó nít'éé'. Neeznádiin nááhaiídą́ą́' dóó níwohdę́ę́' ákót'é. Díí Diné bidiyogí nilínígíí éí dah 'iistł'ó ílnéhígíí éí bił silá. Éí t'ahdoo łahgo áneeh da níléí diyogí beeldléí ádaalyaa yę́ę́dą́ą́' dóó wóshdę́ę́'. Azhą́ shį́į́ bee atł'óhígíí éí łahgo ánáá'niił nidi dóó bee naashch'ąą'ígíí éí łahgo ánáá'niił nidi áádóó ałdó' bee iilchíhígíí łahgo ánáá'niił nidi, íiyisíí diyogí bee íl'ínígíí dóó bee na'anishígíí áádóó baa hane' dóó bik'ehgo atł'óhígíí t'éiyá t'áałáhígi át'é. T'ahdoo łahgo ánéeh da.

    Nihimá dóó nihizhé'é éí yee nihich'į' yádaałti'. T'áá da'íínóhtł'óóh. T'áá níléídę́ę́' nihichóoni' da'atł'óhéęk'ehgo da'ohtł'ó daaní. Dah 'iistł'ó binahji' éí yisdá hóót'i' daaní. Kót'éego éí Diné k'ehji é'él'į. Dah 'iistł'ó nilínígíí éí łahdóó nahaghá bił nít'i' dóó hane' bił nít'i' áádóó saad bił nít'i', Diné bizaad. Áádóó ałdó' ła' hooghan diné háájéé'ígíí, k'é wolyéhígíí, éí ałdó' bił nít'i'.

    Da'atł'óhígíí koji binaanish ádayiilaa. Díí nihimásání deiztł'ó ha'níigo, "woven by the grandmothers" wolyéego danéél'į́į' nilį́. Áádóó naaltsoos bee nidoot'ááł ha'níigo éí ákót'éego da'atł'óhígíí diyogísání deinéél'į́į' dóó yídadoolnii, nihimásání nihichóoni' danilínée ádayiilaaígíí. Díí k'ad kwe'é bee ałch'į' hadasiidzíí' nilínígíí éí t'áá íiyisíí nitsaago nihił da'ilį. Díí hane' nílínígíí kodóó bee nihich'į' hadasiidzíí'ígíí éí nihí baa nitsííkeesígíí dóó binahji' ádeiniidzinígíí áádóó ałdó' nihidine'é baa hą́ą́h niidzinígíí, jó ákót'éego éí hane'ígíí, bee hadasiidzíí'.

D. Y. Begay, Kalley Keams, and Wesley Thomas

CONTENTS

FOREWORD
W. Richard West, Jr.
xi

EDITOR'S NOTE
Eulalie H. Bonar
xv

INTRODUCTION
Eulalie H. Bonar
1

SHI' SHA' HANE' (MY STORY)
D.Y. Begay
13

A CONVERSATION WITH MY FATHER,
KEE YAZZIE BEGAY
D.Y. Begay
28

THE NAVAJO CONCEPT OF ART
Harry Walters
29

SHIŁ YÓÓŁT'OOŁ
PERSONIFICATION OF NAVAJO WEAVING
Wesley Thomas
33

BEELDLÉÍ BÄH HÄNE' (THE BLANKET STORY)
Kalley Keams
43

"MORE OF SURVIVAL THAN AN ART": COMPARING LATE NINETEENTH-
AND LATE TWENTIETH-CENTURY LIFEWAYS AND WEAVING
Ann Lane Hedlund
47

NAVAJO BLANKETS
Joe Ben Wheat
69

A SELECTION OF TEXTILES FROM THE COLLECTION
87

NOTES ON SELECTED COLLECTORS
Eulalie H. Bonar
173

CATALOGUE OF THE COLLECTION
181

NOTES
196

REFERENCES
204

PHOTO CREDITS
210

INDEX
211

FOREWORD

As I first read through the manuscript of the book you now hold in your hands, one phrase in particular jumped out at me: "the spirit line." Here is how contributor Harry Walters uses it: "To make something that is perfect means there is no more room for improvement. . . . If a weaver weaves a perfect rug, . . . she makes a little mistake on purpose—an imperfection. Often we see a little line, which the Navajo call a spirit line, that extends to the edge of a rug through the border. This line is added by the weaver so the rug will not be perfect." This wonderful attitude toward human acts of creation, so antithetical to typical Western notions, is not only characteristic of, but crucial to, the way Native people think about what we call "art." As beautiful and masterful as are the Navajo textiles you will see and read about in *Woven by the Grandmothers*, it is not so much the works themselves that are significant, but rather the process that led to their creation. In the Native universe, the object has always been a secondary consideration to the primacy of the ritual process itself.

This Native sense of aesthetics permeates the world of Navajo weaving and is at the heart of this book as well.

D.Y. Begay comments herein: "Practicing the art of weaving involves my views, my goals, my life. What I do as a wife, mother, artist, business person, and community member, all ties in with my weaving." Indeed, weaving is very much a community and family endeavor: "The process of weaving," says Wesley Thomas, "is communal rather than individualistic. . . . Family members play a continuous role in weaving." The special songs and prayers required in Navajo weaving, Thomas points out, are often not shared beyond the weaver's immediate family. The communal character of Native creations like Navajo textiles is central to their nature—Native objects, in their most profound and ultimate dimension, are statements and reflections of collective values as much or more than they are individual creative statements.

And the community in question here is not simply made up of contemporary people. In Native life, the community extends back and forth in time in a cultural continuum. The past, inhabited by one's ancestors, and the future, represented by children, extend the boundaries of community in ways that are again distinctly Native.

Embedded in the very title of this book is an acknowledgment of the profound importance of the ties between the generations, between all the grandmothers who have gone before and their present-day descendants. The amazing resurgence evident today among Native cultures would not be possible without this lifeblood of tradition, through which the spirit and soul of a people is passed from one generation to the next.

The National Museum of the American Indian, by its very nature, has a passionate commitment to the accurate presentation of Native cultures. The depiction of the universe of Navajo textiles we offer in *Woven by the Grandmothers* is a group portrait, a collaboration among Natives and non-Natives, between the indigenous community and the museum world. The picture you will receive in this book is one that I hope expresses our firm commitment to incorporating a multiplicity of viewpoints and experiences in all of our museum projects. To bring the National Museum of the American Indian into being we conducted two dozen consultations directly with Native communities in the United States, Canada, and Latin America. We have since instituted what we call "The Fourth Museum," a complex of outreach programs and initiatives designed to connect us to the Native world.

Woven by the Grandmothers and the related exhibition of the same name continue along a similar path—in June of 1995, the museum, in collaboration with Navajo Community College (NCC), organized a workshop on Navajo textiles in Tsaile, Arizona. Hundreds of weavers and other visitors from the Navajo Nation came to the workshop to exchange ideas and insights and help us deepen our own knowledge of the works in the museum's collection. It is this kind of interaction with the community that makes *Woven by the Grandmothers* a book that I hope will resonate with a tremor of authenticity.

While we seek to include the Native voice and the collective guidance of Native communities in our books and exhibitions, at the same time we deeply value the importance of sound scholarship in our professional endeavors. There is a crucial dialogue that must be undertaken between scholars and those whose works they study. Such an exchange is greatly to the benefit of both sides. This book, I hope, will not only guide readers along the spirit line, but will simultaneously provide them with a wealth of knowledge, history, and analysis of Navajo weavings, most especially of the incomparable nineteenth-century pieces that we are honored to have among our collections.

Woven by the Grandmothers is the work of many dedicated individuals. We would first like to express gratitude to our Navajo colleagues, their families, and other visitors, many of whom traveled long distances to view textiles from the museum's collection during the workshop at NCC. Their voices, many of which appear in this volume and in the exhibition, gave heart and meaning to the project. They include: Beverly Allen, Rachel Allen, Shirley Arviso Ash, Adam Becenti, Alex Becenti, Andrew Becenti, Dorothy Becenti, Denise Becenti-Buffington, Alice Bilone, Gloria J. Begay, Mary Lee Begay, Nellie Y. Begay, Pamela J. Begay, Sarah Paul Begay, Tillie Begay, Valeria E. Begay, Halena Benallie, Alberta Benally, Joanne Benally, Donna Bizadi, Clara Buckinghorse, Paige Buffington, Irene Clark, Alta T. Clement, Laura Cleveland, Jennie Crawford, Sadie E. Curtis, Virginia C. Deal, Isabell Deschinny, Caroline S. Dick, Elsie Glasses, Ben Hanley, Joy J. Hanley, Glennabah Hardy, Marie Hardy-Saltclah, Martha Harvey, Donna Hawthorne, Irma Higdon, Lorraine Jim, Rita Jishie, Veronica Z. John, Laverne Jones, Adalene Kee, Ethel Mae King, Marcella King-Ben, Bessie Lee, Nellie F. Lee, Alex Lewis, Amelia Lewis, Etta M. Lewis, Lucy Little Ben, Dolly Manson-Montoya, Clara Maryboy, Mary A. Nez, Rose Marie Nez, Sarah Nez, Ellavina Tsosie Perkins, Ella Rose Perry, Marlene R. Perry, Betty B. Roan, Marilou Schultz, Marie Sheppard, Marie Shirley, Mae Smith, Mary H. Smith, Rena M. Smith, Marilyn Staley, Elnora Teasyatwho, Marie Shawn Teasyatwho, Paulene T. Thomas, Rena Tsosie, Rosemary Upshow, Phillip Wauneka, Alma White, Roseann S. Willink, Esther Yazzie, and Inez N. Yazzie.

In addition, we owe thanks to the NCC staff and to all those who contributed hours of dedicated work to make

the NCC workshop possible. Edsel Brown provided everything from display furniture to insightful information
about the blankets. The carpenters of NCC Plant
Operations provided the unique mounts for the display
and workshop. Clarenda A. Begay, Director of the Navajo
Nation Museum, Robert A. Roessel, Jr., and Ruth Roessel
assisted with mailing lists, matters of protocol, and translations. Martinez Begay, Eric Deschine, Winnifred Tsosie,
and Kathleen Tabaha assisted in handling textiles and with
translations. Darren Wagner and Bobby Yoe helped with
installation. Regine Yazzie registered visitors and handled
many other details. We also thank Michael Begaye, who
translated and transcribed text from workshop videos, and
P. J. Coleman, who typed and transcribed texts; as well as
Monty Roessel, who captured the unique atmosphere of
the proceedings with his vibrant photographs.

We would also like to thank the Navajo Nation administration, including President Albert A. Hale and Vice
President Thomas Atcitty, for their support of the project.

Preparation for this book and the accompanying exhibition was the result of the efforts of many devoted contributors, advisors, and NMAI staff members. We particularly thank D. Y. Begay, Kalley Keams, and Wesley Thomas,
contributors to this book and co-curators of the exhibition at the museum's George Gustav Heye Center in New
York. Committed to bringing the "old rugs" to the Navajo
reservation, they worked closely with museum staff to plan
and organize the display and workshop at NCC, and
directed the theme and content of the exhibition and
book, always with a Navajo audience in mind.

Significant thanks go to the other contributing writers
to this volume. Joe Ben Wheat, who first researched the
Navajo blankets in the museum's collection in 1972 and
1973 and returned in 1990 for additional study, brought
his knowledge of the history of Navajo weaving to the
project. Ann Lane Hedlund offered guidance throughout
the project and was enormously helpful as an advisor for
the workshop. Harry Walters, Director of the Ned A.
Hatathli Museum at NCC, was both advisor and co-
sponsor for the display and textile workshop. We are
particularly grateful for the valuable work of Ellavina

Perkins and Esther Yazzie, who quickly and ably provided
translations for both the exhibition script and book text.

Project Curator Eulalie H. Bonar initiated and organized the research that eventually became the Woven by
the Grandmothers project and worked closely with
Navajo weavers to develop the exhibition and this book.
Terence Winch, Head of Publications, guided production
of the book with particular sharpness of vision, and editors
Cheryl Wilson and Holly Stewart carefully preserved the
intent of its authors. Lou Stancari shepherded the book's
images with characteristic attentiveness through numerous
stages of production, and Ann Kawasaki provided meticu-
lous editorial assistance and supported the project in
countless ways. We extend our gratitude to the members
of the director's editorial advisory committee—Olivia
Cadaval, George Cornell, Tom Hill, and Clifford E.
Trafzer—who offered helpful advice and further refined
the book's content. We also thank Gayle Potter Basso,
Carole Broadus, Nancy Eikel, Lynne Shaner, Barbara
Wheat, and Publications intern John McKinn for their
able editing and proofreading assistance. Special acknowledgment to Gene Vecenti of NCC's language department,
for his help in obtaining the Navajo font used in this publication. In addition, we thank Bruce Aronson, of the
Smithsonian's Office of Contracting and Property
Management, for his advice and guidance.

We are especially pleased to collaborate on this book
with the staff of Smithsonian Institution Press, in particular
Daniel Goodwin, Amy Pastan, Ken Sabol, Martha Sewall,
and Jenelle Walthour, all of whom extended themselves in
many ways to meet a very difficult production schedule.
Special thanks are also due to designer Kathleen M. Sims,
who worked diligently and patiently to create the unique
design of this publication.

We owe significant thanks to John and Margot Ernst,
who provided a generous grant that helped make the production of this book possible.

The New York exhibition and NCC workshop were
guided by Project Director Jim Volkert and Project
Manager Andrea R. Hanley, both of whom carefully
directed the complex project through its many stages,

always mindful of its importance to Navajo people. Allan Kaneshiro worked closely with our Navajo colleagues to design the display of blankets at NCC and the New York exhibition. Peter Brill, Stacey Jones, and John Richardson provided planning support and built mounts for both the workshop and exhibition. Susanna Stieff designed exhibition signage and assisted with exhibition script production; Raymi Taylor assisted with label production and installation. Liz Hill, NMAI's Director of Public Affairs, Dan Agent, Lee Anne Fahey, and Tanya Thrasher brought information about this project to the public and, most important, to Navajo people. John Carlin, Lon Saavedra, and John Colonghi, of the museum's National Campaign, helped raise funds for many aspects of the project. Elizabeth Weatherford supplied recording equipment for the NCC event. Scott Merritt, assisted by Mark Clark, made the textiles available for photography and study. Kenneth L. Yazzie assisted with the display and workshop at NCC and coordinated shipment of the textiles. Katherine Fogden photographed weavers and staff at the workshop, and Sharon Dean, Pamela Dewey, Karen Furth, Janine Jones, and Laura Nash provided study slides of the blankets, facilitated research in photo archives, and supplied archival photographs for the book. David Heald produced the photographs in this publication that beautifully capture each textile's brilliant color and weave. Lee A. Callander, Ann Drumheller, Kevin deVorsey, and Mary T. Nooney contributed valuable collection documentation. Douglas Mossman assisted with exhibition production administration, and Jennifer Miller and Andrea Gaines provided valuable assistance with contracts and many other crucial details of the project. Jeanne Brako cleaned and stabilized the blankets; Susan Heald designed blanket mounts for the NCC workshop and supervised the handling, packing, and mounting of the blankets, treating each piece with infinite care. Phyllis Dillon, formerly of the Textile Conservation Workshop, provided valuable input early in the project.

Richard W. Hill, former Special Assistant to the Director, John Haworth, Deputy Assistant Director for Public Programs, and Lee Davis, Assistant Director for Cultural Resources, offered support and advice throughout the project. Charlotte Heth, Assistant Director for Public Programs, and George Horse Capture, Deputy Assistant Director for Cultural Resources, made valuable recommendations along the way. Curators Mary Jane Lenz, Cécile R. Ganteaume, Nancy B. Rosoff, and Ramiro Matos provided support and helped in the review of manuscripts. Research assistant Kathleen E. Ash-Milby provided invaluable contributions to the workshop, exhibition, and book.

At the Huntington Free Library, Mary Davis and library staff members Catherine McChesney and Catherine Sorrell located source material relating to the collectors; Allison Jeffrey identified relevant archival documents; Hugh Conway, T. J. Ferguson, Dennis Lessard, and David Wilcox provided substantial research assistance, and Patrick W. Tafoya assisted with research on the collectors. Jonathan Batkin, Bruce Burnham, J. J. Brody, Nancy J. Blomberg, Bill Malone, Sally McLendon, Lyle G. McNeal, Marian Rodee, Margot Blum Schevill, Laurie Webster, Mark Winter, and Paul Zolbrod shared information about specific textiles and the era in which they were produced. Roland Force, former Director of the Museum of the American Indian-Heye Foundation, and Peterson Zah, NMAI International Founders Council member, provided support for the project.

Special acknowledgments also go to those whose hard work shaped the exhibition: Gwen Spicer, of Spicer Art Conservation, who created the mannequins; Northland Productions, for media and video production; Manny Exhibits and Woodcrafts, Inc., for fabrication and installation services; and A. Sanchez Construction Corp., for painting and construction.

Finally, we owe significant thanks for the generosity of Philip Morris Companies Inc. and America West Airlines, as well as The New York Times Company Foundation, all of whom helped make production of the *Woven by the Grandmothers* exhibition possible.

W. Richard West, Jr., Director
(Southern Cheyenne and member of the Cheyenne and Arapaho Tribes of Oklahoma)

EDITOR'S NOTE

My deepest thanks go to all those staff members, colleagues, and consultants who made this project possible.

D. Y. Begay was a tireless partner from our first day sorting textiles in the Southwest collections at the museum's Research Branch. I am proud to call her a friend—in Navajo, *t'aa 'iiyisii 'ahehee', shik'is*. From Kalley Keams and Wesley Thomas, I learned how to envision the exhibition from a Navajo point of view. Thank you all for sharing your stories and knowledge with me and for including me in your laughter.

It was an honor to work with Joe Ben Wheat, whose knowledge of the history of Navajo weaving is equaled only by his love of the people who created the textiles. I am also deeply grateful to Ann Lane Hedlund for her help and advice, which she consistently offered in quiet but tangible ways.

Thanks to Harry Walters and Clarenda Begay, who kept the dream of a display and workshop for Navajo weavers alive all these years. Thanks also to Esther Yazzie and Ellavina Perkins, who made the Navajo portions of this book possible.

My gratitude extends to Mary Jane Lenz, Cécile Ganteaume, Nancy Rosoff, and Ramiro Matos for their expert guidance and assistance throughout the project. Warm thanks also to Mary Davis for locating resource materials, to Patrick W. Tafoya, who assisted me so ably with the research, and to Brenda Shears, who always listened. It was a pleasure to work with conservator Susan Heald, and with David Heald, who captured the spirit of each blanket he photographed. I am also especially grateful to Clara Sue Kidwell, George Horse Capture, and Lee Davis for many productive discussions. Special thanks to Kathleen E. Ash-Milby, whose day-to-day dedication and assistance went far beyond her staff duties and helped make the project a success.

Finally, a special note of appreciation to W. Richard West, Jr., for his continued interest in the project and support over the years.

Eulalie H. Bonar, Assistant Curator

INTRODUCTION

Eulalie H. Bonar

The collection of nineteenth-century Navajo wearing blankets at the National Museum of the American Indian is one of the largest and most comprehensive of its kind. Known to only a handful of Navajo weavers, scholars, and students of Navajo weaving, the collection comprises textiles made between about 1840 and 1880, primarily for Native use, including intertribal trade. There are more than one hundred and twenty woven blankets, including *biil*, the Navajo woman's two-piece dress; early chief blankets; finely woven sarapes; mantas, worn as shawls or wrapped around the body as dresses; women's striped shoulder blankets; and thick, everyday blankets, or *diyogí*, translated as "soft and fluffy."[1] Designs range from intricate interlocking sarape patterns to the simple bands and stripes of the diyogí; predominant colors are shades of insect-dyed crimson, brilliant indigo blue,

and the natural brown and white of churro sheep wool. Each blanket is the creation of an individual weaver, and no two of these textiles are exactly alike.

This book is intended to document the museum's collection. It also accompanies an exhibition of many of the textiles. Our aim is to share with the public the aesthetics of historic Navajo weaving, the range and variety of the textiles, information about materials, dyes, and construction techniques, and—most critically—the cultural significance of the weavings in contemporary Navajo life, as voiced by Navajo participants in the project. Most of all, we hope that this volume will succeed in bringing images of these masterpieces of weaving, together with information about the collection, into the homes of Navajo weavers, their families, and the Navajo community.[2]

Navajo hogan. (P18129)

I have learned while working with Navajo people that this project can generate profound emotional reactions. Wesley Thomas and Kalley Keams, Navajo weavers and contributors to this volume, as well as guest curators for the exhibition, repeatedly expressed support for the museum's goals. Thomas, asked to consider the philosophical content of the exhibition during a planning meeting, responded, "This is a way of reiterating that we are here. Navajo people in general need to know that this exhibition happened here in New York. . . . to know that there is a part of them elsewhere." Keams's concerns lie in bridging past and present. "My main interest is with the younger generation," she emphasizes. Intent on finding ways to bring young people new information, she says, "It's important that they see the connection between the old and the new."

Also implicit in this book is my own desire to refute the notion that everything there is to say about Navajo weaving has already been said—in part because Navajo people have had little voice in the discourse. Advances continue to be made in our understanding of the events that have influenced the evolution of Navajo weaving, as well as topics such as dating techniques. This is largely due to the pioneering research of Joe Ben Wheat of the University of Colorado Museum. Another misconception sometimes heard in museum circles is that Navajo weaving has been determined to such an extent by the demands of the non-Indian market that it no longer qualifies as indigenous art. Insights offered by Navajo women and men, however, including weavers, anthropologists, and museum professionals, shed new light on the role of weaving in Navajo society and suggest just how much remains unknown by those outside the Navajo universe.

It was in 1986 as a curatorial assistant that I first realized that the museum, then the Museum of the American Indian–Heye Foundation, held a number of historically important Navajo blankets. I had discovered a manilla envelope filled with textile analysis forms on a number of the southwestern textiles in the collection, filed away in one of the curatorial offices. The forms were initialed "JBW"—Joe Ben Wheat—and dated 1972. At first glance, most of them seemed to refer to Navajo textiles. Wheat later told me that because the collection was unusually well documented, it had proved invaluable in helping him establish a framework for dating Navajo textiles. At the time, he was engaged in building the collections of the University of Colorado Museum, where he was Curator of Anthropology.[3]

I was then a new staff member, and the prospect of bringing a number of boldly patterned and beautiful Navajo blankets into the light of day was exciting. When I searched out and saw the first ones, I was hooked; they suggested the roots of a tradition that I could only guess at, and I wanted to know more. I decided to comb the storage vaults at the Research Branch to locate all of the blankets in Wheat's survey—and, perhaps, others. D. Y. Begay, a Navajo weaver then living in New Jersey, agreed to join me in the effort. Little did she know that she had signed on to a project of many years' duration.

Because George Heye, the founder of the Museum of the American Indian, often catalogued objects according to where they were collected, not necessarily where they were made, a number of Navajo blankets were stored with other collections, especially Pueblo and Plains material. One early chief blanket (see plate 21) was found with the Brulé Sioux collections, while a rare fragment of an eighteenth-century tapestry weave manta or one-piece dress (fig. 3) was discovered in storage with Hopi material. A textile with a background woven entirely in indigo blue (fig. 4) turned out to be an early example of Navajo weaving influenced by the Saltillo design system of northern Mexico.

In May 1990, I organized a week-long workshop at the museum to review the entire Navajo textile collection of approximately four hundred blankets and rugs. Could we identify all the items that had been made to wear? I wanted to tackle the project from different approaches and was very pleased when Begay, Wheat, and Ann Lane Hedlund, Associate Professor of Anthropology at Arizona State University, agreed to participate. As an active weaver, Begay brought a new perspective to the discussions, enlarging and enriching them beyond measure. She called into question many Western assumptions about Navajo weaving and encouraged us to reexamine terms commonly used to categorize the textiles. A close analysis of their designs revealed that chief blankets do not fall neatly into four distinct "phases," for example. Hedlund, who had been working with Navajo weavers and studying contemporary Navajo textiles for almost twenty years, was also able to contribute her expertise as a textile specialist. Wheat, whose earlier work in the collections had been the catalyst for the project, brought his unparalleled knowledge of Navajo weaving to the table. The conference gave him an opportunity to review and revise his previous analysis in light of more recent research. By the end of the week, we had also provided him with many more textiles to analyze.

During the workshop we examined the textiles for information about materials, structure, and design. Omitted from consideration were the Navajo woven sash belts, garters, and hair ties in the collection. We were more interested in the way a textile was woven than in its appearance. Begay commented, "The technique, it's just there, it's a part of me, but now I'm looking at it closely, and in

Figure 3

Biil (detail; fragment of one-piece [?] manta dress), 1775–1850 [?]. Handspun wool and raveled yarn. (9.1989)

detail."[4] We were looking for textiles made as blankets, not the rugs produced for a non-Indian market at the turn-of-the-century. Our cut-off date was the early 1880s. We categorized as blankets those textiles that were used for wear, sleeping, and other utilitarian purposes. This was not always easy to determine. By the 1880s, Navajo people had largely replaced woven blankets with clothing made from commercial cloth. They still made woven items for special events, however, and continued to weave blankets for trade to the Pueblos.

In some cases, existing documentation facilitated the establishment of probable dates of manufacture. The chief blankets collected by Samuel W. Woodhouse on the Sitgreaves Expedition are an example of well-documented textiles in the collection (see plates 14 and 15). In other instances, as Wheat remarked, we could "only conjecture, not know[ing] for sure what was made for use or for sale." Some blankets woven toward the close of the period were still heavily napped, showed no signs of wear, and looked freshly cut off the loom, possibly to be sold to a U.S. Army officer eager to pick up a memento of his stay in the

Figure 4

Beeldléí (blanket), 1860–70.
Handspun wool and commercial yarn,
152.4 × 116.8 cm. (9.1990)

Southwest. However, if size and weight did not mitigate against the piece, and if it was in the blanket tradition— soft and draped—it was included.

One textile that posed a dilemma is a late chief blanket collected by Joseph Keppler. This piece, which has the general appearance of an item made for the tourist trade, contains two pictorial elements (a horse with rider and a steer) facing in opposing directions. Despite our doubts, Begay felt it warranted inclusion because the motif that appeared upside down would be upright when the blanket was worn across the shoulders with the top edge folded down, as was customary. Some mantas with brightly colored centers and little evidence of wear may have been sold to Zuni and used only on special occasions, such as a manta also collected by Keppler (see plate 2). Other blankets were probable replica pieces. One biil is decorated with terraced triangles in an early broken-stripe pattern, but the wool is greasy, indicating churro wool contaminated with merino; Wheat believes that the piece was probably not made until about 1880 (fig. 5). Another biil (see plate 10) with a dark brown center and indigo blue stripes along the two short ends is also made in an older style but not in the fine weave of earlier blankets.

At the other end of the spectrum are blankets showing signs of heavy use. The sarapes and chief blankets collected by Douglas Graham at Zuni Pueblo (fig. 6) appear extremely worn; they are stretched out where they curved around the body when worn, and display hand-hold patterns.[5] They were photographed for this book despite their condition. As Begay noted about one blanket in very poor condition, "It is still elegant even though it was worn, and it will be useful for weavers to see."

The museum's nineteenth-century Navajo blanket collection, as it is identified today and represented in this volume, consists of textiles categorized in the literature as falling into two periods: the Classic (prior to 1865) and the Late Classic or early Transition (circa 1865–85).[6] Some variation occurs in the dates proposed by southwestern textile specialists over the years, but the criteria for establishing these time frames are basically consistent. Classic period dresses and shoulder blankets were produced primarily for Native use and arc characterized by the use of handspun and raveled yarns, terraced tapestry patterns originating in basketry designs, and the widespread use of red. Late Classic period blankets reflect influence from the increased Anglo-American presence in the region. Weavers during this period incorporated new commercial materials into their work, including synthetic-dyed Germantown yarn, as well as Saltillo design elements adopted by Spanish-American weavers in New Mexico.

Stylistically, however, Navajo weaving is perhaps best understood as a continuum. As Wheat expresses,

> You get new elements added from time to time and certain pieces can't be younger or older than a certain date, but it's really a continuum in terms of design and design elements. You're likely to get zigzag motifs at the same time you're getting Classic or Late Classic motifs. . . . You start getting broken stripes and checkerboards in the late '60s, and they're the same elements just done in a different way.[7]

THE DISPLAY AND WORKSHOP
AT NAVAJO COMMUNITY COLLEGE

Navajo weaving remains a continuum today, in spite of differences in textile styles and the wide range of new materials available to weavers. This was perhaps the most significant point brought home to NMAI staff when we took twenty-four of the nineteenth-century blankets, mantas, and biil from the collection to the Navajo Nation in the summer of 1995, for a public display and workshop. The event, held at the Ned A. Hatathli Museum at Navajo Community College in Tsaile, Arizona, from 27 June through 1 July 1995, was organized in collaboration with Harry Walters, director of the museum. Begay and I first talked with Walters about the feasibility of such a program ten years ago, but it took the resources of the National Museum of the American Indian to make it possible. More than eight hundred visitors signed the guest book, the majority of whom were Navajo people from all over the reservation and beyond.

Figure 5

Biil (two-piece dress), ca. 1860.
Handspun wool and raveled yarn,
106.7 × 64.8 cm. (9.1960)

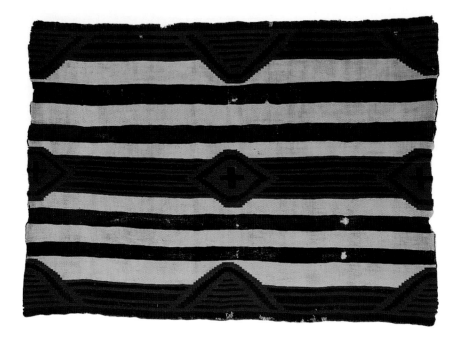

Figure 6

Beeldléí (blanket), 1870–75.
Handspun wool and raveled yarn,
125 × 181.9 cm. (22.7950)

The title for this book and the exhibition came from conversations and interviews with the Navajo weavers and visitors during the display and workshop. We heard, again and again, as in the words of weaver Irene Clark,

> These old rugs were woven by our great-great-great-grandmothers—the grandmothers. We've never seen them, but they did all this work. . . . And I hope that our kids, our grandkids, will continue and pass it to each other.[8]

Weavers spoke about how weaving skills are learned from one weaver to another, one generation to the next. Wesley Thomas saw a woman place her grandchild's hand on a biil, "just like when a weaver finds a nice spider web, takes it down, and washes her hands with it to absorb the knowledge." Although they acknowledged that they found the old blankets very different, many weavers expressed interest in reconstructing textile motifs and design layouts woven more than one hundred years ago. Marilou Schultz, for example, said that her favorite blankets were the blue,

black, and white striped Moki-pattern sarapes and that, even though a lot of her weaving is in the Burntwater style, she still likes to "bring back the classics."

For many of the visitors to the Hatathli Museum, the event was their first opportunity to see a selection of the "old rugs," as almost everyone called them. The blankets were mounted on slant boards placed on raised wooden platforms, permitting a close and unobstructed view. For the workshop, many weavers put on white cotton gloves and, with head loupes, magnifying glasses, linen testers, and picks at hand, carefully examined the textiles, which were laid out one at a time on long tables. They analyzed the structure of the blankets, inspected selvage cords and corner tassels, commented on repairs, discussed processing indigo dye, compared patterns, and considered various possible interpretations of the designs. Isabell Deschinny drew attention to one blanket containing two- and three-ply yarns in addition to handspun wool. "I'm just trying to figure it out," she said, "They must have gotten different kinds of yarns from all over. . . . Just by looking at it I can tell which ones are the three-ply and which ones the single-ply."

It was more than a matter of identifying materials and techniques, however. Esther Yazzie explained,

> You have to have an intimate relationship with the land . . . so that you understand the language and the different shades and the different forms that it comes in. Likewise, you know, it's the same with the rugs. You have to understand the type of fabric, the type of materials, where they come from, how you feel them, how you see them. . . . You have to have that intimate relationship.

For Walters, "It's not only the rugs that we see here, that the Navajos are concerned with . . . there are extensions . . . the affection for the sheep, the vegetation, the grass, the land . . . and the rain that falls." He spoke about the relationship of weaving to the natural elements and how, when some Navajos learn how to weave, they also learn special prayers, songs, and rituals. "The songs and the prayers are instructions," he said. "For example, a weaver should not weave when there's rain or lightning, or at night . . . and she should never make a perfect rug, she should always leave it unfinished, uneven at some point." Edsel Brown, Hatathli Museum staff member, told us that he had said a prayer for the rugs and, he added, "I told them that they're being taken care of very well and I mentioned to them that even though they're away from home, that we haven't forgotten about them, that we as Navajo people feel very dear and strong toward them, and that they represent us."

At times the mood of the workshop was very emotional. In the words of Rita Jishie, translated by Esther Yazzie, "It has a personal effect in the sense that, you know, these rugs were made by your ancestors, people that have woven in the past." Weavers and family members shared their memories and stories with each other and with us. Laura Cleveland, a weaver in her eighties, recalled that her mother was an experienced weaver and that she wove large rugs:

From left: Irene Clark, Glennabah Hardy, Marie Hardy-Saltclah, Eulalie H. Bonar, July 1995. Ned A. Hatathli Museum, Navajo Community College, Tsaile, Arizona. Photo by Katherine Fogden.

> She never wove small rugs. Also my aunt, she still lives with us. I remember they wove large rugs. The loom was so large that it would spread out and go through the roof. The men would stretch the loom from the rooftop. The width of the rugs was from here to the end of that table [pointing to the tables in the room]. Three of my grandmothers would weave. I only helped fill the gaps in the rug. We would weave all summer and finish it before winter. . . . It required three people to load up the rug in a wagon to take it to the trading post.

Marie Hardy-Saltclah translated for her mother, weaver Glennabah Hardy:

> It's her whole life . . . ever since she was a child. She grew up with it . . . and she never went to school . . . and she did all the taking care of the sheep, shearing the wool, and spinning the wool . . . cleaning and carding the wool . . . and finishing the rug. And, she said, everything was so good and easy, but now I just think about it . . . it makes me sad.

Mary Lee Begay and Gloria J. Begay, July 1995. Ned A. Hatathli Museum, Navajo Community College, Tsaile, Arizona. Photo by Katherine Fogden.

With the exception of one piece, all the blankets displayed at the Hatathli Museum also appear in the exhibition, *Woven by the Grandmothers*, on view at the George Gustav Heye Center of the National Museum of the American Indian in New York from October 1996 to January 1997. Many of the weavers' commentaries from interviews and conversations with museum staff were incorporated into exhibition label copy as well as captions for this book.

An important step in shaping the exhibition was asking Begay, Keams, and Thomas to collaborate on the development of the show's thematic content. Rejecting the tendency to display Navajo textiles in chronological sequence and/or by textile type, they organized the blankets in keeping with themes that resonated for them personally, and with a Navajo audience in mind. As the title of the exhibition implies, the emphasis that evolved is on family and community, and on how these create continuity with the future and the past through the textile arts. The display of the blankets on three-dimensional shoulder mounts suggests the way the blankets were originally intended to be seen, while the positioning of the textiles in a circle evokes a large family gathering. This way, the three felt, the enduring human dimensions of Navajo weaving would be made manifest. The emphasis thus shifts away from the historical and technical aspects of Navajo weaving, although it does not exclude them.

THE BOOK

Contributing authors to this book are Navajo and non-Navajo, including weavers, scholars of southwestern weaving, anthropologists, and museum professionals. Each interprets Navajo weaving from his or her own perspective, adding to the body of knowledge about this centuries- old art form. Begay writes as a Navajo woman and a weaver; she recounts her childhood growing up on the Navajo reservation and her development as a weaver and dye specialist. Wheat examines the evolution of Navajo weaving over the past four hundred years, focusing on the introduction of new materials and dyes into the Southwest and their impact on Navajo weaving; he cites many individual blankets in the museum's collection and comments on their larger historical context. Hedlund compares the lifeways of Navajo weavers today and one hundred years ago and finds that salient information about women and their role as weavers has rarely become part of the historical record. Thomas also looks at weaving in Navajo culture today, but in terms of what it suggests to him about the spiritual significance of the textiles over time. In addition, Keams writes about Navajo weaving as an act of personal expression, and Walters examines the possible symbolic content of textile designs. All of the contributors have played critical roles in the museum's project to document, exhibit, and publish the collection.

At least three common threads link these essays. First, Navajo weaving is characterized by innovation and experimentation; individual autonomy is seen as a cornerstone of Navajo culture. Second, in spite of differences in weaving techniques and rug styles, Navajo weaving today provides weavers with a vital link to the blankets made by "the grandmothers," the creators of those blankets. It is the *process* of weaving that is important. As Keams says, "Each time a rug is completed, it is like a birth." Third, implicit in the essays is that for many Navajos, weaving is an integral aspect of everyday life, not an isolated activity occurring outside of the family or community—metaphorically or in actuality. Walters states, "Any attempt to study Navajo art by itself would fail."

Begay's compelling essay is a "personal account." She and her husband have built a hogan, a traditional Navajo home, on land occupied by her family on the Navajo reservation for more than one hundred years. Begay recalls stories of her ancestors, including an account of her great-great-great-grandmother, who was among those Navajo imprisoned in the 1860s by the U.S. government at remote Bosque Redondo, in east-central New Mexico. Begay learned how to weave by watching her mother. Her work with dyes, documented here, is in the tradition of Navajo weavers but also exemplifies her personal interest in experimenting with new colors, materials, tools, and patterns (see figs. 7, 8, and 9). Begay writes that she lives in two worlds. She continues to fulfill family responsibilities on the reservation but, with her husband, who is Anglo-American, lives half of the year near Phoenix. Raising their son, Kelsey, in a way that acknowledges both of his parents' heritages, is a primary goal. Begay's life seems to mirror the Navajo world today—rooted in part in the old ways but also multifaceted and modern, with new and complex options at every turn.

From left: Sadie E. Curtis, Alice Bilone, June 1995. Ned A. Hatathli Museum, Navajo Community College, Tsaile, Arizona. Photo by Monty Roessel.

Wheat's chapter introduces the history of Navajo weaving and leads to a fuller appreciation for the role of the textile arts in contemporary Navajo life. He places Navajo weaving within the context of two other southwestern textile traditions, Pueblo and Spanish-American. Both of these traditions continued to influence Navajo weaving well into the nineteenth century, just as Navajo weaving continued to influence Pueblo and Spanish-American weaving. Early Spanish trade records indicate Navajo blankets of wool and cotton were highly prized trade items as early as 1706, and Wheat describes many of the woven garments in the museum's Navajo collection that derive from the early 1800s or earlier. Wheat combines his knowledge of the structure of Navajo textiles with the evolution of materials, techniques, and design elements, and charts his course using individual blankets from the museum's collection as markers.

Hedlund uses nineteenth-century Navajo wearing blankets as a starting point with the intention of comparing the textiles and lifestyles of weavers one hundred years ago and today. Her time frame is from the mid to the late nineteenth century, and from the mid to the late twentieth century. In the comparison, many similarities and contrasts

Rita Jishie, June 1995. Ned A. Hatathli Museum, Navajo Community College, Tsaile, Arizona. Photo by Monty Roessel.

emerge. As Hedlund observes, and as many weavers commented at the workshop at the Hatathli Museum, it is remarkable that even during their internment at Bosque Redondo in the 1860s, Navajo weavers continued to produce such handsome blankets—tangible symbols of survival and cultural continuity. Events occurring after the release from Bosque Redondo transformed Navajo lives forever. These included the establishment of the Navajo Indian Reservation and the arrival of the railroad, trading posts, and U.S. government schools. In the late twentieth century, the political activism of the 1960s, an economic development plan established by the Navajo Nation, and a resurgence in the arts and crafts market nationwide also signaled shifts in Navajo lifeways and the production of textiles. A smaller percentage of the population weaves today, but women, as the principal caretakers of the home and primary carriers of the culture, remain, in the words of Navajo scholar Ruth Roessel, "the heart and center of our society."

Thomas's chapter focuses on the act of weaving. He defines the complex relationship that exists between a Navajo weaver and her or his tools and rug, or *dah'iistł'ó*, a Navajo term for weaving, translated as "the process of integrating the warp and weft in the art of weaving on a set-up loom." Thomas draws on his experiences learning how to weave from his mother and grandmother and from research he has conducted on the Navajo reservation. He writes that Navajo weavers, especially older weavers, imbue textiles with life through a process of personification. The agents of personification are special weaving songs and prayers, which vary from region to region and weaver to weaver. A weaver will also talk to her or his dah'iistł'ó because it must be nurtured like a child; it *is* the child of the weaver and will remain a part of the weaver, even after completion.

Like Thomas, Kalley Keams and Harry Walters address weaving as an act of creation. Keams writes, "I was told that the loom is like a child, that my tools are an extension of me, that the weft strings are parts of my life, and that the warp is the foundation of my soul." She considers weaving akin to language in the sense that it is a form of communication linking families together; the rugs also link Navajo people to the weavers of the past. Weaving, then, is both a foundation for and a means of transmission of Navajo culture, as well as the personal expression of the weaver.

Walters is interested in defining the role of weaving in Navajo culture. He points out that Navajo people do not consider weaving as "art" in the Western sense but, rather, "Art in Navajo society is considered alive. It is like a person. It has feelings. It has power—healing power." Further, this art extends not only to a person's work, but to the way a person conducts his or her life. Songs and prayers reestablish a weaver's relationship with his or her art and, by association, with nature. The parts of the loom, the rug designs, and the colors all relate to elements in nature and also reflect male and female principles. When everything a weaver uses is in balance, harmony prevails. "The word that we use is *hozho*," Walters writes, "Hozho means 'I will walk in the Beauty Way.'"

We have tried to provide as comprehensive a set of information about the textiles as possible. To that end, the essays are followed by a plate section illustrating a number of the blankets, with commentaries; biographical information about collectors of the blankets; and a catalogue (annotated object list) of the collection.

The textiles illustrated include those blankets determined to be the earliest and best-documented; they also represent the variety and depth of the collection. As noted above, captions for the illustrations were drawn from comments made by weavers and other visitors to the display and workshop at Navajo Community College. There are also interpretations of the blankets by Begay, Keams, and Thomas recorded during their work for the exhibition. In addition, NMAI Navajo staff members Kathleen E. Ash-Milby, Andrea R. Hanley, and Kenneth L. Yazzie have offered some of their stories and reactions to the blankets, which we are especially pleased to include.

The catalogue of the collection includes every known nineteenth-century Navajo wearing blanket in the museum's collection. It provides provenance, information on materials and technique, and the approximate date of manufacture of each textile. It is based on analysis of the textiles recorded by Wheat in 1972 and 1990, with additional test results on some of the dyes noted at later dates. Wheat's forms were edited by Ash-Milby, who also provides an explanation of terms and symbols. The sequence of terms follows in the tradition of southwestern textile studies, specifically the model developed by Kate Peck Kent.[9]

Finally, the collectors of these textiles are also a part of the story. The section that describes them was included largely in response to inquiries from Navajo weavers and visitors to the museum wanting to learn how the blankets ended up in New York, so far from home. Some of the collectors were U.S. Army personnel stationed in the Southwest in the 1800s, including Gen. William Tecumseh Sherman and Gen. Nelson A. Miles; others, including John Wesley Powell and Samuel Woodhouse, were scientists accompanying the U.S. mapping expeditions; U.S. Indian agents; western artists; or anthropologists. Not surprisingly, dealers and private collectors of Indian art, active in the early years of the twentieth century throughout the

Nadespa (Navajo) wearing a *biil*, 1892. Arizona or New Mexico. Photo by James Mooney. Courtesy National Anthropological Archives, Smithsonian Institution. (#2396-B)

country and in Europe, were also sources of textiles in the museum's collection.

Today this collection has taken on new life. For the first time, these blankets are being studied and interpreted by members of the Navajo community. Perhaps some of the old design motifs will be adapted by contemporary weavers into new and innovative patterns, or maybe there will be renewed interest in the color combinations that characterize nineteenth-century sarapes. Whatever the outcome, Navajo people clearly consider the blankets not mere emblems of a remote and forgotten past, but rather part of an ongoing story.

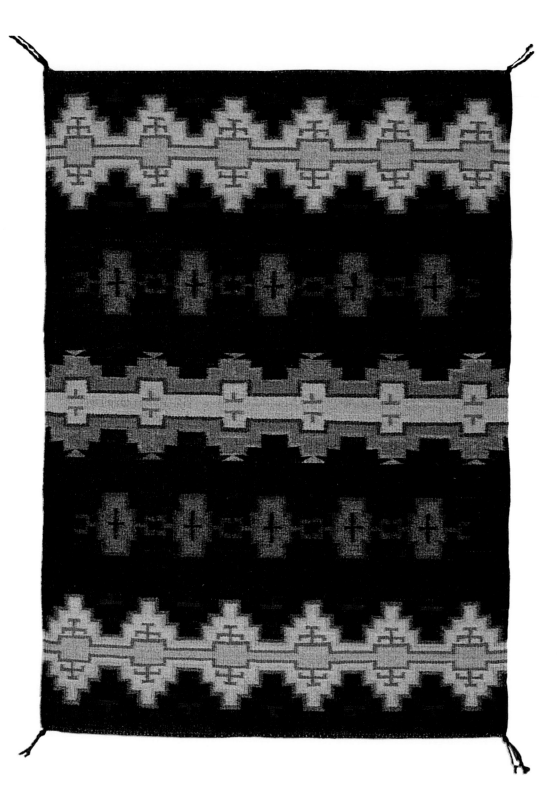

SHI' SHA' HANE'
(MY STORY)

D. Y. Begay

I am born to Tótsohnii, the Big Water people, and born for Ta'chii'nii, the Red Streak Earth people. My mother's clan is Tótsohnii, and she is born for Tséni'jikini'. My father's clan is Ta'chii'nii, and he is born for Ashiihi'. My maternal grandmother is born to Tótsohnii and born for Tódich'ii nii, and my maternal grandfather was born to Tséni'jikini' and born for Tlizilani'. My paternal grandmother is born for Ta'chii'nii and born to Ma'iideeshgiizhnii, and my paternal grandfather was born for Ashiihi' and born to To'ahani'.[1]

The sky, the Lukachukai Mountains, and the piñon trees at the "middle road" fill my memories of childhood. These are my roots. The middle road, A'taa ha ii'tiin, was my grandfather's Navajo name.

A'taa ha ii'tiin identifies our family, who we are, and where we live. If I am walking down the road and someone asks me, "Where do you come from?" I could say "Tselani," but that would not explain where my family comes from. But if I say the "middle road," that identifies me.

My mother tells me that her grandmother told her that the Big Water family have always lived here. My great-grandmother (Big Water Woman) spent about three years in captivity in Bosque Redondo. She was taken away during the gathering of the Navajos about 1863, in the "time of fear," and she made the Long Walk. She escaped from the camp when she was about eight months pregnant and returned to her home and land— land still occupied by my family.

Life was very simple when I was a child. I remember a lot of things—playing in the trees, picking juniper berries and piñon nuts, and making mud toys. My Aunt Stella and I were the youngest of the children, and we were always left behind. Our brothers and sisters and cousins would take off and hide from us and we would wander around looking for them and end up getting stuck in the trees! We made toys out of whatever we found around the hogan. We made horse hooves out of evaporated milk cans, put them on our hands, and ran around pretending we were horses! We also made telephones out of cans and talked to each other in the trees.

My first memory of a loom is when I was about five years old. My mother was weaving a pictorial rug. She was copying the Indian chief's head pictured on a can of Calumet baking powder. I watched her and wondered how she could follow the pattern without any guide. My memory of the reddish background color she was using is still vivid today.

Sometimes as a child I would tag along when my mom gathered plants for making dyes. She would collect the plants in buckets and gunnysacks, crush the plants, and throw them into a pot with hot water and the raw fleece. Sometimes she would leave the wool in the dye bath for days; maybe she forgot it was there, like I do sometimes. But my only interest in weaving as a little girl was in watching my mother. I remember being awakened early in the morning by the tapping of her weaving comb. I would peek out from under the blankets and watch her change the colors in the rug she was making. Sometimes I would fall back to sleep. I didn't pay much attention to my mom's weaving techniques or to the designs she wove.

My mother used to talk about things that are important to a Navajo woman. It begins in the home. You must rise with the sun and begin the everyday chores. You must cook the meals and care for the children and livestock. You should know how to weave.

My brother and I were kept occupied from the time we got up until we went to bed. We participated in cooking, chopping wood, hauling water from the spring, and herding the sheep. I learned how to cook when I was very young. I remember making my first batch of potatoes, which mostly burned. Independence is stressed at an early age. When we were little, we took care of each other. I'm the second of ten children and the oldest of the girls so I was given a lot of responsibility. I looked out for my brothers and sisters and gave them advice. We still consult with each other about our problems and concerns.

Many of our mothers and grandmothers say it is important to be brought up Navajo. Some young people do not understand the importance of traditional Navajo values, and this worries our elders. My parents, who do not speak English, notice that their grandchildren are being raised to learn English as well as Navajo. They tell us, "Just make sure they speak Navajo and know their clans."

SHEEP IN NAVAJO CULTURE

In Navajo families it is important to have sheep. A Navajo woman is expected to know how to care for the sheep. It is part of knowing how to weave. Sheep provide food for the family and wool for weaving. I have known how to care for sheep since I was a little girl—when to take them out, when to bring them in, when to take them to the watering hole, and what to do during lambing and shearing.

Our family had two flocks when I was a child. My grandfather, A'taa ha ii'tiin, had a herd for his family, and my Uncle Benny had a herd. My mother's sheep and my father's sheep were included with my uncle's herd, and we also had a few head with my grandparents' herd. In 1970, my mother inherited a grazing permit from Uncle Benny. These permits, issued by the Navajo tribe, allow families to own and raise a certain number of sheep, goats, and horses. After acquiring the permit, my mother separated her sheep from my uncle's herd and started her own herd.

When a young couple gets married, their families usually give them sheep, horses, or cattle to begin their new life. My father is from Tachee, which is west of Black Mountain and three miles north of Blue Gap Chapter House. When he moved to Tselani, my mother's community, he brought with him twelve head of sheep and one horse. That is how our family started our sheep flock, and today we have over one hundred sheep and goats. My Uncle Eugene is the main caretaker of the flock. The grazing permit will be kept in the family, and when my mom is no longer able to oversee the sheep, one of the children will take custody of the permit.

Woman with fleece, 1904. Chaco Canyon, New Mexico. Photo by George H. Pepper. (N2471)

EDUCATION

I spent a lot of time away from home as a child. Most Navajo children started school when they were six or seven years old. The year my Aunt Stella and I went to boarding school was not a happy one. We were taken away to Chinle at about age six. I cried the whole way. We were allowed to come home for the holidays and sometimes on weekends, but the miles of dirt roads to our home made this difficult. My parents, who did not have a truck at that time, had to depend on relatives to get a ride into Chinle to pick us up. In the winter travel was especially difficult because of the snow and mud. During the 1968 blizzard, my grandfather, my dad, and a neighbor, Ben Tsosie, who had a pickup truck, made it to Chinle to bring us home for Christmas. I remember how deep the snow was and how hard it was to see the road. It was a long ride and very cold, and we had to walk the last mile to our house.

My first memory of boarding school is that the dormitory aides wanted to cut our hair off. Most of the new girls had long hair, which we wore in braids or ponytails. The aides told us, "You don't know how to take care of

your hair," so almost everyone had her hair cut—to the same length and in the same style. I didn't get mine cut because I screamed! I really carried on. I was scared. Nothing at school was familiar. There were times when we weren't allowed to speak Navajo, but we didn't know English yet. It was hard learning English because all our teachers were Anglo. Every night I would hear someone crying, which made me sad.

In time, I became familiar with the school environment and started accepting some of the things we were learning. There were routines we had to follow. All of the students had to eat together in a big hall. Recreation was held only on certain days and at certain times. We had duties in the dormitories, including scrubbing and polishing the floors and folding the laundry. Our school clothes were sent out in bulk to be washed, and every Friday the clean clothes and linen were returned; whoever had laundry duty had to spend many hours sorting, folding, and distributing the clothes to the proper dormitory wing.

I still had a hard time with English skills because I didn't understand what we were learning. Then, in the fifth grade, I had a really good teacher, Mrs. Fletcher. She took the time to explain what we were learning. She made a big difference in my education. Although she taught many subjects, she always stressed reading. Her lesson plans incorporated many elements that were familiar to us and cultural activities that we enjoyed. She might ask, "What do you do in the morning, at home, with your mom and dad?" We would say that we had tortillas and potatoes for breakfast, and that after breakfast we took the sheep out. Then we would write a nice sentence. Mrs. Fletcher taught on the reservation for twenty-eight years. I still write to her, as do many of her former students, and recently I visited her in her home in Texas. She still speaks of her students and how much she loved living on the reservation and teaching Navajo children.

At the end of every school year I was anxious to get home to my family. During the summers I would go over in my mind what I had learned in school. I was especially proud that I could read and interpret letters that came for my parents. My parents encouraged my brothers and sisters and me to continue our education. My mother was placed in a boarding school when she was very young, but she refused to go back after one of her visits home. Dad always told us, "Go to school," because he never had the opportunity.

It was also during the summers that I began to help my mother with her weaving, and each year I learned a little bit more. I made my first rug when I was about twelve years old. It took me almost all summer to weave, but it paid for a new dress for me for school.

After Chinle Boarding School, I attended St. Michael High School, a Catholic boarding school near Window Rock. I was encouraged by my art teacher, Sister Franceline, to pursue my interest in weaving, and I began to read about weaving with different materials, including cotton, linen, and wool, and about different weaving traditions. I was especially interested in Chilkat blankets from the Northwest Coast.

I spent my freshman college year at Rocky Mountain College in Billings, Montana. The art classes were exciting because the instructor, Mr. Morrison, encouraged me to draw from my own culture and background. I painted scenes from the Southwest and incorporated rug patterns in my design projects.

In my sophomore year, I transferred to Arizona State University, where I received my teacher's certificate. I began to focus on Navajo weaving, but I still wanted to learn more about other kinds of weaving, so I took fiber art classes requiring detailed studies of different weaving techniques, processes, and materials. One of my professors, Rowen Schussheim Anderson, was also a weaver, and she inspired me to continue my own weaving. I did some weaving to help pay my college expenses, but I didn't market or show my work. After I finished college and began to teach, I continued to weave part-time.

A WOMAN'S ROLE

I am a Navajo woman—a Navajo weaver—but I also live in the Anglo world. I live both in and outside of my community. I spend the winter months outside Phoenix, where my husband, Howie Meyer, works, and our son, Kelsey, attends school, but our home is in Tselani, west of Chinle, on the Navajo reservation. We have also lived on the East Coast and have enjoyed all the conveniences available off the reservation, but I am most comfortable living where I was raised. It's all a part of me and my weaving. Practicing the art of weaving involves my views, my goals, my life. What I do as a wife, mother, artist, business person, and community member, all ties in with my weaving. I am a Navajo woman, with roots where I was raised.

I have many roles. I juggle two cultures—Navajo and Anglo—because my son, Kelsey, is both Navajo and Anglo. It is important to me that he speaks Navajo and English. With my parents, other family members, or friends, I may speak Navajo or English, or a combination of both.

Woman spinning wool, 1904. Chaco Canyon, New Mexico. Photo by George H. Pepper. (N2480)

Sometimes it is difficult to manage all my different roles. I have many family responsibilities on the reservation, including participating in ceremonies. There are also tasks such as working on the hogan my husband and I built, or driving twenty-five miles into Chinle just to do the laundry.

Navajo women are expected to have large families. I have friends and relatives with children who take in other family members as well. Navajo women are the caretakers. A woman's pride reflects who she is, what she has, and what she does. My mother makes the important decisions; for example, she is the person to say, "Let's sell all the sheep," or, "Let's produce more lambs." She is respected by her children and other family members because she is able to keep the family unity. A woman's role is to maintain and pass down the traditional values to the next generation. Knowledge about raising children, teaching your children about their clans, and maintaining your relationship with the people in your community, is very important.

When a young girl comes of age she has a *kinaaldá*, or puberty ceremony. At that time her mother will select a relative, usually an aunt, to serve as a role model. Recognized for her knowledge of Navajo culture and womanhood, she will guide the girl through her ceremony. Weaving and the importance of knowing how to weave are stressed at this time. Many of the relatives attending the ceremony bring personal belongings to be blessed, and among the items are weaving tools, as well as jewelry, purses, cooking utensils, and Pendleton blankets. This helps the girl think about what she will need to furnish her home. She will learn about all the important aspects of womanhood.

My mother was raised primarily by her grandmother, who taught her many of the old traditions. She taught her how to weave, how to herd sheep, and how to cook. My mother was married when she was fifteen or sixteen years old, and her marriage was planned by her mother and father. She says that in those days you did not disagree with your mother's decisions. She did not have a choice.

My mother and grandmother always said, "A woman has to weave." To be a complete person, a Navajo woman should weave or have some knowledge of weaving. Weaving is important for your thinking. Weaving is communication. It is like speaking Navajo. It enables me to communicate with weavers, my family, and my friends. Even when I lived back East, I continued to weave. Weaving brought me back to my roots. My mother says that she doesn't think she would ever feel comfortable weaving away from home. Unlike weavers today, she did not have the opportunity to travel to demonstrate weaving or to talk about her work. She says that she is glad that I am able to weave somewhere else, that I don't feel uncomfortable weaving in a different environment.

LEARNING TO WEAVE

I learned how to weave by watching my mother. She never said, "Sit down, this is what you are going to learn about weaving today." I watched and listened. I remember memorizing the warp count for the heddles for a diamond twill weave. As I became more experienced, I began asking my mother questions such as, "How come you spin this way? How come you card this way? Why do you weave?" Sometimes I got an answer, and sometimes I didn't.

Kóó t'éego means allowing people to watch and to learn from watching. Teaching is showing. Passing on knowledge is a weaver's responsibility. A young girl may pick up weaving at an early age just because she is around weavers—maybe her mother, grandmother, or aunts. She can participate in many ways, whether it's herding the sheep, adjusting the warp tension of a rug on the loom, or putting the weaving tools away. My twelve-year-old niece, Debbie, is already weaving. She weaves in the Two Grey Hills style, the style that her mother, Roselyn, prefers. Debbie makes sketches of weaving patterns at school and brings them home. She had her kinaaldá in the summer of 1995, and my sister Bernice was chosen to be the role model. My mother wanted all the children, especially the younger nieces, to witness the ceremony. When I asked my mother and my sisters how the kinaaldá went, their response was, "The woman's ceremony was good." It made me feel very proud.

Weaving also involves a sense of modesty. We are taught as children not to point, stare, or be loud. We are a private people. It might be okay to be thought of as a teacher, but not to be labeled an expert, someone who knows it all. Several years ago I was invited to conduct a series of workshops with Navajo weavers in Ramah, New Mexico. I felt somewhat uncomfortable at first because many of the women were older than me and much more experienced as weavers. But we had a lot in common, and the Ramah weavers—Annie, Nadia, and many others, became an inspiration to me. I felt motivated to be more involved, and they made me aware of how I speak about weaving.

We covered many topics. We processed indigo dye baths to acquire colors ranging from blue to green. We talked about cochineal dye and how the insects are processed for the dyes, and we experimented with exotic plants such as brazilwood and madder. The weavers were interested in learning about the plants, especially what parts of the plants are used to obtain the colors.

We also talked about improving spinning and weaving techniques. I emphasized that the materials used will determine the quality of the finished textile. There was also considerable interest in marketing techniques—what styles, designs, and colors are the most marketable. I shared my opinions, my reading, and my personal experiences, which include talking to collectors and gallery owners and going to art shows, art auctions, and conferences.

Working with these weavers was one of the first times that I taught weaving. It was intimidating because the workshop was in Navajo, and I was nervous that I might mispronounce words or not explain dye recipes well. But it would have been difficult, if not impossible, to conduct the workshop in any language other than Navajo. Some of the technical terms and many of the underlying principles cannot be translated into English. A full understanding of Navajo weaving demands a knowledge of our language, because the activity cannot be separated from the Navajo words and beliefs from which it arises.

WEAVING BRINGS RESPECT

There are many exceptionally talented weavers working today. Although weavers may compete with each other, they don't talk about it. We always want to do a piece that will knock somebody's socks off, but we don't verbalize it in public. I have a lot of respect for weavers like Mary Lee Begay and the late Rose Owens. Rose Owens was one of the originators of the round rug, and she produced some of the finest work of her generation. Mary Lee Begay's textiles display quality in techniques and designs. These women, both traditional weavers, remind me of my paternal grandmother who lives and practices the Navajo way.

I see weavers as powerful. They bring respect to their families. Weaving conveys the power to support a family.

Power can be thought of as status in the community, how people look at you, whether they hold you in honor. Wealth in the form of land, livestock, vehicles, or homes conveys power. It gives a person a place in society. If a person is a leader in his or her community, if he or she speaks up at community meetings, that person is also respected.

Weaving brings goods to a family. Pauline Esitty, a young weaver, once told me, "These hands earn money so I can provide for my family." When my mom started a family, her weaving was an important source of income. My father worked for the railroad, but it was a seasonal occupation, and at times he was away for weeks or months. The railroad would also lay off workers for long periods of time. My mother's weavings provided for the family's needs. My maternal grandmother, Yanasbah, also wove for economic reasons. Both my mother and grandmother traveled by horse or wagon to the trading post to sell their rugs.

Weaving has provided me with an income, too. I sold one or two rugs when I was twelve years old, and, with the money I earned, purchased fabric to make school clothes. In college I sold a few weavings to my art teachers and one or two pieces to Hubbell's Trading Post, in Ganado, Arizona. Today, weavers will travel considerable distances to get the highest prices possible for their rugs. Recognized weavers sell their textiles directly to private collectors and art galleries, at rug auctions, or to trading posts. As we gain marketing skills, we will be exposed to new ideas that will impact on our weaving, and we will be better compensated for the work we produce.

WEAVING TODAY: AN INDEPENDENT APPROACH

My weaving involves experimenting with new materials, new designs, and different techniques. I read as much as I can and visit museums to see textiles from all over the world. I am affiliated with weaving guilds and participate in fiber conferences across the country. I have always been very independent. When I went off to college I never asked for any money. My parents did not have the money to pay my living expenses. I worked as a waitress and at odd jobs, and sometimes I wove a rug to pay the rent.

One of my dreams in high school was to travel to Vancouver to see Chilkat weaving. My friend, Peggy Maher, a volunteer teacher at St. Michaels Elementary School, traveled with me to Canada. We drove her pickup truck and camped out at night. Sometimes we would pull up to a camp and make fry bread, which we sold for gas money. Today we laugh at the things we did. Once it was very cold and all we had to eat was a can of sardines and some instant coffee, and we couldn't even get a fire going. But we made it to Vancouver and saw Chilkat blankets with our own eyes.

I used to wonder how the Chilkat weavers could weave without tension on the warp threads. Chilkat weaving is like finger weaving—it is actually twining. With Navajo weaving there is constant tension on the warps—the foundation of the textile—and a weaver is in control of the tension at all times. In Chilkat weaving, the warps are strung over a bar and the warp ends hang loose, held down only by weights. That is all the tension there is. I asked one weaver how she controlled the warp tension, and how she kept the edges of the blanket straight. She simply said, "Oh, there's no problem." I was fascinated by the color combinations and the designs of the blankets, and I have incorporated some of these ideas into my own work.

WEAVING TOOLS

Navajo weaving tools—the loom, batten, and comb—have a place and a purpose in Navajo origin stories. They were made by the Holy People for us to use. They are very precious, not only to women but also to medicine men, who may use a batten to smooth out the surface of a sandpainting in a healing ceremony.

Woman carding wool, early 20th century. Chaco Canyon, New Mexico. Photo by George H. Pepper. (N33110)

In Navajo, there is no precise word for loom. Weaving terms are descriptive of how space is filled, of how parts of a loom occupy space rather than of the parts themselves. I use *bikaa dah n' atlohi'*, which means "weaving done on top." To describe the whole loom, I have to make reference to each part of the loom. The top frame is *wödahji'ni'ahii* ("on top, it stretches across, like a stick"); the bottom frame is *wo'yahji'ni'ahii* ("on the bottom, it stretches across, like a stick"); the side posts are *abaahgi'ni'ahii* ("on the side, it sticks upward, like a stick"); and the loom's legs are *bikáá' dah náttohi'bijáád* ("on top weaving's legs").

Although Navajo weaving techniques have stayed basically the same for the past three hundred years, there have been some changes. For example, women no longer set up a loom between two trees or wooden poles. Some weavers now make their looms from old metal bed frames or road posts, but they probably always constructed looms from whatever was available. Today, top warp beams and tension beams are often made from metal pipes.

Looms vary in size. My large loom is about eight feet high by seven feet wide and reaches from the floor to the ceiling. My husband made it out of poplar wood. This loom can support three weavings at once. I can set up a large rug on one side and two smaller pieces on the back. I sit in a small swivel chair with casters so I can roll back and forth across the loom as I weave, and thereby avoid weaving in sections. I am always at eye level with the area on which I'm working. I use a portable loom for weaving demonstrations.

In Navajo weaving, the warps are laced in pairs on the loom and attached to the top and bottom warp beams. A weaver must control the tension of the warps at all times. This was once accomplished by pulling and tightening the rope strung between the top warp beam and the tension beam. Many weavers today use metal turnbuckles, which work very well and can be purchased at a hardware store. They are attached to the top warp beam and the tension beam. If I am not going to be weaving for three or four days, I can loosen the warps by just turning the buckles a few times.

The *bee nik'i'nilt ish'*, or batten, is said to be the sun halo. It is a flat, straight piece made of juniper or oak. The batten is inserted between the warps to open and maintain the shed, through which the weft is passed. A weaver usually owns several battens of different sizes and shapes. A good weaver's batten shows a lot of wear, including teeth marks from the warps. I did not know this as a child, and once when I was playing with my mom's battens, I sanded one of them! I did not know many of the customs for caring for weaving tools until I was older. For example, you should not point with your batten, or poke another person with your weaving tools, or leave them in the shed opening.

In our stories, the *bee' adzooi'*, or comb, is made out of white shell. Weaving combs are used to pack the weft into place on the portion of rug that is already woven. They are carved from hard wood and require a great deal of time and skill to make. They come in many sizes and shapes. My personal weaving tools, my battens and combs, are made by my brothers. I have also inherited some tools from my mom and my *nalí* (grandmother), Desbah Nez, my dad's mother. I also collect tools from other places; I received one as a gift when I conducted a weaving workshop in Australia.

Spinning is the most important part of the weaving process. The quality of a rug depends on how well the wool is spun. It must be spun evenly and tightly, and it must be uniform. I use two types of spindles, *bee adizi*, a hand spindle, and a Louet spinning wheel, which is made in Holland. The spinning wheel is more efficient. I can spin a ball (about five ounces) of warp in about three hours on a spinning wheel, whereas it would take me almost a whole day to spin the same amount of warp with a hand spindle. I enjoy using the hand spindle because it is the tool I used when I first learned to spin.

Bee ha'nilchaadi', or hand carders, are small, rectangular pieces of wood with metal teeth, which are used to clean and straighten the wool fibers in preparation for spinning. The type of carder we use today was first provided by traders. Before there were trading posts, many women—especially the young girls—used to pick through the wool, separating and straightening the fleece by hand. After my great-grandmother went blind, she would sit on her bed and unravel the fringes of her Pendleton shawl and tell us that this is how you work with the wool.

Shades of gray and brown are also obtained by carding different colors of wool together. I use Clemens hand carders, but I have also experimented with the larger drum cards. Drum cards are made of two barrels with the teeth set up against each other. You crank the handle to feed the wool through the drums. Carding is the easiest part of the weaving process. You clean, pick, and sort the wool, and then you wash it and card it. When I was a little girl, I despised carding, but one of my chores was helping my mom prepare the wool for spinning. Today, you can purchase wool rovings by the pound, already cleaned and carded. This is convenient for many women who do not have running water.

MATERIALS

I like to experiment with different kinds of wool to see how manageable the fibers are and to compare the quality of the finished piece with other textiles. The texture and body of the fibers depend upon the breed of sheep. I like to work with churro fleece because the fibers are long and pliable. Spinning churro wool is especially enjoyable, and rugs woven with churro wool have a lot of body and a smooth surface. Rugs woven with merino wool sometimes look and feel dry. Merino fibers are shorter and kinkier than churro wool, so more effort must go into the spinning. I'm always pulling at the fibers or checking to see if the skein is evenly spun. I often mix merino with other kinds of wool to add body and to improve the flexibility of the fibers. Skeins of machine-spun wool are also available.

I look for different characteristics in wool. I use wool from my family's flock and also commercially processed wool from outlets such as trading posts, arts and crafts centers, and fiber supply stores. My family's flock is a mixture of Rambouillet and merino sheep. Rambouillet and merino sheep are meatier animals than the churro, but churro sheep produce more wool. My family sells most of the wool that they shear, but I pick through the piles and take what I can use. The back of a sheep is the place to get the best wool, because that is where it is the longest. I hand-process a lot of the wool that I use. It takes a great deal of time to shear, clean, card, spin, and dye the wool for a project, but the visual appearance of a rug reflects how much care was put into preparing the wool.

Pure black wool is hard to find. One of my sources is in Durango, Colorado. The sheep on this farm wear Australian sheep covers to prevent their coats from

Woman pulverizing black alder bark for red dye, 1904. Chaco Canyon, New Mexico. Photo by George H. Pepper. (N2468)

bleaching in the sun. Many weavers like to use as black a wool as possible. On the reservation, "black" sheep are really a dark brown. When the sheep are out all summer long, the sun bleaches their outer coats. It's hard and very time-consuming to trim all those bleached areas, so many weavers overdye brown wool with synthetic dye to make it black. I recently acquired three churro sheep, two black and one white. I plan to cover these sheep to obtain some pure colors.

Like many weavers, I also work with commercially processed wool that is already washed, carded, spun, and dyed. Sometimes I respin store-bought wool, because by the time I get it into my hands—after handling, crating, and shipping—the wool has unraveled. My friend Helena Hernmarck, a Swedish weaver, introduced me to wool produced by Berga, a Swedish company, and to wool from Walstedts, a third-generation, family-owned business in Sweden. The Walstedts raise sheep and sell the wool to a number of weaving outlets as well as to individual weavers. They do custom work as well as raising sheep

and spinning and dyeing wool. I order red wool from them and it's consistently uniform in color. I use Swedish wool because of this excellent consistency from one dye lot to another. When I went to Sweden I got some catalogues from the different outlets, and I still order from them. The Swedish wools are very nicely spun, for machine-spun yarn.

Today, when I ask weavers where they get their materials, some of them say that they order from mail-order catalogues. They also buy commercial yarn at stores on the reservation as well as from large retail outlets and wool manufacturers throughout the country. Churro sheep wool can be ordered from the Navajo Sheep Project at Utah State University, and raw wool is also sold on the reservation. Recently my mom picked up some brown wool at the Gallup flea market. Many weavers used to handspin their warps, but today many of them work with machine-spun warp. For the past few years I have also noticed weavers using commercial yarn for warp. They respin the yarn, and many weavers say it is much stronger under tension. Cotton string was popular for a while, but probably only a few weavers use it today. There are many different kinds of wool and synthetic yarns available, and weavers experiment with them and with different brands. I don't limit myself to churro or merino wool. I use various types of wool, even mohair, or a combination of mohair and wool. There are no limitations to the materials that weavers can use.

DYES

I am very interested in re-creating some of the colors used by Navajo weavers one hundred years ago—indigo blue, for example, or cochineal, or some of the other colors produced at the turn of the century and earlier. It's a challenge to re-create the colors and designs used by my great-grandmothers. Maybe in time these colors will be reproduced, but right now not too many weavers are interested in processing indigo vats, for example. It's a complex technique involving chemicals and a great deal of time. Indigo (*Indigofera*) is the oldest known blue dye and the oldest of all dye plants. The dye comes from the leaves of a plant that usually grows about five feet tall. The color is extracted by placing the leaves in large vats and allowing them to ferment. The oxidized solution forms a blue powder or cake, which is what is sold in stores. Oxidized indigo is insoluble in water, and special techniques must be employed to extract the blue color. I did my first experiment by preparing the solution for producing true indigo blue. I spent a lot of time researching the plant and learning how to prepare the vat solutions. I prepared hydrosulphite and indigo sulphate vats, which meant working with sulfuric acid, boric acid, oxalic acid, sodium hydroxide, cream of tartar, and washing soda. Once you have the solution prepared, it goes a long way. It must be stored in airtight glass containers and discarded properly.

I will always remember one of my visits to my nali. She was collecting plants, and she told me that she used them to make the colors for the wool she used in her weaving. I think that's when I became interested in dyeing. She boiled some water, put in some plants, and then added the wool, which she left soaking for a long time. When she took the wool out, it was a beautiful yellow. I think she was using snakeweed.

I collect plants from all over the reservation to see what colors they will produce. A lot of my work with dyes is just experimentation; sometimes the most beautiful plant yields no color at all. I prefer natural to synthetic colors, but that's just a personal choice. There are more choices in commercial colors, but I can use these any time. Many weavers don't have running water so it's easier for them to go to the store and buy commercial yarn. I have always had access to running water so I prefer to wash and dye the wool myself. To wash the wool I use Orvus, a commercial, biodegradable detergent. Weavers used to wash their wool in yucca suds. Natural white wools can be put out into the sun to bleach—which also cleans the wool.

Once, when my mom was visiting me in New Jersey, I was soaking brazilwood (*Caesalpinia echinata* or *Haematoxylon brasilletto*), which looks just like wood chips, in a bucket in the basement. My mom saw it and asked, "Why are you soaking the wood?" She thought that it was kindling. Then I told her about my experiments with brazilwood. I used to buy it at a local weaving shop, where it was sold by the pound, as sawdust, or in extract form. The extracted material comes from the heartwood of the redwood tree and produces lavender-red, shades of pink, and a variety of colors ranging from violet-blue to purple. I always save the dye bath to produce different tones and shades of the colors.

There are many different native dye plants, and I am still learning about all the colors that they produce. Around Tselani there are a lot of juniper trees, whose wood, bark, or berries can be used to make dyes of various colors. You can also use mistletoe, a fungus that grows in the branches of trees. Juniper from another part of the country may produce different colors. I have also made dyes from pine cones and prickly pears. I've used rabbitbrush to make yellow and sagebrush to make a muddy green and an off-brown. I've used Indian paintbrush roots, but you have to pick a lot to get a strong rose color, and the plant does not grow in abundance around Tselani. The color also depends on the mordant, a reagent used to set the dye. Also, soil, climate, and rainfall all affect the colors that the plants produce.

Other plants I have used are madder (*Rubia tinctorum*), cutch (*Acacia catechu* or *Uncaria gambier*), logwood (*Haematoxylon campechianum*), and bloodroot (*Sanguinaria canadensis*). The roots of the madder plant produce red; the color comes from the core of the roots and the outer bark layer. I purchase madder roots by the pound from weaving outlets. I have always enjoyed working with this plant because extracting the dyes does not require a specific recipe. After soaking the roots for days I get a nice orange-red and sometimes a deep red shade. Often I save the dye bath and reuse or combine it with other dyes. During the

From left: Ann Lane Hedlund, Cherileen Teasyatwho, Elnora Teasyatwho, D. Y. Begay, Marie Sheppard, Keevin Lewis, Irene Clark, July 1995. Ned A. Hatathli Museum, Navajo Community College, Tsaile, Arizona. Photo by Monty Roessel.

winter I place the madder roots in a big glass jar with water that I put in the sun to extract the color. Cutch comes from the wood of an acacia tree native to Burma and India. Extracted cutch is sold in stores in a hard crystallized form that is just the resin from the tree. It produces rich browns and tans. Logwood comes from the heartwood of a tree that grows in Central and South America, and it can be purchased in a powdered form or as bags of chips. I use it over and over again until there is no color left. In a dye bath with chrome mordant, logwood can produce a beautiful blue-purple. Bloodroot is a tiny plant with white flowers that grows in wooded areas on the East Coast. I use the roots to get different shades of rose. A woman who owns a weaving store in New Jersey introduced me to the plant. When you splice the root, which is about the size and color of a finger, it bleeds and looks just like you have cut your finger. I have taken the plants home and soaked the roots, which produce a rosy shade of red.

Cochineal is a dye made from the dried and pulverized bodies of tiny insects (*Dactylopius coccus*) that live on certain cactus plants. The female yields the most dye after she has been fertilized and before she lays her eggs. Processed cochineal is very expensive. It takes about two ounces of these tiny insects to dye one pound of wool. I like using cochineal because you can always count on getting a beautiful crimson as well as purple and green. My mother also collects dye recipes. She has been told that you can use sheep manure, and that it produces a tan-brown. My son, Kelsey, suggested that I try Kool Aid. He experimented and left a small skein of wool in a cup of strawberry Kool Aid; it turned a beautiful red and smelled very nice. He gave it to me to put in my collection.

I have many boxes of dyes and plants in storage. I have been collecting and learning more about some of the native plants that produce dyes, especially those that grow locally. I am going to collect mahogany roots with my dad in the fall. I have never used the plant but I know the roots can produce orange-red, a deep purple, and lavender. My dad is going to show me where to go and how to pick the plants. We pay respect to the plants that we take from the earth by blessing them with corn pollen. Many of the plants that I use to make dyes have other uses. For example, sagebrush (*Artemisia tridentata*) is an herb sometimes used for curing a headache or stomachache. There are many stories about the different plants that I use, and I try to record them as I learn them.

DESIGNS

When I begin a rug, I think of the design first. I think of new ways to construct a pattern or to combine colors. My mother and grandmother wove designs that were familiar to them. My mother created new designs and changed colors by working from the pattern of a rug that she had previously made or by using designs from rugs she had seen in the trading post. My mother does not weave much today, although occasionally she will make a small rug and ask me for ideas or want to talk about different designs and colors.

In the late 1800s, hoping to create a new market for Navajo weaving, traders began encouraging weavers to incorporate new designs into their textiles. Often they provided sketches and paintings for weavers to copy. I imagine that it was a very exciting time. Other design sources included books and magazines as well as a wide variety of images from labels on commercial products. New features in the landscape, such as the railroad, inspired the weavers to incorporate novel images into their work. I have always found it a challenge to try to weave new designs.

My work is strongly influenced by nineteenth-century Navajo wearing blankets. I have learned about the history of Navajo weaving from studying these textiles. I have come to recognize different styles and techniques and to be a better judge of quality. Analysis of these textiles inspires me to re-create certain styles and combinations of colors in what I hope are new and innovative ways. Weaving involves being open to new design sources and new materials. I think that's what makes a weaver creative.

Some trading posts continue to suggest certain styles, colors, and sizes for rugs and wall hangings, and some art galleries have followed their lead. I prefer to have an order that leaves me to my own devices, although once in a while it's rewarding to work with somebody else's ideas. Some days I feel more creative than others. At times I come up with great ideas, wonderful designs and color combinations, but, at other times, I'm ready to start a piece and have no specific design in mind. I keep a book of sketches and continually jot down new ideas for designs. I record patterns and colors I've seen in magazine articles, newspapers, posters—even movies. I draw sketches of rugs I've finished, but I also have them professionally photographed and I add the photographs to my portfolio. Maybe someday these notebooks will be a resource for other weavers.

There is a Navajo phrase, *aashi bi'bohlii*, which means, "It's up to you." When my mother uses this term, she is saying that there are no formulas in weaving. Weaving allows us to create and to express ourselves with tools, materials, and designs. It's up to you—up to the weaver. It's your choice. There are no rules as long as you know the basic techniques, and the basic techniques will not change; our mothers, grandmothers, and great-grandmothers have been practicing them for years.

Once, at Indian Market in Santa Fe, I met an older, very traditional Navajo lady. She was looking at my work for a long time, perhaps half an hour. She kept looking at one rug, turning it over and studying the selvages. I thought she was going to tell me that something was wrong, or ask why did I do it this way? Finally, in Navajo, I asked her if she had any questions. She smiled and said, "No." Then I asked, "Do you like it? What do you think?" She replied, "It's very different. Obviously you can make a living doing this." That was her opinion. She liked it. It goes back to aashi bi'bohlii.

MY GOALS

Today I realize how important it is to document stories about Navajo weaving techniques, materials, dyes, and tools. I record interviews and conversations with Navajo weavers of all ages and backgrounds as well as personal accounts of places I have been and people I have met and with whom I've worked. This information can be helpful to many young Navajos, especially novice weavers.

Someday I would like to organize a facility to collect and maintain information about weaving techniques, styles, dyes, plants, sheep, and individual weavers. It would make available relevant publications as well as video tapes and photographs. It would also offer weaving workshops for Navajos and non-Navajos.

Often I hear our elders talk about how life was in the early days when there were no turnbuckles or weaving supply stores. My mother is impressed with all the different types of dyes available today for obtaining a wide range of colors, and finds it amusing that I keep notebooks

Figure 8

D.Y. Begay (b. 1953), *Three Points*, 1994.
Handspun wool, natural white
and black; warp, machine spun wool,
151 × 103.4 cm.
Artist's collection.

of weaving suppliers with numerous color cards, sample wool and yarns, and addresses and telephone numbers. Today many of the schools on the reservation stress the importance of cultural enrichment programs. Parents' committees check for appropriate lesson plans and projects for the students, and weaving is frequently taught. My aunt, Marie Sheppard, who is also an accomplished weaver, taught beginning Navajo weaving at Chinle High School, and she says that she found it very rewarding to share her knowledge with the students.

I also hope to study other kinds of weaving. I am especially interested in the arts and cultures of South America, and I particularly want to learn about the Peruvian people and their weaving traditions. I am interested in their weaving techniques, in the different materials they use, and in the dyes they produce from local sources. Perhaps we have more in common with the Native peoples of Peru than I know. Learning about another weaving tradition will be an adventure and will enrich my own work.

Today I am busy setting up a business to sell Navajo rugs woven by family members and friends. I believe that Navajo weaving should be presented, sold, taught, and preserved by the Navajo people, and I have found a lot of support for this approach among weavers and friends. I have witnessed too many transactions in which an elderly person agrees to sell a weaving for too little money. A grandmother whom I often visit will weave a rug just so she can purchase soda and candy for her many grandchildren. She is hindered from marketing her rugs by her language and age, but businesses that promote Indian art are in a position to assist artists like her.

The most important thing to me is raising my son, Kelsey, Navajo. He is growing up in two cultures, Navajo and Anglo, and I have to work at balancing both worlds—to give him the best of both. My husband and I decided after Kelsey's first birthday that we would raise him the Navajo way. I want my son to experience the way that I grew up and the place where I was raised. Kelsey's maternal grandparents are getting older, and I want my son to learn from them. My father stresses that it's important that

Kelsey speaks Navajo and participates in our ceremonies. And he wants Kelsey to ask questions and to listen to Navajo stories.

Navajo people are culturally rich. We have maintained our language and traditions. We still hold ceremonies to restore ourselves when we are out of balance with our thoughts, work, children, or community. My brother Nelson made a special trip home last year to have a Blessing Ceremony. His family and his job are in Oklahoma, but he wanted to have the ceremony so he could continue his work and his life in good health and thoughts.

Scholars say the Navajo learned the art of weaving from our neighbors, the Pueblo people. But I also respect the stories that our grandmothers and grandfathers tell us about how the Dine'é came into the world, and how they came to weave. I am proud of the beliefs and customs that our parents taught us. I will carry on the language and the traditions. I keep an open mind and heart to learn. Navajo life is a continuation of learning.

Our stories come from the home—from our grandmothers, grandfathers, mothers, fathers, aunts, uncles, and children. Our stories do not speculate, revise, or reinterpret technical and historical points. They are stories that we live. Weaving is not just a matter of sitting at a loom and weaving; it is not only about weaving techniques and rug designs. My weaving reflects who I am. It incorporates my beliefs, my family, and my community.

A Conversation with My Father, Kee Yazzie Begay

D. Y. Begay

As my father says, *k'e* (family structure) is very important. K'e identifies you. K'e implies respect and gratitude for your relationship with many people and with your community.

In Navajo life, many events and things occur four times. There are four sacred directional colors: white (east); blue (south); yellow (west); and black (north). Dine taa (Navajoland) is encompassed by four sacred mountains: in the east, Sis Naajini (Blanca Peak); in the south, Tsoodzil (Mount Taylor); in the west, Dook' o' oosliid (San Francisco Peak); and in the north, Dibe Nitsa (la Platte Mountain). The Dine'é originated from four clans. Changing Woman formed the Kinyaa'áanii Clan by rubbing the skin from her breast; the Honágháahnii Clan by rubbing the skin from her neck; the Tódích'íí'nii Clan from the skin under her right arm; and the Hasht 'ishnii Clan from the skin under her left arm.

My great-grandfather, Ta'chii'nii Yazi, told my father that we are the real Ta'chii'nii. Our clan's name describes a location and homes built into the hills where the Ta'chii'nii people lived and worked. The hills had red streak clay deposited in the earth. The people from nearby Dook' o' oosliid saw fire off in the distance toward the north, about where Tachee is located in the mountain ranges. This happened three times and each time the people went to find the fire, but, having no luck, they returned to Dook' o' oosliid. The fourth time, the people searched for the fire again. They stopped where they thought they saw it, but they still did not see any sign of fire. There was a man sitting there in the shade sewing moccasins. He said, "We are the Ta'chii'nii and we live here." He folded up a skin and behind it was a cave, and inside there were many elders, women, men, and children working. He explained that they were the real people, Ta'chii'nii.

Figure 9

D. Y. Begay (b. 1953), rug, 1994.
Handspun and commercial wool, plant-dyed.
118.4 X 70.8 cm. Private collection.

28

The Navajo Concept of Art
Harry Walters

The Navajo do not have a word for "art." Art is not seen as separate from other cultural components like music, philosophy, religion, or history. To study Navajo art, one must study the whole culture. Any attempt to study Navajo art by itself would fail.

What is called art in Western culture is viewed differently by the Navajo. Art in Navajo society is considered alive. It is like a person. It has feelings. It has power—healing power. This is something that a Navajo person learns; it is not something that you are blessed with or that you inherit. Like a person, your art has to accept you.

Art must be approached with the right attitude, and, to maintain it, you must communicate with it or else it will disassociate itself from you. When art turns away from you, you have run into a block or you have lost your talent. Periodic blocks are a natural part of being an artist. To maintain good relations with art, there are ceremonies and prayers that you learn along the way, and you use these to renew your talent and to reestablish your relationship with art. These ceremonies, songs, and prayers refresh your skills, as well as your knowledge of and your appreciation for art. This is what is important.

Like every cultural component, art has a negative and a positive side. The negative side keeps you in line; it is what the Navajos call *ajitni*. Some Navajo scholars call this the "prostitution way," which refers to both a ceremony and a way of life, but it has nothing to do with prostitution. The term often refers to someone indulging in a sexual relationship to excess, so this is how the word "prostitution" came about. What it actually means is that art has a side that is very seductive. It is beauty, and this beauty can be misleading. It is the icing on the cake, but it does not have

substance. It should be taken for just what it is—not to be indulged in but rather to be used to a certain degree and no more. If you look at art only for its beauty, it will be misleading. Our songs, prayers, and rituals are very important for this reason because they give art substance.

The Navajos say that if you are a fine weaver, you have been blessed with this talent by the Holy People, and they are responsible for the art. You must acknowledge them, and you must live right on this earth. Whatever you receive in exchange for your work, whether it is money, livestock, or food, you must use it right—to feed your family or help people. If you use the money, or whatever it is, for something like alcohol or to gamble, it is said that art will withhold itself from you, and you will lose your talent. Art extends not only to your work but also to your life, to the way you conduct yourself.

Navajo weaving is directly related to nature—dawn, day, twilight, and night; mountains, trees, animals, and insects; earth, air, and water. All of these are holy elements, and they are all present in Navajo weaving. These elements have power, and when we depict them in weaving, they have the same power. When a weaver is weaving a rug, she receives these powers. When she has good feelings and good communication with her weaving, she will receive these powers, or blessings, in return. And when she sells her weavings, she will receive the profit from her work.

There are different parts to the Navajo loom—beams, dowels, shed rods, heddles, and warp—and to the Navajo designs—diamonds, bars, and steps. All of these come directly from nature. In Navajo weavings, they are male and female rain clouds; rain and straight and zigzag lightning; sunbeams and rainbows. The colors in the weavings are

also the colors in nature. White represents the dawn and is associated with east; blue represents day and is associated with south; yellow represents the sunset and is associated with west; and black represents the night and is associated with north.

Colors are also viewed in terms of male and female. The male and the female not only signify sex, but principles. There are male principles and female principles, and the male and the female should have equal power. When they work together in balance, they establish harmony and peace. The word that we use is *hozho*. Hozho means, "I will walk in the Beauty Way." When a weaver makes a rug, she has to maintain this view. Everything that she uses must balance male and female. White represents male and blue represents female. Black represents male, and yellow represents female. When a weaver distributes these colors evenly, and the design is working together nicely, there is balance. This is how the weaver maintains a good relationship with her work. Weavers learn about these things through ceremonies and rituals.

All ceremonies, all rituals, and everything in Navajo is based on the natural order. Everything in the world subscribes to this natural order—birds, plants, animals, insects, and even people. All living things behave a certain way at dawn, during the day, in the evening, and at night. They also behave a certain way in the spring, summer, fall, and winter, as well as during a new moon, a full moon, and so forth. This life cycle of all living things repeats again and again, and art is a part of all this. When a weaver knows this, there is balance and harmony and peace in her work.

Today, most weaving is created for sale. Weavers have lost a lot of knowledge about the weaving process. Many of them approach weaving with an aesthetic from Western art and have forgotten the ceremonial connection. But in some nineteenth-century Navajo weavings, like those shown here from the National Museum of the American

Figure 10

Beeldléí (blanket), 1865–75.
Handspun wool, raveled and commercial yarn,
181.3 × 131.5 cm. (22.1688)

Indian, something more is at work. For example, in one Second Phase chief blanket (see plate 15), the white and black stripes reveal a series of black warps. You might wonder why a Navajo weaver would put these designs where they were not likely to be seen, but it was not done for the sake of design. It was done so that the weaving would maintain relations with the elements. The warp is rain. Rain comes down from the sky in a series of dark and light bands, often of different colors. To maintain a connection to this natural process, a weaver applies the same elements to her weaving.

To make something that is perfect means there is no more room for improvement, but it's important always to want to improve. This is what makes life worth living. If a weaver weaves a perfect rug, she will not have anything to compare with a future weaving, so she makes a little mistake on purpose—an imperfection. Often we see a little line, which the Navajo call a spirit line, that extends to the edge of a rug through the border. This line is added by the weaver so the rug will not be perfect. In one weaving (see plate 26), there is a series of bands and three red streaks with cloud designs and zigzag lightning. On the left side of the bands, the white and black bands are perfect, and on the right side, in the middle, the bars are large. Why would a master weaver make a mistake like that? It was done on purpose so that the weaving would not be perfect. A Third Phase chief blanket (see plate 18) displays the same technique. The stripes at the top are even; in the lower half, however, the black line is even at the left side but the top bar narrows, becoming thin toward the edge. Again, this was probably done on purpose so that the rug would not be perfect. These are some of the things a weaver learns.

Weaving also extends to the sheep. Sheep are part of the natural world. How the sheep are cared for plays an important part in weaving. Weaving also extends to the

land. You take your livestock to a place where there is plenty of grass, plenty of water, and you care for them and talk to them. There are songs and rituals that involve the sheep, and they also extend to the land—to Mother Earth. Weaving is nothing without all these other elements. This is how the Navajo approach weaving.

Canyon de Chelly, Arizona, ca. 1875. Photo by Timothy H. O'Sullivan. (P1744)

SHIŁ YÓÓŁT'OOŁ

Personification of Navajo Weaving[1]

Wesley Thomas

In the Navajo world knowledge is constructed of a combination of thought and speech.[2] Furthermore, voice is constructed with a combination of language and speech. *Nilch'i* (air) is the agent for voice.[3] When voice becomes the medium, the agents are songs and prayers. The later two—air and voice—in turn, initiate personification in Navajo cosmology.

The act of weaving does not merely produce a product for sale or display. Employing the constructions described above, Navajo weavers of the past envisioned an entity with a life of its own as they wove. To a certain extent this is still so today, especially among older weavers. The personification of textiles is activated by the weaver through construction. From a traditional weaver's point of view, the act of weaving and the whole process of preparation and laboring is exhilarating. To a Navajo, weaving is an act of love and desire—desire in the sense of wanting and longing. A margin of weavers do weave out of need. As a traditional weaver constructs a textile, she imbues it with part of herself through talking, singing, and/or praying as she weaves.

By singing, praying, and talking, weavers complete the process of personification, just as the Diyin Dine'é, "Holy People," thought, sang, and prayed the world into existence at the rim of the place of emergence.[4] Traditional Navajo weavers give life to their weavings through the weaver's actions, the weaving fork, the batten, the spindle, the prayers, the songs, and the dialogues.

Throughout this essay, Navajo weaving will be referred to the majority of the time as *dah'iistł'ó*, which is the appropriate term for weaving in the abstract. In Navajo discourse, dah'iistł'ó is a verb referring to the process of integrating the warp and weft in the art of weaving on a set-up loom. The word does not change even when the weaving is completed and removed from the loom. The term dah'iistł'ó applies during the full life of the dah'iistł'ó.[5]

"Sacredness begins at the tip of our tongues and we are to be careful when speaking. We are told, we create our world around ourselves with our words."[6] Certain words in the Navajo language are considered to be more powerful than others, especially if they are part of songs and prayers. In this particular case, weaving songs and prayers used by weavers influence the process of weaving. Words of power used in songs and prayers are not part of "day-to-day" conversation.[7] Navajo oral history, particularly the Creation stories, teach Navajo people that as speech is a manifestation of thought, it is inherently powerful. Tradition teaches that the combined powers of thoughts and words were used to construct the reality of Navajo life.

The title of this chapter, Shił Yóółt'ooł, "it is weaving me with it," is a line in one of the weaving songs my grandmother told me, a song inherited from her grandmother. My great-great-grandmother, T'aadezbáh, passed on in 1959, when I was a small child. I recall being by her side as she was dying in her small hogan, the traditional Navajo home. The only other recollection I have of her was her funeral service. T'aadezbáh taught my grandmother most of the weaving stories with which she was familiar, but only a handful of songs. When my grandmother recalled one particular weaving song, the verse "shił yóół-t'ooł" was repeated forty-eight times. Each time I questioned her about the weaving songs and stories, she cried out of gladness that one of her grandchildren yearned for such knowledge. There are many weaving songs. I personally know of twenty-four separate weaving songs, which are differentiated according to specialization—sash weaving, basket weaving, loom weaving, and so forth.[8] According to my grandmother, my great-great-grand-

mother knew sixteen of them. Between my grandmother and me, we know even fewer than that.

I still vividly remember hearing throughout my childhood the thumping sound of my mother's and grandmother's weaving forks as they wove. Weaving was a routine activity for them. The weaving fork produces rhythmic sounds that bring me home to my family and relatives in New Mexico, no matter where I am. The sounds made by the weaving fork are equivalent to the drumbeats heard at any urban or reservation powwow. There, it is often said, "The drumbeat is the heartbeat of Mother Earth." Here, I say the sound of the weaving fork at the loom is the heartbeat of the dah'iistł'ó. I first heard this sound in my grandmother's home. Now, I hear the same heartbeat in my own home.

My maternal grandmother was taught how to weave by her grandmother. My grandmother lost her mother when she was an infant, so her grandmother raised her. My grandmother in turn taught my mother how to weave. In addition, my mother learned various methods of weaving by observing different weavers. More than a decade ago, my mother and grandmother began to teach me how to weave. They agreed to teach me in order to carry on the tradition of weaving in our family, and only after they found no one else near their homes who wanted to learn.[9] Even with that length of time and experience in weaving, I still feel uncomfortable identifying myself as a weaver,[10] as I am only partly aware of the knowledge, powers, and ambiguities associated with traditional Navajo weaving. My discomfort derives from my lack of knowledge of weaving songs and prayers, the fundamental source of Navajo cultural power. Since I do not have full knowledge of the cultural power, I have to maintain a certain distance from the realm of traditional Navajo weaving subjects, for the sake of my "soft mind." As my grandmother says, "Your mind and thoughts are soft. You need constant protection from outside forces."[11] All Navajo people are considered to have soft minds until they obtain a certain level of cultural knowledge or awareness. Navajo cultural knowledge lends protection.

Over the last decade, due to her age and the limitations of her eyesight, my grandmother has given up most of her work, including weaving and some of her matriarchal duties. The duties are in transition and slowly, over the past five years, most have been inherited by my mother. Unknowingly, I was evaluated by my grandmother every summer when I was home. The "tests" included determining my continued interest and commitment to weaving, in learning more weaving stories, and in improving my weaving techniques. During the early summer of 1993, I formally inherited some of my maternal grandmother's weaving tools and her loom. The weaving tools were evenly divided between my mother and me, since we are the only weavers in my family. My mother was given the weaving finishing tools, and I, the "starting" tools, because I am still a beginner.

After a decade, my grandmother saw I was fit, responsible, and mature enough to have her weaving tools and carry on her art. Since receiving the gift of my grandmother, and departed grandmothers, I have repeatedly embraced her desire. I use the term "desire" here to refer to a continuous craving and longing for weaving to continue endlessly for me. My days are filled with thinking of combining new colors. I look outward on my daily life and its activities, and they invoke new ideas and designs. I act upon those designs when I sit at the loom.

My matrilineal and patrilineal grandfathers were instrumental in the construction of my weaving loom and some of my tools. Although not weavers themselves, my grandfathers taught me songs and prayers associated with weaving. They taught me how Spider Woman and Spider Man constructed the first loom in the third underworld, as well as many other weaving stories. These stories or parables explain the construction of my loom and tools as a metaphor for teaching, and tell why they are needed by the Navajo people. The tools are our mothers, since they provide for us—the creation of blankets provides warmth for our bodies. Such stories are shared at every stage of a weaver's development.

Figure 12

Beeldléí (blanket), 1865–70.
Handspun wool, raveled and commercial yarn,
110.9 × 72.6 cm. (23.922)

Through the actual construction of the loom and the process of weaving, I learned about one form of Navajo spirituality. A weaver must have clear and positive thoughts while weaving, thereby creating a "sacred space" around the loom.[12] Negative thoughts or bad words are not to be spoken near the loom and most definitely not while it is in use. My mother reminds me that the loom and the dah'iistł'ó will hear me, should I express such thoughts or words. My grandmother constantly tells me that my weaving tools are my defenders, my weapons against hunger or any form of "hard times." They are never to be used as weapons to cause physical harm to a human or animal because weaving tools provide for and protect life. They are nurturing tools, mothers.

The power, strength, and endurance of Spider Woman are ever-present in the weaving tools and in the community that surrounds the weaver. As a potential weaver, I am repeatedly told never to lose or put aside my weaving tools for any length of time; to do so would be to risk losing part of myself and jeopardizing my identity as a Navajo person, especially my identity as a weaver. The process of weaving is communal rather than individualistic. It involves more than the weaver. Family members play a continuous part in weaving. It is literally a "family affair." The wool and mohair used to make warp and weft come from sheep and goats maintained by the family members, some of whom are sheepherders. Children of all ages help gather plants and vegetables for dyes; siblings help process the wool and mohair in various phases of preparation. Numerous acts by family members are invested in the whole process of weaving, not only the acts of the weaver. It is not possible for a weaver alone to produce a dah'-iistł'ó. Weaving teaches me that these elements are incorporated into the continuum of Navajo life. Just as weaving has many parts—tools, wool, loom—life has many parts.

In the academic world, especially in anthropology and similar disciplines, there is a constant need to determine how "other" people construct their ideas of "personhood" or "selfhood." This profound curiosity stems from the apparent lack of a sense of "wholeness" or "completeness"

in some Euroamerican cultures: academicians are preoccupied with finding the most minute parts of themselves through various explorations, for example, in studies of the structure of DNA. The process of "seeking the part of a whole" is the preoccupation.[13] In Navajo culture, however, a sense of "wholeness" or holism is primary.[14] Countless parts and functions in the structure of Navajo culture make up the whole. For example, as mentioned before, various people play different parts in the process of weaving, and the weaver employs many tools. All these people and things play an important role in completing or maintaining the "whole." Traditional Navajo weavers create wholeness from multiple parts—wool, mohair, the manipulation of tools, and human labor. The Navajo world view emphasizes experience and performance over abstract theory.

In Navajo culture, theories are of marginal interest because they do not have life forces, be'iina. An entity of any form has to have be'iina. It is imbued with be'iina through the process of creation. Theories are considered to "have no life of their own" and, therefore, can not make any valuable contribution to the lives lived by traditional Navajo people. To be beneficial, thinking must be brought to life. It is given life through overlap with empirical concepts that make thoughts absolute and real. They become tangible. Entities of all forms and shapes need be'iina. Thoughts and plans become real when coupled with speech, song, prayer, or action.[15] When an idea is introduced in a Navajo family it is discussed very little. If it is not feasible, it is merely dismissed. If it is strong and has the attention of family members, it is reinforced and discussed further. Before it is lost in the midst of discussion, an idea is given a "life" that is viable and can be acted upon. In the case of a dah'iistł'ó, it is given be'iina through songs and prayers by the weaver. This allegiance of "idea" (creation) and "enacting" (labor) is experienced daily by traditional Navajo weavers.

My grandmother tells me that "a song was initiated when the weft was laid first at the lower right corner and the weaver continued weaving until the song was completed. When you begin to weave always start from the right, never from the left."[16] Today, and probably in the past, the use of weaving songs, prayers, and dialogue with dah'iistł'ó occurs on an individual level. Weavers use weaving songs and prayers in a dialogue with their dah'iistł'ó as one form of creation. Treatment and caring for their dah'iistł'ó is equated with nurturing human children. The three agents—songs, prayers, and dialogue—are intertwined and conveyed with maternal instincts and emotions. Care is needed in weaving, in order for the dah'iistł'ó to grow, just as care is needed for an infant's growth. As the warp is being set up onto the loom, it is addressed by the weaver as "my child." Desire and respect are created in the sacred space of the loom, to express and project these human emotions. An incomplete dah'iistł'ó is analogous to a child, insofar as it is considered immature and in need of care and nurturing. A dah'iistł'ó is not fully matured until it is finished. When it is completed, it is thought of as an adult, having responsibility for itself. In some ways, however, it will always remain a child of the weaver. The weaver and the dah'iistł'ó are considered to be an undivided self, and a completed dah'iistł'ó is further considered a reflection of self—a reflection of the weaver.

Not only are songs, prayers, and dialogue needed in the personification of weaving, which ones are used and how they are used varies from weaver to weaver and from region to region, as with any social practice. Songs are used for first setting up the loom, preparing and constructing the warp, and spinning; another song is used when the first weft of yarn is placed in the warp, and on through every step in the weaving process. Songs establish a pace and rhythm. Weavers usually sing softly to themselves or simply hum. Setting a pace and establishing a rhythm is said "to shorten the time spent weaving."[17] Confidence is enhanced by learning the songs and prayers, and helps the weaver's work. Moreover, knowledge of the songs and prayers enhances positive thoughts and actions toward weaving, family, kin, and Navajo culture.

The majority of the weaving songs were not and are not sung in public. Songs are not readily expressed or

Havasupai man wearing *diyogí*, 1907. Photographed and presented by F. S. Dellenbaugh. (P10731)

given to students of weaving. In a few rare cases, they are offered to apprenticing weavers. Many times, weaving songs and prayers are the domain of the weaver's immediate family and are not shared outside the family. Only a handful of weavers retain this knowledge and they are constantly asked to share their songs. It is unusual to hear of one weaver publicly sharing her or his knowledge, especially songs. Then again, everything does have a price.

At public events, such as conferences or ceremonial gatherings, Navajo people express their opinions. Speakers give themselves to listeners through their speeches, knowing they are protected by their songs and prayers. The protection offered by the songs and prayers allows speakers to expose their thoughts and voices, since "the speakers live in the public realm where chaos exists."[18] When children are first learning to ride a bicycle or roller-skate, we shield them in a shell of protection—a helmet, knee guards, elbow guards, and so forth. The shield for our thoughts is songs, prayers, and ceremonies. These protections provide immunity against those who wish to inflict harm—not only harm to us, but to others in the spiritual domain.

I can only theorize that a weaver's singing, praying, and having dialogues with her dah'iistł'ó derived from the time when our ancestors wore *biil*—woven dresses—like those shown in this book (see plates 8 and 23). In that time, the mid nineteenth century, the Navajo people were in a nearly constant state of war. Hunger and chaos prevailed. Songs and prayers were embodied in biil while they were being woven. In a similar way, other American Indians in the late 1800s used songs and prayers in constructing Ghost Dance shirts.[19] Through the process of weaving, weavers personified their biil to be their shields of protection. These invocations included requests that the biil be immune to arrows and bullets. Not only did weavers personify their woven dresses, but at the completion of the weaving, they wore them. Wearing or "existing within" a biil provided protection from hunger and various forms of chaos. The biil became the weaver. The human body in the biil represented the final and

complete personification of the biil. In this manner, the biil fulfills its purpose.

My mother and grandmother, and those before them, learned weaving differently from how I did. My mother and my grandmother began learning how to take care of the sheep and goats as young children. In their early years they learned how to shear sheep for wool and goats for mohair. In addition, they learned how to gauge the quality of wool and mohair. Weavers in my generation find it is much easier to obtain wool for weaving from stores. Moreover, wool is available in an array of different colors, some of which are quite astonishing; this was not true for my mother and grandmother. Weavers with twenty or more years of experience, like my mother, literally got their wool and mohair off the backs of sheep and goats. They not only did the shearing, they cleaned the wool by washing and rewashing it. Then they sun- or heat-dried it, which was done by placing the wet wool on the ground around the fire stove located at the center of the hogan. The idea of getting a variety of colored wool from one location was the farthest thing from their minds. Our mothers and grandmothers dyed their own wool, and carded and spun the wool by the light of kerosene lamps into the late hours of the night, just to arrive at the point where they could begin weaving. Carding and spinning were permitted to be done at night since they were preparatory stages, while weaving is in the final domain of creation. The next major task was to spin the mohair into strings, which would serve as the warp on the loom. Today this whole process has been eliminated from weaving in most regions of the Navajo Nation.[20] Shearing, cleaning, carding, and so forth are now considered too time-consuming.

However, it is important to note that through the process of shearing, of obtaining wool from a living being, personification was taking place: the sheep gave up its wool to be used by the weaver. Personification has always been part of Navajo culture, although, due to influences from the "outside," such personification is not obvious today. The elimination of these rituals and other technical aspects of weaving has led to weavers having a disorganized and divided sense of self. The division of self contributes to the lack of interest in continuing Navajo weaving, as it was learned and practiced by our parents, grandparents, and ancestors.

The weaver is the key person who empowers her or his dah'iistł'ó through singing the weaving songs or praying while she or he is actually weaving. Another form of empowerment is derived from having a dialogue with one's dah'iistł'ó while weaving. The technique, the weaver, and the weaving tools create a boundary of be'iina, or life.

It is said that dah'iistł'ó have be'iina. The weaver's task is to create the shell for the be'iina of dah'iistł'ó. The be'iina already exists; it is not created by the weaver. My grandmother says, "When your loom is set up with a dah'iistł'ó, you are never alone. Communicate with your dah'iistł'ó by talking to it." The be'iina of a dah'iistł'ó is the created one; the weaver is not the one who creates or designs her or his dah'iistł'ó. That is why it is said that the traditional Navajo weaver does not design her or his dah'-iistł'ó. The design is thought to exist on the loom at the conclusion of the initial construction of the dah'iistł'ó. The weaver simply acts upon it. The design is further projected into the weaver by the be'iina of the dah'iistł'ó. Many weavers have a desire or a need to create, because of the energy provided by the be'iina of the dah'iistł'ó.

Weavers have to be careful, however, because all things have limitations. Excessive creativity and designing with intricate details is living on the brink of chaos. In a Navajo traditional sense, this particular type of chaos is equated, at times, with greed. Only through the winter ceremony of the Ye'ii' Bichaii dance can this be corrected, by re-creating the normal world of the weaver.

Ceremonies, such as Hozhoo'ji, or Blessing Way, are conducted for weavers to pray for the continuity of their skills and materials (tools). Personal actions and cultural rules enhanced by weavers through other cultural practices further perpetuate weavers' skills and techniques. My

Figure 13

Diyogí (utility blanket), ca. 1870.
Handspun wool,
173 × 126.7 cm. (20.5584)

grandmother once instructed me, "When you come upon a precise-patterned spider web, you are to gently and delicately remove the web with your right hand and rub it into both of your hands."[21] I am to use my right hand, because that is the creative side of my body.[22] This act enables me to incorporate the energies of the spider into my being as a weaver. Moreover, it is suggested that this task be done in the early morning, after the Diyin Dine'é, Holy People, have passed through the spider web.

In the past, individual songs and prayers were available for each weaving tool, including those used in the preparation of the wool and throughout the process of weaving.[23] Each of the weaving tools has a place in the Navajo origin stories, especially the weaving fork or comb, the batten, and the spindle.[24] Weaving tools are made from various types of wood, which may vary due to their availability in different regions, or more often, according to the weaver's preference. Weaving tools are never stored separately or left alone in a closed container; they are always kept together. If they are not in one place, the weaver's thoughts may scatter.

Weaving tools are not used solely to create dah'iistł'ó; they have broader uses in various Navajo ceremonies. For example, the weaving fork is used in the *kinaaldá* ceremony, the girls' puberty ceremony, as a sign of femininity and industriousness. The use of the weaving tools to mold a girl during the ceremony conveys that she will become a fine weaver. At times, the batten is used in smoothing the sand for ceremonial sandpaintings. Furthermore, the weaving comb is often used as a gauge in the configuration of ceremonial sandpaintings or other designs associated with Navajo ceremonialism.

For many weavers, and for traditional Navajo people who tell origin stories, the weaving fork or comb is made of white shell.[25] The first such tool was made at the request of Spider Woman. Allegorically, this tool, which is used to pound the weft solid, functions in the role of the father and/or grandfather; the family members responsible for teaching Navajo children the meaning of life. As

each loose weft of yarn is laid through the warp, the weaver pounds it into its proper place in rapid repetitive motion. This is the heartbeat, the thumping sound, I have heard since childhood. Teachings are internalized, and we build experiences upon them. From experiences, we learn not only of ourselves, but also of our surroundings—our environment—and those with whom we share it. Each weft of yarn is an experience. The weaving fork secures and finds a place for each weft in between the stream of warp within the construct of the dah'iistł'ó. What we see with our eyes in a completed dah'iistł'ó is layers and layers of weft, one on top of another—an accumulation of experience.

The batten is said to be the "sun halo" by some, while other weavers say it is the sun. I say it is the sun because the sun is the core of the halo, and it is mobile. When the batten is inserted into the warp and angled, the sun is providing heat and light for the dah'iistł'ó to grow. With each weft of yarn laid, the sun is there to provide light and to oversee the growth of the child. When the batten is removed, the sun is no longer there. Among some weavers, the batten is never left in the warp, even un-angled, during the night, or when the weaver is not at the loom, because the dah'iistł'ó is entitled to rest during the night as much as other living beings.

The spindle, used to spin wool and mohair into yarn and warp strings, was constructed in the fourth world. It was initially called, *yodi yił nalwoł*, (turns with material goods).[26] The top or tip of the spindle is the center of the zenith; the bottom point is the nadir. The disk is the earth. Spider Woman instructed the female deity, referred to as Chief Medicine Woman, "You must spin towards your person, as you wish to have the beautiful goods come to you . . . or the beautiful goods will depart from you."[27]

In view of the "intimate" connection between a weaver and her or his dah'iistł'ó, how can Navajo weavers sell their dah'iistł'ó? What procedure or process does a long-time weaver experience in detaching from a dah'iistł'ó? What emotions are involved in the separation? Is it the same as saying goodbye to a human child who is moving away for the first time? How hard, confusing, and chaotic is it to give up one's protection? The protection is generated from the minds of the weavers—the thought processes interwoven into each biil and dah'iistł'ó. What accommodations do weavers make that enable them to separate a source of protection in exchange for tangible items or money? How was selling one's "thought" first negotiated by weavers?

My grandmother said, "It is only natural to experience the utmost need to find a good and safe home for one's child"[28] when a temporary separation is to occur. The same types of emotions are experienced by traditional Navajo weavers with their dah'iistł'ó when it is completed. At times, I would see and hear Navajo women cry, not out of sadness, but in celebration or happiness and a sense of reunion, when they recognized one of their dah'iistł'ó in a book or at someone's home or in a museum. Many times these weavers return to a museum or gallery periodically, if not often, to check up on their "children." Many older weavers keep photographs of their weavings, like photos of their own children. If the weavings are illustrated in a book or magazine, the weaver will have more than one copy of the publication. On a few occasions, I have seen elderly Navajo women have long dialogues with their dah'iistł'ó when the weavings were on display in galleries in Santa Fe and Phoenix. To people milling around them who are unaware that this dialogue is taking place, the conversation probably seems one-sided.

My maternal grandmother told me that there is an "ending song." This particular song was sung as the final weft was inserted at the conclusion of the final weave. It is a form of detachment. A finished dah'iistł'ó is seen as being similar to a human adult child who is separating— moving to another location to marry, begin a career, or go to school. At the completion of the weaving, the separation is acknowledged, both verbally and in thought. A message is conveyed to the child, or dah'iistł'ó that "he" or "she" is always part of the weaver, the self. This relationship

From left: Kenneth L. Yazzie, Keevin Lewis, Byron Benally, Neva Lee, Calvin Yazzie, Wesley Thomas, July 1995. Ned A. Hatathli Museum, Navajo Community College, Tsaile, Arizona. Photo by Katherine Fogden.

is never spiritually ended; therefore, the self remains undivided. Prayer is another form of comfort at separation. A prayer is said before the dah'iistł'ó leaves its "sacred space," just as is done when an adult child leaves a mother's home.[29]

The voice and words of a weaver, translated into print, through my fingers, on a keyboard, have addressed you, a possibility that was granted to me by my matrilineal kin. This is one of many ways to communicate. If I were sitting at my loom, I might have woven a weft instead—one layer onto another, not all the way across, but in parts. I experience life as such. One thread onto another, many in parts, weaving my own way through time, attempting to create a whole. The practices, beliefs, and traditions described here establish a sense of continuity with history. In the Navajo world, they form a whole that constructs and reconstructs cultural experience in an infinite cycle.

Figure 14

Diyogí (utility blanket) 1875–85.
Handspun wool,
171 × 116.5 cm. (24.7842)

ACKNOWLEDGMENTS

This chapter is dedicated to my weaving instructors, my maternal grandmother, Elizabeth Tom Yazzie, and my mother, Katherine K. Thomas, both of Mariano Lake, New Mexico, located in the southeast corner of the Navajo Nation.

Thanks to my mentors and committee members, Gary Witherspoon, Ph.D., who cautioned me from the outset to insist on my right to conduct research from my cultural perspective and to never lose connection with Navajo concepts and language; Sue-Ellen Jacobs, Ph.D., for constantly "pushing" me along and making me explore my curiosities; James D. Nason, Ph.D., for "simply" and continuously being there for me as I make each step, however small; and finally, K. Tsianina Lomawaima, Ph.D. (University of Arizona), a role model one could only attempt to emulate, for seeing my "potential" from the start, when I first returned to school in 1991.

Special thanks to Catharine Beyer at the English Writing Center, University of Washington, for continuing to teach me proper English writing mechanics, and for providing comments on previous drafts of this paper. Deep gratitude and thanks to Maureen Trudelle Schwarz, Ph.D., for her consistent support throughout my academic studies, instilling in me that I can finish my Ph.D., sharing much-needed criticism and, most of all, helping me through the awkwardness of writing English.

Back on Dine' Bi'keyah (Navajoland), *ahehee'* (thank you) to Robert A. Roessel, Ed.D., for saying "you have to tell the world about Navajo weaving as a weaver," when I gave this paper at the Navajo Studies Conference in Farmington, New Mexico; and to Harry Walters, Director of the Ned A. Hatathli Cultural Center at Navajo Community College, Tsaile, Arizona, for continuing to teach me the fine line between anthropology and Navajo culture.

Beeldléí Bäh Häne' (The Blanket Story)
Kalley Keams

Navajo weaving is a personal expression of life. It is an art form created by combining tangible materials with fibers of the soul. Each time a rug is completed, it is like a birth. I do not believe it was any different one hundred years ago. The same basic principles and thoughts inspired the paths to weaving a Navajo rug then, as now.

Weaving is a family affair. Each member of the family has a role in the weaving process. While a weaver works, someone has to bring in the sheep, shear the wool, feed the lambs, card and spin the wool, and finally, take the rug off the loom. Someone has to make the loom and tools. Someone has to generate the money to buy the weaving materials. If the weaver is elderly or without a vehicle, a family member has to provide transportation. No one is excluded, not even visiting relatives and friends.

My reasons for weaving differ from those of my grandmother and mother, but the values instilled in me by them remain the same. I still weave to fill a need in the family. In the past, weavers made blankets to be worn as clothing, for sleeping, and for everyday uses. Today, when I finish a rug, I sell or trade it to provide for my family. My rugs pay for food, college tuition, ceremonial and medical expenses, and the mortgage. These reasons are very similar to the reasons why rugs were made one hundred years ago.

The persistence of Navajo weaving is perpetuated by the process of weaving, which remains unchanged. A weaver might create a rug with a computer-generated design, but it is woven with the same techniques as that of the grandmothers. My mother and I shear the wool, and we card, spin, and dye it as my grandmother did. The

Bessie Lee, June 1995. Ned A. Hatathli Museum, Navajo Community College, Tsaile, Arizona. Photo by Monty Roessel.

44

weaving materials are different, the designs are always changing, the colors are more abundant, but the principles and techniques of weaving in the Navajo way continue unchanged. This simple yet significant lesson is handed down from one weaver to the next.

Beyond the tangible form of a Navajo rug lies the soul of the weaver. This personal side eludes most collectors of Navajo rugs. For many of us, a blessing ceremony is necessary to continue weaving. There are stories, songs, and prayers linked to all aspects of weaving. I was told that the loom is like a child, that my tools are an extension of me, that the weft strings are part of my life, and that the warp is the foundation of my soul. I was taught not to pass objects through any loom, not to leave the batten unattended, not to weave at night or while pregnant. Like my grandmother instructed, my weaving area is neatly kept to keep my mind clear and balanced. "Rules" like these, used to maintain harmony in weaving, are observed in traditional weaving homes.

Every time I look at an old or new rug, I feel a kinship toward it. To my family, these rugs encompass our people's stories. They help us connect to the grandmothers who gave us this extraordinary gift of communication. My daughter and I enjoy visiting museums to see their collections of "Grandmother's rugs."

These old blankets can empower our children with pride and self respect to help them face the two worlds they must live in. The rugs can be used to eliminate cultural and generation gaps. I believe nimble weaving fingers and the need for artistic self-expression will keep our weaving culture alive and growing.

Women weaving under summer shade, 1907. Tuba City, Arizona. Churchill Collection. (N26609)

"MORE OF SURVIVAL THAN AN ART"

Comparing Late Nineteenth- and
Late Twentieth-Century Lifeways and Weaving

Ann Lane Hedlund

You can't find any information about the artists [back then] because back in the old [days], it
was more of survival than an art. In fact, that is what it was—it was clothing. When the trader
was impressed enough with a [blanket] he would buy and that was used for trade. There was no
money exchanged and it was a trading thing for survival, for food. And, of course, it was used—
a blanket in the doorway, a blanket to sleep with, a blanket to wear.

—*Kezbah Weidner, 1990*[1]

How do the lives of Navajo weavers in the late nineteenth century compare with those of weavers today? Would a blanket weaver of the 1860s recognize connections between herself and a rug weaver of the 1960s? And conversely, what links do modern weavers make when they look at the work and lives of their ancestors? By combining both historic and modern viewpoints, what can we learn of the place of weaving in Navajo lives, then and now?[2]

First, the diversity of weavers' approaches makes it difficult to generalize about a group of creative people whose cultural values have always stressed individual autonomy. Despite many outward changes in Navajo lives, the most important Navajo values have remained substantially the same over the last century. Indeed, weaving embodies and serves to preserve a complex set of values linked with the land and livestock, families and spirituality. It represents a proper way to make a living or, putting it more exactly, to live. Weavers continue to be patient and self-reliant, using sheep's wool and native plants; caring for their families, homes, and herds as they work at their looms; and remembering sacred stories, prayers, and songs that "go with the weaving."

From 1860 into the 1890s Navajo woven products and their marketing changed significantly, evolving from wearing blankets to floor rugs, and from Native use and intertribal trade to a national market. One hundred years later, from the 1960s to the 1990s, Navajo weaving made equally dramatic transformations—from anonymous floor rugs known by regional style names to wall hangings associated with individual artists and from local trading posts to a global market.[3] Through a series of historical sketches we can explore two times of dramatic flux, a century apart.

The reason for selecting these two periods, 1860–90 and 1960–90, lies in both their similarities and their differences. Practically speaking, the mid to late nineteenth century is the earliest time from which complete Navajo textiles survive (some excellent examples from the NMAI collection are presented in this volume). Moreover, the decades of both 1860 and 1960 were political watersheds. The American government established the original Navajo reservation boundaries in the 1860s. The Navajo government asserted itself and moved toward sovereignty (in principle if not in actual practice) in the 1960s, even as Navajo lifestyles joined mainstream America. In the late 1800s weavers responded to influences that stemmed from incursions of the U.S. Army, the railroad, new settlers, and trading posts. Today, weavers work with community schools, museums, and art galleries and feel the rapid pace of life in the Information Age.

In Navajo culture, then and now, women are the principal weavers, spinners, and dyers.[4] Weaving is passed down through the generations on the woman's side of the family. Women, in their roles as mothers and grandmothers, are culture bearers and embody important cultural continuities. This essay, therefore, focuses on women's lifeways and those family and household activities that reveal individual choices and concerns.

Where do we turn for firsthand accounts about women weavers? We are confronted with a challenge in pursuing Navajo women's stories, because sources for information are limited in number and in the extent of their coverage. Most southwestern history, based upon Euroamerican male-oriented accounts of strategic events, contains only broad generalizations about daily life, and less about women, their roles, and their perspectives. Original observations, travelers' notes, government reports, translations from Spanish to English, and subsequent interpretations are all constructed predominantly by men. The pronouns used both in Spanish and English are almost always the third-person plural forms—"ellos" and "they"—that obscure indications of gender. Nevertheless, some sources are worth scouring. Early Spanish documents provide sketches of early Navajo lifeways. Personal accounts from Anglo-American travelers occasionally provide glimpses into weavers' lives. Reports from military personnel stationed in Indian Territory comment on the Southwest scene.[5] Franciscan Father Berard Haile's *Ethnologic Dictionary of the Navajo Language* (1910) is an exceptional work, the earliest that preserves everyday linguistic information as reported by Native people. More recent biographies and a few autobiographies shed light on earlier times through reminiscences and stories shared among generations,[6] and reports by southwestern anthropologists describe Navajo household activities and compare the past and present. Few firsthand accounts by Navajos themselves have been published;[7] reminiscences by Tiana Bighorse and Son of Old Man Hat and those collected by Ruth Roessel (1973) are remarkable exceptions.

From such accounts, we can learn about major events and trends, such as the growth of trading posts and the evolution of a cash economy on the reservation. We can also reconstruct the historical development of textiles from wearing blankets to floor rugs and wall hangings.

Tragically, weavers' attitudes and desires, their ways of perceiving and categorizing, were rarely documented in the nineteenth century.

Caution must be used when reading descriptions about the late twentieth century as well, for naturally, biases arise regarding culture and gender. Fortunately we have essays relating Navajo perspectives written by individuals such as Ruth Roessel and Harry Walters. Luci Tapahanso[8] adds a poet's personal views of her own childhood and her elders' teachings. Publications of the Rough Rock Demonstration School, Navajo Community College, and the Navajo Tribe discuss historical and cultural issues. Many articles authored by Navajos are built upon earlier Euroamerican work, but their unique value emerges when the authors express personal points of view and draw upon knowledge held by Navajo elders. Most importantly, women working at their looms today carry memories of their elders' stories and continue the craft of weaving. Much of this knowledge is held privately and shared within family circles.

Many weavers' statements quoted were gathered during interviews that were conducted by me on and around the Navajo reservation since 1978. As a museum curator, anthropologist, and former tribal employee, I have worked with families and individuals from many parts of the reservation and neighboring areas. I have learned the most through participant observation, the classic method of interacting with people in their homes and workplaces on a daily basis. Some of my research involves viewing photographs of blankets with weavers in order to understand their perceptions, co-curating exhibitions with Native weavers, and participating in conferences that have brought together weavers, scholars, collectors, and dealers. I make no pretense to speak *for* the Navajo women with whom I have worked. As an Anglo ethnographer, I can only speak *about* them, describing their lives as I see and interpret them, and citing their own words to amplify and personalize my observations about their lives.

The Navajos are an Athapaskan-speaking people related to the Apaches and to northern Athapaskan Indians living in Canada and Alaska. Through a complex narrative, many Navajos locate their origin in a series of four (or more) worlds that conclude in their ultimate southwestern homeland. Before humans walked the earth, animal and insect people interacted with influential supernatural beings. Structure and reason, harmony and balance, slowly emerged from a disordered and confused existence.[9] Archaeologists theorize that Navajo and Apache people may have entered the Southwest sometime during the 1400s, after a lengthy migration from the north. The Navajos found Pueblo Indians settled throughout the area and made their own homes in present-day northwestern New Mexico. From the earliest times they hunted, gathered wild foods, farmed, and worked animal hides for clothing and accessories. Little is known about their early social relations or family structure, although Navajo narratives suggest that women played a strong role as community advisors and family leaders.

As they settled in parts of northern New Mexico and, eventually, northern Arizona, Navajos adapted many Puebloan practices, including dry farming and loom weaving. Many Anglo scholars believe that other traits, such as the female-centered social structure and the system of clans, and certain religious rituals and narratives—including stories about Spider Woman, who brought weaving to the first Navajo people—may have derived from Pueblo sources as well. Sixteenth- and seventeenth-century Spanish observers reported that Navajos alternated between their cornfields and more distant hunting grounds and actively traded meat, hides, and mineral products with the Pueblo Indians.[10] Most activities described—hunting, leadership by headmen, warfare—were presumably male-oriented; women's roles in homemaking, working hides, and trading were rarely detailed.

Woman and children outside of hogan. The David C. Vernon Collection, presented by Laurance S. Rockefeller. (P21237)

Pueblos—Zuni, and perhaps Jemez and Tesuque—where Native women may have been the principal weavers.[13] Alternatively, Navajo women may have learned from Pueblo men through crosscultural marriages or possibly through intertribal exchange as servants. However weaving knowledge was transmitted, Navajo women pursued weaving vigorously throughout the next centuries.

For practical purposes, nineteenth-century Navajo history can be divided into three periods. Historically, we may distinguish the time before Navajos went to Bosque Redondo (pre-1864); the Bosque Redondo Period (1864–68), when Navajos were interned at Fort Sumner, New Mexico; and the Early Reservation Period (1868–1900), following the creation of Navajo reservation boundaries. Blanket weavers were directly influenced by such historic movements; their work changed with the times even as it retained certain ties to the past. Thus, parallel but somewhat broader divisions are useful when discussing Navajo weaving history: the Classic Period (pre-1865), the Transition Period (1865–95), and the Rug Period (since 1895).[14]

What *were* the women doing? In the small, widespread rancherias that the Spaniards described, women were most likely raising their families, clothing them, socializing them, and playing a considerable role in the evolution of Navajo culture. Some families practiced polygamy.[11] In most households, it is likely that several generations of women from the same family shared household tasks.

Proficient Navajo weavers must have been working at their looms by 1650, judging by a Spanish report issued in 1706 that Navajo blankets were already highly valued and widely traded.[12] The earliest Navajo weaving, which remains as archaeological fragments dating to the 1700s and early 1800s, shows technical and design features that suggest Navajos borrowed and adapted the craft from Pueblo sources. Based on isolated Spanish reports, it is assumed that men were the weavers in most of the Pueblos, including those known on the Hopi mesas. Navajos, however, may have learned from one of the few

LATE NINETEENTH-CENTURY LIFEWAYS AND WEAVING

By the nineteenth century, Navajo culture was well established in the Southwest and continued to reflect the Navajos' northern Athapaskan origins, as well as the influences of neighboring Pueblo, Mexican, and Spanish-American groups.[15] In addition to farming on a small scale, herding and raiding became common pursuits as Navajo families acquired growing numbers of sheep, goats, horses, and cattle. Much of Navajo culture, materially and ideologically, revolved around the importance of these animals.[16]

Navajo families lived in scattered clusters of one-room houses surrounded by smaller sweatbath houses, sheep corrals, and summer ramadas made of poles and brush. Several different styles of houses, all called hogans, were constructed—the forked-pole, rock-ring, and five- or six-sided log hogans. All usually had entrances facing east, toward the morning sun. Special ceremonial hogans and "dance grounds ringed with brush" were also built.[17]

Before the establishment of the centralized tribal government of the twentieth century, Navajo leadership operated on a regional level, with headmen governing small, localized groups.[18] Their female relatives undoubtedly contributed actively to community government. As Mary Shepardson describes, "Men were the leaders in public decision-making, but women were consulted. Men were . . . the mediators in disputes. . . . However, even these areas were not completely closed to women."[19] Juanita, the wife of Navajo leader and spokesman Manuelito, accompanied a Navajo delegation to Washington in 1874. Given the preference of Euroamerican males to interact with Navajo men rather than women, it is difficult to tell to what extent women's political roles in the tribe were suppressed or not reported in early records.

Navajo society was, and remains, predominantly matriarchal, with women making decisions in most Navajo households. Domestic responsibilities were loosely divided by gender and age, with men and women pitching in to complete a job. Daily activities for most women were defined by their domestic roles as grandmother, mother, wife, and daughter. They prepared food, reared children, hauled water and firewood, herded livestock, and farmed. Making blankets, baskets, and pottery was women's work, while hunting, preparing the fields, and making saddles were men's duties.[20]

Women held relatively high status within their families and their communities during the mid nineteenth century. An army surgeon reported in 1846, "The women of this tribe seem to have equal rights with the men, managing their own business and trading as they see fit, saddling their own horses, and letting their husbands saddle theirs."[21] Ten years later he noted that women wielded considerable influence both inside and outside the home because they controlled the children, the homes, and the herds.[22] During the same time period, David Meriwether observed,

The Navaho tribe of Indians differ in some respects from any I have seen. They treat their women with more respect than any other Indians, are more cleanly in their appearance, and the women hold property separate from their husbands. All the sheep and wool belong to the women, and you can't buy either from any man in the tribe.[23]

Navajo society was, and is, organized into dozens of clans, each with a distinctive name (for instance, the Bitter Water, Towering House, and Many Goats Clans) and a distinct cultural history. Even today, belonging to one of these clans defines many social relations for a Navajo person and provides a network for social and economic support. Each person is born into his or her mother's clan and is said to be "born for" the father's clan. One should marry outside the mother's clan and any other clans said to be related to it.

Not all families were equally situated: they varied widely in their wealth and relative status, which was gauged principally on the number of sheep and horses owned. Although not locked into a rigid system, well-to-do families with much livestock—often called by the Spanish term *ricos* (rich)—commanded more respect and power within a community. Those of lower circumstances, the *pobres* (poor), often worked for their wealthier neighbors and relatives.[24]

By the 1800s, women worked at their looms either inside their one-roomed homes or, in good weather, outdoors under a shady arbor. No evidence in the early records indicates that weaving was a restricted or specialized activity; in fact, it was probably practiced by most, if not all, women. As with other elements of Navajo culture, weaving passed from grandmother to mother to daughter, in matrilineal fashion. Weavers belonging to the same clan and living near each other would have given technical advice and aid. To some extent designs and materials may have been shared among family and clan members. An integral part of daily life, weaving served to clothe the family, provide bedding and horse blankets, and produce items for barter. It must also have represented considerable understanding of proper Navajo behavior and beliefs, women's roles, and work ethics. In contrast, midwivery, ritual consultation, political decision-making, and other specialized activities were supplementary tasks that required special knowledge possessed by relatively few women.

Navajo clothing changed dramatically during the late nineteenth century. In the mid-1850s, men still wore animal hide as well as wool garments. As one Fort Defiance surgeon recorded in 1855:

> Some [men] wear short breeches of brownish-colored buckskin, or red baize, buttoned at the knee, and leggings of the same material. A small blanket, or a piece of red baize with a hole in it, through which the head is thrust, extends a short distance below the small of the back, and covers the abdomen in front, the sides being partially sewed together and a strip of red cloth attached to the blanket or baize, where it covers the shoulder, forms the sleeve, the whole serving the purpose of a coat. Over all is thrown a blanket, under and sometimes over which is worn a belt, to which are attached oval pieces of silver plain or variously wrought. . . . The men, as a rule, make their own clothes. These articles constitute the only covering, together with the breech-cloth and moccasins, that are used. Many are seen who wear nothing but a blanket, and some in summer, nothing but the breech-cloth, and we have seen some with no covering but moccasins and a cotton shirt, which the mercury was below zero. . . . The [women] wear a blanket fastened about the waist, and sewed up the sides for a skirt. The front and back parts being attached over either shoulder, a covering is obtained for the front and back portions of the body. The skirt comes down below the knee, about half way to the ankle, the leg being well wrapped in uncolored buckskin. . . .[25]

The wide range in quality of wearing blankets made from the 1860s through the 1880s, including coarse striped blankets (see plate 36), fancy sarapes (see plate 31), and refined chief blankets (see plate 18), suggests that weavers with varied abilities and backgrounds were aware of functional differences in the textiles and social differences in the wearer's status. Most likely local male and female leaders wore higher-quality blankets and *biil* (two-piece dresses; see plate 8) with fancier designs than did *pobres* and servants.

A modified form of slavery—holding lifelong family servants—was an integral part of the Southwest's social system during the nineteenth century.[26] Well-to-do Navajo, Spanish, and Anglo families acquired Indian servants by "taking captives during raids, trading with Indian tribes for them, adopting orphaned Indian children or those placed by their parents who felt they could no longer care for them."[27] Many servants became Christianized and intermarried with the families who took them in.

Navajo servant girls and women helped with the shearing, carding, spinning, dyeing, and weaving of blankets for local family use. Although assimilated into their adoptive society to a considerable degree, these individuals left a legacy of documented "servant blankets" that combine Navajo and Hispanic traits.[28] Some were woven with uncut selvages on Navajo upright looms, yet the Hispanic influence is evident in the color choices and subtle changes of yarn. Others were created on Hispanic floor looms, which resulted in cut warp selvages, and incorporated Navajo designs such as crosses and stepped diamonds and triangles. A blanket in the NMAI collection (fig. 16) contains serrated motifs, pastel dyes, cut-warp fringe, and simple side selvages that suggest Hispanic influences, yet the single-ply warps and the spacing and firm texture of the weave are both Navajo in style. Originally catalogued as a "slave blanket," it may well have been woven by a Navajo woman living in a Hispanic household in New Mexico.[29]

In addition to local consumption, the Navajos traded their homegrown and handmade goods with neighboring Indian tribes. By at least 1706, Navajo basketry, leather, and woven fabrics of wool and cotton were bartered with the Pueblos and Spanish for other goods.[30] In the early 1800s Navajo blankets were a popular trade item among

Plains Indians. Some exchanges occurred in areas where the Navajo lived, but Navajo families also traveled to regional trade fairs.[31]

While Navajo women were responsible for making the textiles that Pueblo, Plains, and Spanish peoples wanted, were they involved in the actual trading? Historic documentation does not mention gender divisions of labor in this regard. Certainly most Spanish and Anglo buyers were men, and perhaps they preferred to deal with Navajo men rather than women. Most reports suggest that women stayed at home weaving, while men went on trading trips, just as they also conducted raids and hunts, but it is difficult to know.

Traditionally, each Navajo was responsible for his or her own business affairs. Women often owned land and livestock. Those early itinerant traders who visited Navajo camps to make deals most likely had opportunities to negotiate directly with women for their woven goods. Records of trading and visits between Navajo and Pueblo families attest to women's involvement at a social level at the very least.[32] Families participated in large regional trade fairs with the Plains tribes (the Comanche trade fair at Pecos Pueblo in 1786 is an early example). And entire families occasionally represented Navajo culture at major expositions, such as the Chicago Columbian Exposition in 1893.[33] Certainly by the early 1900s, when trading posts were well established, women took charge of marketing their own blankets and rugs.[34] Thus it is questionable whether men dominated even the early trading days, especially when blankets woven by women and from the wool of female-owned sheep were involved.

In 1864, in an effort to end the frequent conflicts between the Navajo and recent settlers to the Southwest, the U.S. government forced thousands of Navajo men, women, and children to leave their homes, fields, and flocks, and to move on foot and horseback to eastern New Mexico. The Long Walk—over three hundred miles by foot, on horseback, and in wagons—terminated in the 1864–68 internment of Navajos at Fort Sumner, known as Bosque Redondo in Spanish and Hwééldi in Navajo.

While there, more than 2,500 people died from smallpox and other diseases, exposure, and starvation; others suffered extreme homesickness and depression. Lives were indelibly altered, as Robert Roessel notes:

> Nothing in heaven or earth could have been more terrifying and traumatic to the Navajo than the experience of the Long Walk. They were a free people who lived in their own country with its sacred mountains and familiar landmarks. They were people who were independent and self-sufficient: a people who had a way of life that was satisfying and meaningful. They were people who related to Navajoland in a spiritual manner since it was given and made safe for them by the Holy People. To be forced to leave their beloved land with its sacred mountains and shrines, and to cross three rivers, all of which their traditions warned them never to do, was to subject the Navajo to unparalleled anguish and heartache. When this anguish and heartache is combined with the unequaled physical suffering experienced at Fort Sumner, a faint glimpse of the impact this tragedy had, and continues to have, for the Navajo may be realized.[35]

At Hwééldi, the Navajo were forcibly introduced to white people's ways, with their different clothing, foods, and tools, and strange customs and concepts. Once again, although the historical events and economic issues concerning the Navajos' stay at Bosque Redondo are well-documented, little is known of individuals and families, and even less about women and children.

During the 1860s, commercial cotton cloth began to replace hide and handwoven fabrics. With newly acquired sewing skills, women adapted the long-sleeved tailored blouse and full, gathered skirt derived from Victorian fashion in Europe and America. Men shifted from hide breeches to short cotton trousers, usually slit up the legs for increased movement. Blankets worn wrapped around the shoulders remained very important for both women and men. By the 1880s, however, handwoven sarapes were more often replaced by commercial blankets woven by Oregon's Pendleton Mills and other manufacturers.

Seated group, several individuals wearing commercial blankets, 1903. Keams Canyon, Arizona. Churchill Collection. (N26600)

Hard-soled shoes gradually supplanted moccasins. Prominent silver ornaments and jewelry—rings, bracelets, buttons, brooches, necklaces, and belts—became a sign of the wearer's wealth.

Histories passed down in families and recounted in later autobiographies provide the richest descriptions of daily life during the 1860s.[36] Several books, ironically all focusing on male protagonists, provide insight into women's lives during this stressful period, yet none describes weaving as any more than a background activity that women performed to benefit their families. All emphasize the persistence and resourcefulness of Navajo women in the face of extreme hardships; their roles as culture bearers prevail over all the changes wrought by the Long Walk.[37]

The stories of Gus Bighorse, recounted by his daughter Tiana Bighorse, illustrate Navajo life and values during this period. Through Chief Manuelito's messengers, reports of life at Bosque Redondo reached Bighorse and other

Navajos who had escaped to Canyon de Chelly. "The Navajo are like slaves to the soldiers. Build houses, chop wood—whatever chores they want them to do, the people just have to do it. The soldiers just live in those houses. But the Navajos have to live outside in the cold, in the holes in the ground."[38] He remembers meager food and water supplies, Navajo solidarity and prayerfulness, and intertribal hostilities. "They don't have no blankets. All they have to sleep with is gunnysacks."[39]

It is remarkable in all respects that, during this disruptive period in Navajo history, women wove many of the striking blankets that appear here and in museums worldwide. Despite hardships, weaving during the Bosque Redondo period advanced the earlier garment-making tradition and the blanket trade.[40] Even though dispirited by the loss of home and relatives, women set up looms and created blankets of strength and beauty. Blankets were woven with yarns raveled from government-issued wool fabrics and with commercial wool and cotton yarns, as well as with handspun sheep's wool. Weavers added serrate diamonds and other patterns borrowed from Mexican and Hispanic-American blankets to the earlier striped and stepped designs.

Army personnel often acquired Navajo blankets (many came directly from Hwééldi) and returned home with these handwoven souvenirs, some of which eventually made their way into museum collections. A weaver named Paulonia and her husband were not sent to Fort Sumner, but instead were detained at Fort Wingate by Lieutenant Colonel Chavez, so that she could weave blankets for him there.[41] Weavers were reportedly working for Maj. J. V. Laudervale at Fort Wingate in 1875.[42]

The forced relocation to Bosque Redondo failed. Gus Bighorse recalls his feelings, when he learned that the survivors were returning to Navajo country.

Our people are released from a land they never will call theirs. They will never forget what happened to half of their people in front of their very eyes. They had

handmade, all-natural goods, while Native artists drew on crafts traditions and explored new forms and media. By the 1990s Indian weaving and jewelrymaking, as well as potterymaking, basketry, beadwork, and painting, composed vital sectors of the international art market. Today, Germany, Belgium, France, and Japan are important consumers of Indian art, including Navajo rugs and tapestries.

Between 1868 and 1960 the Navajo population expanded almost nine-fold, from an estimated 9,000 people in 1868 to 79,587 in the 1960 census.[56] Since 1960, the population has nearly tripled to an estimated 233,000 people.[57] Meanwhile, the landbase has grown to encompass 17.2 million acres (nearly 7 million hectares).[58]

Navajo political life has also changed dramatically over the past century. The Navajo Nation, with its capitol in Window Rock, Arizona, is now an enormous bureaucracy with numerous departments and enterprises, thousands of employees, and a budget exceeding $29 million. It is divided into 109 chapters, each with an elected representative who is a member of the Tribal Council. Similar to community centers, chapter houses within each chapter sponsor community programs that range from administering grazing permits to providing childcare and nutritional meals for the elderly.

In the 1970s, the tribal government established the Office for Navajo Women, indicating official as well as popular concern for women's roles in society, business, and government. Many Navajo women work to support their families (about one quarter of all Navajo families are headed by women without husbands). Primary responsibilities for the majority of women remain in the home, as they are the principal caretakers of children and the elderly in a household. Many women are landowners and stockholders, both of which confer considerable status. As community members, some women contribute actively to decision-making and command respect for their specialized cultural knowledge.

The matrilineal clan system is still honored in most parts of the Navajo Nation, but in many areas the large extended family no longer plays as central a role as it once

did in everyday life. More young people and couples choose to live apart from the extended family and seek support principally within a smaller nuclear family.[59] In contrast to the earlier pattern of widely separated households, many Navajos today live in reservation communities where homes, schools, clinics, stores, and other facilities are concentrated together. First clustered around trading posts in the early part of the century, these communities expanded as government services and commerce increased. In the 1970s, the Navajo government designated eight primary and a number of secondary "growth centers" across the Navajo Nation, each representing a focus for continuing major development.[60]

Despite the importance of the hogan, the most common main dwelling today is a simple one-story, two-room frame or stucco structure.[61] When they can afford it, or when the Navajo-Hopi Relocation Commission supplies them, many Navajo families live in modern multistory or split-level homes, often located within housing developments that supply utilities. Modular and mobile homes are increasingly common. Standing alongside these newer homes, hogans are frequently used for ceremonies or as secondary dwellings. Each year fewer families move with their sheep and other livestock to a separate summer camp, usually in the mountains where the cooler climate provides good grazing areas.

The oft-noted strength and status of women in contemporary Navajo society continues to derive from their centrality within the family and community. Navajo poet Luci Tapahanso writes that a mother is one's "home."[62] Ruth Roessel emphasizes the culture-bearing roles that women play. "We women are the heart and center of our society. If there is no teaching of Navajo life to our children there will be no future for the Navajo people."[63] As she reflects upon her own childhood, her schooldays, and becoming a woman in Navajo society, she credits strong female role models for her guidance. Acknowledging the respect and social standing that Navajo women have always enjoyed, she emphasizes present-day problems such as the loss of Navajo language and culture, alcoholism, abuse and

Figure 17

Rose Owens (1929–94), round rug, 1981.
Handspun wool, 109 cm. diam.
Gift of Gloria F. Ross. (25.637)

social diseases, jealousies, and other divisions that threaten Native lifeways. The search for personal and cultural identity, Roessel believes, succeeds when women integrate past strengths into their present-day lives.

Despite weaving's cultural importance, a smaller percentage of Navajo women weave now than ever before. Not every family has weavers, nor does every woman assume that she will weave, although many say they wish they had learned. Nevertheless, from the total population of almost a quarter million, perhaps over 20,000 women weave today. In addition, almost every reservation community seems to include at least one or two men or boys who weave.[64]

Individual circumstances, including a woman's level of education, the location of her home, and the number of children she has, play an important part in why and how a weaver works today. Some weave for money, for creative expression, for pride in their Native heritage, or because their mother and grandmother wove before them. Incentives of economics and cultural preservation are frequently combined. While the importance of each of these issues differs from individual to individual, four major overlapping orientations reflect Navajo weavers' essential motivations.

Household weavers are the most conservative group and weave because it fits into the traditional role of Navajo women as keepers of the household, fields, and flocks. These weavers work at home, usually where they watch their children, grandchildren, and the sheep and goat herds. Producing rugs that range from excellent to mediocre quality, household weavers make and sell a rug approximately every one or two months, providing a steady, if moderate, income to the family.

Professional weavers place their craft high among their priorities. They produce rugs of superior quality and may weave full-time. Their names are often well known in collecting circles, and they frequently keep waiting lists of prospective buyers. Their large rugs may take as long as a year or more to complete and may cost many thousands of dollars. These weavers occasionally attend conferences and are most often hired to demonstrate their work at museums and galleries.

Occasional weavers may have learned to weave in their youth but did not continue as they grew older, or they may have learned later in life but quit when other activities competed for attention. Earnings from their rugs are small but often much needed. Moreover, because Navajo culture recognizes thought as an active and creative element in life, tantamount to action, the fact that these individuals consider themselves to be weavers—because they know how to weave, regardless of how much or how well they actually weave—makes this group significant.

Revival weavers do not weave out of strong financial motivation, but because the craft is an integral part of Navajo heritage and is a marker of their ethnic identity. Only a few revival weavers keep their rugs or give them to family members to keep, but those who do acknowledge the cultural and spiritual significance of weaving. One woman, who is wealthy by her community's standards, learned to weave when she was in her forties because, she says, "I want my grands [grandchildren] to know their grandma knew how to do this." Another weaver keeps the equivalent of a "hope chest" for her daughter and son; she stores away each of her rugs as part of the family legacy. Recognizing that the roots of weaving are deep in Navajo culture, this group may represent a major trend for the future.

For many household and revival weavers, weaving represents knowledge of traditional stories as well as of time-honored practices. For some professional weavers, work is also linked to the outside world of employment and worldly recognition. The increasing practice of signing one's pieces—sometimes by weaving or embroidering one's name, initials, or insignia into a rug—signals an outward-looking attitude. Women achieve recognition through weaving as a way to carry on tradition and through weaving practiced as a modern career. Both demonstrate how weaving can accord social status to a woman.

Rose Owens weaving an innovative round rug at her home in Kinlichee, Arizona, 1986. Photo by Ann Lane Hedlund.

Beginning in the early years of this century, weavers in certain communities began to develop distinctive rug styles. Rugs produced in the Ganado area, for instance, contained more red in strong geometric forms. Around Two Grey Hills, New Mexico, rugs became strictly natural colored with intricate stepped motifs and interlocking borders; in Wide Ruins, vegetal dyes and banded, borderless patterns became the rule. Local traders encouraged this regionalization and marketed the styles by their community names. By the 1960s and 1970s, more than a dozen regional rug styles were readily recognized, and each decade has seen a few new styles invented. Now, as weavers travel and draw inspiration from distant sources, styles are woven all over the Navajo Nation, far from their originating communities.

For many weavers, the specific tasks involved in making a rug have become specialized. In earlier times, weavers created their blankets from their own sheep's wool, which they sheared, carded, spun, and dyed. Today, some women focus, for instance, on spinning yarn or dyeing it with vegetal colors and then supplying it to others. Those who are financially able to purchase their yarns weave without preparing any raw materials. Looms and other tools, constructed by the weaver or her male relatives in the past, are not always built by the family; often they are purchased ready-made or special-ordered.

Almost all weavers work at home, whether in traditional hogans, modern houses, or mobile homes. Most work inside, although in good weather some women still enjoy working on looms set up outdoors. Professional and some household weavers may use a separate hogan as a weaving studio, a special place to store wool and yarn and to display works for sale. Weaving takes place in a variety of institutional settings as well, in school classrooms and dormitories; in community meeting rooms; and in trading posts, galleries, and other demonstration centers.

The designated growth centers and new housing developments simultaneously compete for weavers' attentions and simultaneously aid their efforts. On one hand, women have greater access to alternative training and jobs, yet on the other hand, growth centers provide easy access to commercial weaving materials and to rug salesrooms. And women living in close proximity may collaborate on a project, with one serving as master designer and others contributing to the tedious background weaving.

Almost one-third of all Navajo people live off-reservation, where housing, jobs, and schools are more plentiful. Approximately half of those live in rural and suburban areas surrounding the Navajo Nation; others live in cities such as Los Angeles, Chicago, Minneapolis, Denver, Phoenix, and Albuquerque. Many women regularly travel back and forth between the two worlds and return to their mothers' homes each weekend, where they can weave in good company and pick up local supplies. Other weavers who live far from their homelands provide expertise to urban museums and Indian cultural centers by demonstrating their craft, lecturing, and consulting on exhibitions.

The period from 1960 into the 1990s saw increased Navajo involvement in the reservation educational system at both secondary and higher levels. Where previously the Bureau of Indian Affairs controlled the schools, local communities gained more say in their education, and more schools incorporated Navajo language and culture materials into their curriculum and recruited Navajo teachers. Simultaneously, the number of students attending post-high-school technical training programs and off-reservation colleges has risen each decade.[65]

In general, schools have not altered the matrilineal pattern and family-centered way in which weaving is taught, but the number of schoolgirls who weave has diminished, partially due to schooling. Typically a girl would first watch her mother work, perhaps helping card wool or winding the yarn into balls. Some women remember making "toy" looms and sneaking away to play with snippets of yarn. Others were given the beginnings of a small rug and told, "Here, finish it." Still others, sitting next to their mother, imitated her every step. These introductions to weaving continue, but only as a girl's time permits. In addition, community center workshops, work programs, and school and museum classes provided limited opportunities to learn. Since it opened in 1969, Navajo Community College has offered Navajo studies courses that include weaving and other traditional crafts. Nevertheless, girls are not learning to weave at the rate they did one hundred years ago. Their educational and recreational activities compete directly with weaving time, and the pressure to finish school and get a paying job is considerable.

The division of labor between men and women, always relatively loose in traditional Navajo society, has reflected trends of the surrounding Euroamerican society. The women's liberation movement affects Navajo women and men just as it does Anglo society. By the 1960s, women's roles broadened considerably, with more women completing high school, pursuing higher education, joining the outside workforce, and raising families as single parents. Navajo Nation families today make their living through a "mixed economic strategy." That is, many households are supported by a combination of activities, with men and women working outside the home seasonally or part-time, as well as performing subsistence activities that directly provide food and supplies at home. Wage labor and salaried jobs provide the majority of cash (92.5 percent of all personal income in 1991), with government assistance furnishing a small additional amount (5 percent). Estimates for the contribution of sheepherding, raising livestock, small-scale farming, and other traditional subsistence practices appear much less (2 percent),[66] but these activities, including handcraft production, require the largest amount of time and energy from the Navajos.

Weavers come from all socioeconomic levels and make wide-ranging contributions to household expenses, from eking out a meager living to drawing substantial income from rug sales. Navajo weavers work largely for external buyers, marketing their own rugs and continuing the centuries-old tradition of active commerce. Very few make woven goods for internal consumption by Navajo people. An occasional saddle blanket, dress, floor rug, or sampler is kept or given to friends or family members, but everything else is made for sale to trading posts, curio shops, galleries, museums, individual brokers, and collectors. Only a very small number of women can afford to weave principally as a hobby.

Each decade of the late twentieth century has represented new trends in the practice and products of weaving. During the nationwide Indian arts and crafts boom of the 1960s, regional rug styles became sharply differentiated and weavers focused on refining patterns from their families and communities. The appreciation of ethnic arts on a national level encouraged Native weavers to maintain solid technical and design skills. New kinds of floor rugs, saddle blankets, and wall hangings were created. Increased tourism in the Southwest reinforced the craft market and strengthened the weavers' primary outlets— local trading posts and border town rug galleries.

Weaving in the 1970s, in contrast, became more exploratory and expansive. Weavers experimented with new materials and moved away from the standard regional styles to try new combinations of color and pattern. As prices rose for rugs and tapestries, pillow covers and smaller items began to form a secondary market. In concert with the growing acknowledgment of nineteenth-century Navajo weaving through scholarly study,[67] public display,[68] and rising prices, the importance of a modern, living art form was recognized.

The decade of the 1980s continued the trend toward increased eclecticism, moving away from objects that "look Indian." Often referring to themselves as artists, rug weavers employed a more personal mix of materials, colors, and styles in their rugs. Very large and absolutely tiny textiles appeared in greater numbers; superfine tapestries with weft counts over ninety threads per inch (per 2.5 centimeters) characterized one corner of the market. Weavers also responded to the spread of the "Santa Fe style," with its emphasis on pastel pinks and purples. They

Figure 18

Larry Yazzie (1955–95), raised outline rug, ca. 1994. Processed and commercially spun wool. 125.7 × 74.9 cm. Gift of Gloria F. Ross. (25.4375)

ventured farther from their communities to sell rugs and began attending Indian markets held in Santa Fe, Phoenix, and Los Angeles. Urban art galleries and museums showcased Navajo weaving, and rugs were almost exclusively hung on walls as tapestries.[69]

In the 1990s, like the 1890s, interest has turned to the end of the century. What will the future bring?

VIEWING NINETEENTH-CENTURY WEAVING

Separated by a century, weavers from the late nineteenth and late twentieth centuries would easily relate to each other's tools and textiles and to their respective roles as homemakers. Major elements of Navajo culture—values concerning families, the land and livestock, and spirituality—persist into the late twentieth century. Both late nineteenth- and early twentieth-century weavers battled social and economic hardships with resourcefulness and creativity. Beyond their daily activities, nineteenth-

century weavers might not recognize many roles that modern women now play outside the home, but they would appreciate how they are enacted. Both groups of women often appear forthright yet responsive, self-sufficient yet supportive, productive yet unhurried. The attention that weaving receives as an artform and the separation of art, culture, and religion today would seem alien to those weavers of long ago, just as they do to many Navajos today.

More than anything, both groups would agree that all of the time-consuming and thought-provoking processes—the days of collecting herbs for dyeing, nights of dreaming designs, weeks at the loom creating—are equal to, if not more important than, their finished products. These processes help weavers cope with surrounding change. To understand Navajo weaving, then and now, we must look beyond the products and into the lives and values of the makers.

Until recently few living Navajo weavers had handled nineteenth-century blankets, but opportunities for weavers to examine such textiles are growing. Museums in Arizona and New Mexico that surround the Navajo Nation display their own collections and host traveling exhibitions. Periodically, the Navajo Nation Museum and the Ned A. Hatathli Cultural Center showcase early Navajo blankets and rugs. Museum collections are published and available in southwestern bookshops. Indian art galleries also carry antique textiles. Many of these places have invited Navajo weavers to view and comment on the older work.[70]

The past is very much a part of the Navajo world today. In a society reliant on oral history, the past—ałk'idą́ą́'—is actively relived and revitalized through the repetition of stories, religious narratives, and shared language and culture. Being flexible and quick to adapt new cultural items to their needs is not incompatible with having a strong sense of beginnings and roots. Ruth Roessel expresses it aptly: "The Holy People left us a way of life—one that takes into account change and progress. Navajo culture is the key that unlocks our problems and gives us a future."[71] John Farella elaborates on this theme, ". . .the Navajos are not change oriented but rather. . .they are changing in order to remain 'traditional.' Specifically, they are altering their technology to maintain their epistemology."[72]

Even so, individual perceptions and understandings vary widely when Navajo people look at nineteenth-century blankets. One weaver may draw on in-depth historical and cultural knowledge, perhaps acquired through elders, her own reading, or, in rare cases, formal schooling. Some weavers apply their particular technical knowledge to interpreting earlier textiles. Others may bring direct market experiences. As Navajo scholar and ritual specialist Harry Walters acknowledges, Navajo people are now in the process of "reconstructing the weaving tradition."[73]

Rarely are Navajo weavers overtly judgmental about other people's work, whether from the past or present. Their criticisms are subtle and often couched in sympathy. For example, women almost never say a textile looks ugly. Instead they may comment, "That woman

Larry Yazzie at his loom in Tuba City, Arizona, 1991. Photo by Ann Lane Hedlund.

was distracted. She had too much on her mind when she made that. But that's up to her." Another explains a lopsided design: "Maybe the weaver could not see too well. Maybe she was elderly, or handicapped with some difficult disabilities."

Many weavers today relate nineteenth-century weaving to their own family lineage: "This is just like ones my great grandmother made," and "It remembers [reminds me of] our great-great-great-grandmothers that we've never seen." A granddaughter translates for her grandmother in her eighties: "A lot of men used to wear blankets like that a long time ago, just simple and striped and not very many colors. . . . [She knows because] her mother and grandmother used to tell her." Viewing blankets from the 1870s prompted eighty-one-year-old Grace Henderson Nez to reminisce, "Our maternal grandmothers survived by means of weaving, with the rugs that they made. Our maternal grandfather used to weave and his name was 'Atł'óhí (Weaver). He is remembered for his weaving. What he was remembered by I also am now doing."

Sadie E. Curtis weaving a revival-style chief blanket, Kinlichee, Arizona, 1981. Photo by Ann Lane Hedlund.

The *biil*—a matched pair of rectangular fabrics with brown-black mid-sections flanked by red end panels containing rows of dark indigo blue motifs (usually stepped triangles, diamonds, crosses, or some variation of these elements)—forms the woman's traditional two-piece dress and is almost universally acknowledged as a special garment. Some women recall wearing one themselves for their *kinaaldá*, the girl's puberty ceremony, and for other special events. (Most remember, too, that a biil is scratchy on bare skin.) Others have made them for their daughters or other young women. Only a small number know details about the symbolism of the biil designs and their important relationships to basketry patterns and other cultural elements.[74] The chief blanket, although no longer worn on any occasion, is almost universally recognized, in part because its distinctive pattern is reproduced on many rugs today. Older weavers call it *hanoolchaadí*, which refers to the pattern but also means "carded," as in carded wool.

Linguistic distinctions between textiles other than the dress and chief blanket—for wearing blankets versus rugs, for instance—are often blurred. Among bilingual weavers, the English term "rug" is used for almost all textiles, regardless of time period or function. In Navajo, the parallel term is *diyogí*, literally meaning "shaggy," "bushy," or "coarse," and used for both nineteenth- and twentieth-century textiles. A separate word is sometimes used for blankets—*beeldléí*. Despite the crossover of terms, most weavers distinguish textiles' different functions as wearing blankets, ponchos, saddle blankets, floor rugs, and wall hangings.

At varied levels of specialization, weavers focus on physical features that relate to or contrast with their own work. One excellent spinner exclaims, "How did they make their wool so fine?" Another expert weaver, looking at a different blanket, comments, "I think the designs were easy [then]. I guess that it was all handspun at that time. And at that time the wool was different. They're all in big bumps and kind of rough." They easily become involved in seeing where the weaving started, how patterns are joined together, and other procedural details. Side cords, tassels, and any irregularities are closely examined. Remarks emerge about the yarn and weave structures, color combinations, and how motifs are balanced in a particular layout. Many weavers especially notice the sheep's wool in old blankets. They comment on the natural colors—browns from *dibé łich'íí'* (red sheep) and greys from *dibé dotł'izh* (blue sheep). They compare the old-style churro sheep's wool to the mohair goat's wool that is available today. Others are fascinated with unusual techniques no longer used. Employed only from about 1870 to 1890, the wedge weave (see plates 11 and 42), for instance, is almost unknown among weavers today.[75] Many weavers puzzle over its construction.

Also of interest is the care of older pieces. Concerned about repairs in antique textiles, the grandmother of one weaving family remembered, "People used to say, 'Don't restore rugs, just leave them as is.' That's what I heard a long time ago. Just let it wear and tear." Because of the emotional energy and thought that a weaver invests in her work, this family felt danger might befall another weaver if she were to restore a worn blanket because she would not be in the same physical or psychological condition as the original weaver. "It's kind of like there is the spirit of the original weaver still woven within the weaves of these rugs."

The Navajo identity of many nineteenth-century blankets is not obvious to weavers more familiar with modern rug patterns. Since many wearing blankets exceed the fineness of recent rugs, weavers without a basis for comparison often do not consider such weaving Navajo. Likewise, an unfamiliar color or yarn (raveled threads, for instance) is suspect because weavers today do not use it. A few weavers wondered whether a poncho in the NMAI collection (see plate 3) was Mexican. Looking at photographs of nineteenth-century wearing blankets rather than at actual textiles, few weavers rate older work as being better than their own; most consider it inferior to modern products. "Maybe back then they didn't design too much. They made their blankets in their own way. They designed

somehow, but not very well," says one weaver of large and elaborate pictorial images.

Many weavers today relate to earlier weaving in economic terms. They want to know how much that blanket was originally worth. How much is it worth today? How much if I now weave one just like it? Some resent the fact that older blankets sell for far more than their own rugs do: "These long-ago blankets are worth a lot, I'm told. Now the price [for today's rugs] is lower."

Contemporary weavers vary greatly in their knowledge and opinions about the meaning of blanket designs. A number of weavers provide names for specific motifs—stepped triangles are often referred to as clouds, and zigzags are called lightning, snakes, or mountains. Some weavers assert a strong connection between Navajo religious motifs and woven designs; others deny them. Several suggest that men's knowledge of the religious sphere is crucial to interpreting designs, even though it is women who create them.

The hardships Navajo people have endured—domination by military and government forces, impoverishment, lack of modern technology—are reflected in the blankets, according to many weavers who identify closely with the weavers who came before. Looking at two blankets of contrasting quality, a college-educated weaver says, "This weaver [of a fine blanket] might have had the opportunity to get the best yarn . . . [and] all the supplies she needed. Versus that kind of weaving [of poor quality] where the weaver must have lived in a more remote area, poverty-stricken, [and without] a comfortable nice home."

According to many weavers, traditional values and positive aspects of life—family togetherness, closeness to the land and livestock, resourcefulness, harmony with nature—are embodied in early blankets and expressed in the weaving process, which is connected with sacred activities. "We have our stories, songs, that were told by our grandmothers, our mothers and fathers."

Blankets are thought to have intrinsic power, imparted by the weaver, and associations with people who are now gone. One weaver comments in Navajo, "By [seeing these blankets and touching them], you extend your ability to do your weaving. [This experience] becomes a part of you. It becomes a part of your thought, your dreams, your vision, your prayers, and meditation. It's a process of relearning. We're relearning the old ways."

Viewing older work often makes many weavers feel nostalgic. One weaver recalls, "My grandmother and my great grandmother were weavers too, but I never saw their rugs [or] how they used to weave." Some wish they knew more and could pass on the weaving culture more surely. "Today, our children—daughters and grandkids—we should teach them all that goes into these rugs," entreats one weaver and teacher. Another accomplished weaver notes, "My mom has a song about rugs but I don't know it. That's one thing I haven't done. My mom's getting old, and I should learn it. I should learn how to sing it and sing it while I weave."

WEAVING THE PAST

Visible reminders of the past abound in rugs and tapestries woven today. Weavers reproduce entire blanket or dress patterns; others borrow isolated motifs, a color scheme, or a suggestion of layout. They incorporate banded and borderless layouts from early striped blankets, as well as crosses and stepped diamonds from Late Classic sarapes. The modern use of allover zigzags and other eye-dazzling geometric patterns refers to Transitional period styles when Germantown yarns became popular.

The woman's two-piece biil represents continuous use of a basic pattern since at least the early nineteenth century. Remnants of a two-piece dress found in Massacre Cave in Canyon del Muerto show that the Navajo were weaving and wearing such garments by 1804.[76] Photographs taken during the last quarter of the nineteenth century establish that women still wore such dresses, at least for special occasions. Today these dresses are made for Navajo use—kinaaldá, powwows, parades, and other special events—and for external sale as collectors' items and

curios. Recently woven dresses may have different colors, such as turquoise and black, or new design motifs along the end panels; some even have a float-patterned sash-belt woven across the middle. Even so, connections to the past remain important.

Over the past century, the adaptation of entire blanket and dress designs to make contemporary reproductions has become popular. During the late 1880s and especially in the 1890s, weavers in the Ganado area were encouraged by trader J. L. Hubbell to create new versions of chief blankets, biil dresses, and sarapes. Moving away from the array of new synthetic colors that had just gained popularity, these weavers returned to the more subdued natural-colors-plus-red color scheme from earlier in that century. In the 1920s, an interest in older blankets again led traders such as Cozy McSparron at Chinle to obtain red and blue Du Pont dyes for local weavers and to encourage weavers to make banded, borderless designs associated with earlier blanket styles. During the heyday of regional rug development, through the 1960s and into the 1970s, fewer revivals were woven. By the end of the 1980s, however, a third period of renewed interest in older blanket designs emerged. Breaking from the standard repertoire of regional rug styles, many weavers are seeking new patterns by consulting museum catalogues with illustrations of nineteenth-century blankets.[77]

Revival patterns are rarely slavish copies of actual nineteenth-century textiles. Rather, weavers combine traditional layouts with appropriate motifs and color schemes of the period, reinterpreting the patterns in their own manner. Suitable for floors or walls, these rugs are much heavier and stiffer than the early, drapable wearing blankets.

Weavers' attitudes toward revival weaving vary considerably. Many women comment that making the same pattern more than once should be avoided to limit excessive behavior or to reduce boredom. There are also strong feelings that one person should never weave the designs of another. Since contact with materials associated with the dead is considered dangerous to one's well-being, reviving ancestral patterns is not always encouraged. Nevertheless, some people honor the past by preserving the old patterns. For them, revival rugs represent important symbols of their cultural heritage. Finally, popular demand and simple economics provide a strong motivation to make revival patterns.

Perhaps the past actually has less to do with the products weavers make, than with the ways they approach their work. Weavers today value their independence and individuality, even as weaving permits them to support their families and stay close to home. They focus on innovation and pragmatic action rather than rigidly following rules and copying. As in earlier times, new designs are easily initiated and materials readily adopted. By their very flexibility and interest in adaptation, Navajo weavers reflect their heritage and carry on their cultural traditions.[78]

Eclecticism is ultimately the hallmark of Navajo weaving, visible in both process and product. Nineteenth-century weaving reflects indigenous Navajo aesthetics (especially as known from their early basketry and pottery), combined with Pueblo technology and design, Spanish layout and motifs, and incipient Anglo market preferences. Later, even Oriental carpet designs provided inspiration. Twentieth-century weaving draws from these significant roots, while it demonstrates further evolution in style and technique. Weavers today respond to a variety of stimuli, old and new, as they experiment, collaborate, and create a wide range of textiles.

CONCLUSION

As might be expected, considerable differences define lifeways from a hundred years ago and now. Navajo people moved from seminomadic activities to localized sheepherding and, most recently, to a broader mixed economy. From widely dispersed and independently operating family groups, Navajo society evolved to incorporate centralized systems of education, business, and healthcare. No longer dominated by the U.S. government nor isolated from the rest of the world, Navajos govern themselves to a larger extent and participate in national and international affairs.

Navajo values of honoring the family, the land, and animals; autonomy; and spiritual harmony represent a continuous, if not always an evenly spun, thread to the present. These values provide mainstays for Navajo culture and for Navajo weaving. Regardless of changes in the outward appearance of its products, weaving retains important cultural elements, some shared by people separated by a century of change. Some values are imbedded in the very processes of weaving; others emerge as modern weavers discuss earlier work.

The past is a powerful source of inspiration for weavers. Their responses to it may be secular or spiritual in nature, continuous or disjointed through time, and direct or indirect in practice. Elements carried forward from the nineteenth century range from the basic structure of the loom and certain design styles, to songs that are sung to underscore the religious significance of the craft. Several features, especially weaving methods, have been passed down through generations, while others, such as designs, have been lost but periodically rediscovered and revived. Many weavers have a sense of earlier weaving, and they may unconsciously incorporate into their work specific behaviors and attitudes from the past.

Not surprisingly, weaving can be both traditional and innovative. In the nineteenth century, Navajo people fought for their very existence. Weaving became an important survival tool, providing clothing, shelter, and goods for exchange. In the midst of modernization, Navajo people continue to assert their Native identity and hold fast to their unique cultural heritage. Weaving remains a survival tool that conveys crucial concepts of Navajo identity and personal expression.

NAVAJO BLANKETS

Joe Ben Wheat

Many millennia ago, the first peoples in North America almost certainly carried with them as part of their cultural baggage some knowledge of interlacing various plant fibers into mats or light and pliable bags and baskets. Cordage rolled or twisted from the same fibers was used to tie things together and, by manipulation with the fingers alone, to weave some simple fabrics.

By about two thousand years ago cotton and, probably, the narrow backstrap loom were introduced to some of the peoples living in what is now the southwestern part of the United States. Only narrow fabrics such as belts and kilts could be woven on this loom. A wide loom, upon which larger textiles could be woven, was developed some time around A.D. 800 and was widely used throughout the Southwest to produce a variety of

garments and blankets. Belts and other narrow fabrics were still woven on the narrow loom. Cotton quickly became the most widely used fiber for weaving.

When Spanish explorers first came into the Southwest in the sixteenth century they found a number of village-dwelling, agricultural peoples, nearly all of whom were weavers. These villages were called pueblos by the Spanish, as were the villagers themselves. Around and between the pueblos lived a number of less settled tribes, mainly Athapaskan or Apachean groups, but including some Ute and Paiute Indians to the north. Most of these peoples depended on hunting, gathering wild plant foods, and raiding for their livelihood. However, one Athapaskan group that lived north and west of Santa Fe and along the Continental

Woman at loom, seated on wedge weave blanket, ca. 1885.
Photo by Ben Wittick. Courtesy of the Museum of New
Mexico, Santa Fe. (#16269)

common sheep of southern Spain, whose long clean
fleeces ranged in color from creamy white to dark brown.
The Spanish introduced indigo, and perhaps other dyes,
and adopted some of the native plant dyes used by the
Pueblos. Soon the Spanish built European-style horizontal
looms from local materials to weave cloth and blankets to
use themselves and to sell to the Spanish miners in
northern Mexico.

Within a few years all of the Pueblos, who by now had
been missionized by the Spanish, were given sheep. Soon
churro wool began to replace cotton for much of Pueblo
weaving. By 1638 both Spanish and Pueblo blankets and
cloth, along with other goods, were assembled by the
Spanish governor and packed off for sale in northern
Mexico.[1] In addition to the articles of cloth, there were
several baskets attributed to the unsettled Indians, most
likely Navajos or one of the other nearby Apachean tribes.

Probably the first sheep obtained by the Navajo in the
early 1600s were used as food. About 1640, Navajos began
to raid the large flocks of sheep owned by the Spanish
along the Rio Grande.[2] During this period, a number of
Pueblo Indians went to live among the Navajo to escape
Spanish rule. Sometime during the middle of the seven-
teenth century, Navajos began to use the ancient wide
loom of the Pueblos and to weave many of the same kinds
of garments and blankets. When the Pueblo Revolt began
in 1680, the Navajo helped drive the Spanish down the
Rio Grande out of New Mexico. The Spanish began a
reconquest of the valley and its pueblos in 1692. It took
four years, to 1696, to complete the reestablishment of the
Spanish government, and many more Pueblos fled to the
country of the Navajo. Ten years later, in 1706, Governor
Cuervo y Valdez remarked that the Navajo "cultivate the
soil with great industry, sowing corn, beans, squash, and
other seeds, such as those of chili, which they use, having
found them in the towns of our Christian Indians of this
Kingdom. *Yet this is nothing new among these Apaches, for
whenever they are sedentary they do the same things. They make
their cloths of wool and cotton, sowing the latter and obtaining
the former from the flocks which they raise."*[3]

Divide did some farming as well. These were called
Apaches de Navajú, or "Apaches of the Big Fields." Later
they were simply called Navajo.

In 1540 and later when the Spanish began to explore
the Southwest, they drove herds of sheep with them for
food. When they settled the Rio Grande Valley in 1598
they brought sheep and goats to provide both meat and
wool for weaving, together with tools, plants, and other
supplies needed to subsist in the new territory they
named New Mexico. These sheep were the churro, the

Several reports in the Rabal Manuscript,[4] compiled by the Spanish governor of New Mexico, Codallos y Rabal, in the mid eighteenth century, describe Navajo culture as observed during Spanish visits into the Navajo country between 1706 and 1745. These relate that the Navajo were weaving quantities of cloth and garments of wool and cotton, and much basketry, which they traded to the Christian Indians and to the Spanish of the Realm. One observer noted that there were about two hundred Pueblo Indians living among the Navajo. Some Navajo men dressed in tanned deerskin, but in general they and their women wore the same kind of clothes as the Christian Indians. Women's garments included a one-piece dress or manta, held around the waist by a sash belt, and a second manta worn as a shawl, while men wore poncholike shirts and also used the manta as a shawl.

Pueblo mantas were wider than long, as measured along the warps, and were usually woven in some variety of balanced or warp-predominant twill weave with a strong selvage of three two-ply cords woven around the edges. Early Navajo blankets were woven much the same, but changes in the details of the way they were woven began to occur by the mid 1700s. The selvage changed to two three-ply cords, and Navajos began to weave their textiles in segments, leaving diagonal join lines, often called lazy lines, between them.

Spanish blankets were usually long and relatively narrow. The edges were reinforced by extra warps, but they did not have selvage cords, and the ends were tied off in various knots and fringes. Heavy twill cloth was woven by the Spanish, but their blankets were normally woven in weft-faced and tapestry weaves. Decoration of Spanish blankets and sarapes, or wearing blankets, usually consisted of various patterns of stripes alternating the natural wool colors with each other and often with indigo blue. Red was rarely used. More complex figured designs were woven in tapestry weave.

In Pueblo weaving, decoration was often achieved by the texture of various twill weaves alone. Other patterns, such as stripes, were woven in. Painted and embroidered designs were also used. While Navajos continued to weave and wear mantalike blankets, they soon began to emphasize the longer-than-wide proportions of the Spanish sarape. They adopted weft-faced and tapestry techniques even for their diagonal twills.

Before the Spanish arrived, Indians from the Great Plains used to bring their products, skins, and dried meat to trade with the Pueblos for cotton blankets and corn. After the Spanish settled New Mexico, commerce was carried on in trade fairs at the pueblos where Plains Indians, Pueblos, Spaniards, and Navajos convened to exchange their various products with each other.[5] Each year goods from the local trade fairs were collected by the merchants of New Mexico. In late fall these merchants formed a caravan to take their merchandise to a major fair in Chihuahua, in northern Mexico, where they exchanged it for goods from throughout Mexico, as well as goods from Europe and the Orient. For these caravans, the Navajo provided their share of blankets and baskets.

Throughout the eighteenth century, Navajos continued to develop their weaving skills and, with this, their share of the market. After the Pueblo Revolt, most of the Pueblos along the Rio Grande valley continued to weave their ceremonial and domestic garments of cotton or wool, but they acquired most of their better blankets through trade with Navajos. When the Navajo were at peace, the Spanish also traded indigo, knives, and bridles for the finer grades of Navajo blankets and baskets. By 1788, the Navajo were making "the best and finest sarapes that are known, blankets, wraps [mantas], cotton cloth, coarse cloth, sashes and other [things] for their dress and sale." The woman's "dress is of two blankets of black wool with a colored [red] border and they arrange it in the form of a blouse and skirt."[6] Since the Navajo had no good red dye, they were clearly raveling bayeta, or baize, which the Spanish Indian Fund had been issuing to the Navajo "at peace." Bayeta was to achieve a major place in Navajo weaving for the next hundred years.

While we have numerous references to Navajo weaving during the 1700s, we have very few textiles that can be

Figure 20

Biil (two-piece dress),
1850–60.
Handspun wool and raveled yarn,
131.5 × 86.8 cm. (20.7820)

reasonably dated to that period, and most of these are from archaeological sites.

By the beginning of the nineteenth century Navajos were weaving shoulder blankets, utility blankets, fine sarapes, women's mantas and two-piece dresses, and men's shirts. Nearly all of these were woven in weft-faced and tapestry weave. Even in weaving twill mantas, Navajos began to emphasize weft-faced technique in contrast to the open, balanced twills of the Pueblos. While various kinds of stripes continued to be a major kind of decoration, more and more fabrics were being decorated with geometric figures such as triangles, diamonds, and zigzags, all carried out with stepped edges. Most of these terraced designs were probably borrowed from Navajo basketry, where the nature of the foundation and sewing elements dictated stepped-edge figures. In cloth, even the most complicated patterns were woven by simple manipulation of terraced figures and, importantly, the negative spaces that were left between.

The earliest sort of Navajo woman's dress was the single-piece manta, very similar in form to garments worn by Pueblo women, such as one finely woven fragmentary manta (see fig. 3). Woven in weft-faced weave, this manta dress is characterized by clustered stripes in red, blue, and brown with a center of natural brown wool. This one-piece dress was ancestral to the eighteenth-century biil— the two-piece dress so identified with Navajo women. By tradition, the earliest two-piece dresses were woven in natural brown wool with simple decoration in indigo blue. While the nature of the wool used to make the dress shown in plate 10 suggests a date in the 1880s, in form and color this dress strongly resembles an early biil.

About 1800, a very fine threaded cloth called 100-thread bayeta (one hundred threads to the inch) was introduced to southwestern weavers. For the most part, the threads were S-spun, that is, the direction of the twist was parallel to the center stroke of the letter S. This bayeta was woven of smooth, worsted wool and was piece-dyed crimson red, usually with the dye lac, an Asian relative of cochineal. This variety of bayeta was widely available until

Figure 21

Beeldléí (blanket),
ca. 1875.
Handspun wool
and commercial yarn,
109.2 × 145.4 cm. (6.302)

about 1863, when larger-threaded kinds of bayeta, often woven with Z-spun (parallel to the center stroke of a *Z*) fuzzier woolen yarns, began to replace them. Cochineal dye and, later, synthetic dyes tended to impart scarlet or orangey reds rather than crimson. There are three dresses, or biil, in the museum's collection woven using natural black wool for the center, with designs in indigo blue on crimson backgrounds of fine raveled bayeta (see fig. 20 and plates 8 and 23). The terraced, open diamonds across the center and stepped-edge triangle borders in these dresses are early forms of decoration in biil as well as other Navajo weaving. They were probably woven in the 1850s or early 1860s.

One biil (see fig. 1), woven about 1870, was made of a softer and larger-threaded bayeta that forms the ground for terraced zigzag lines across the center, with triangles bordering the top and bottom of the panels. After 1870, more and more Navajo women began to wear sewn dresses of calico and other cotton fabrics, and with that the everyday use of the wool biil declined, but some older women still wove and wore biil. One dress in the collection (11.8066) represents this later period, with a pattern of stepped zigzags and a simple cross atop each crest. The rounding of the steps in the design is an unusual treatment.

When Navajo women changed from wearing the one-piece to the two-piece dress, sometime in the late 1700s, they continued to weave a similar fabric of tapestry twill, which they wore as a small shoulder blanket or shawl. In contrast to the Pueblo twill manta, the decoration of the one-piece Navajo manta was the same as that of the two-

Ute group with individual wearing chief blanket. W. H. Jackson catalog 963. (NMAI P426)

through them were used on the manta shown in plate 9, with a ground of later, coarser red bayeta dyed with synthetic dyes. Handspun wool and four-ply yarns were used in the manta illustrated in fig. 21, which has a row of crosses with flagged corners, sometimes called a Spider Woman's Cross. After this style of cross was introduced about 1864, it became a very widely used element in Navajo weaving of the 1870s and 1880s.

Navajo woven shirts for men were very similar to those worn by Pueblo men, but were woven in tapestry twill instead of balanced twill. Although these shirts were a standard item of clothing, they were never worn as commonly as were two-piece dresses for women. Some shirts were woven, like ponchos, as a long narrow fabric with a hole for the neck cut into the center. The folded center formed the shoulders when the shirt was worn.

Worn far more commonly than these shirts was the wider-than-long shoulder blanket. During the 1700s, decoration on these shoulder blankets consisted basically of stripes clustered only slightly into zones. By 1800 a pattern had evolved, which consisted of two zones of broad black and white stripes with wider black bands at the ends and a double-wide panel across the center. The end bands were embellished by pairs of narrower stripes of indigo blue, with two pairs across the center. Although it is a misnomer, this pattern has been given the name First Phase or Ute chief blanket. These rather somber blankets were in great favor among the Utes and, by 1833, many were being traded to the Indians of the Great Plains, as far north as the Blackfeet. One blanket, collected in South Dakota by artist DeCost Smith, was further decorated with Plains metal buttons and tassels (see plate 21). This simple style continued in popularity until the middle of the century. Toward the end of this Phase I period, some blankets were further embellished by the addition of a few wefts of bayeta yarn along the edges of the blue stripes. One of the earliest documented Navajo blankets was a "red-lined" First Phase blanket collected by Samuel W. Woodhouse while on the Sitgreaves Expedition in 1851 (see plate 15). Collected at the same time was a similar

piece Navajo dress, with a black center and identical designs in blue on red end panels. Occasionally mantas had centers of colors other than black, and sometimes different colors were used in the decoration as well. While the mantas were frequently worn by Navajos, many of them were traded to the Pueblos, as they were heavier and more decorative than the plain mantas made by Pueblo weavers. The manta shown in plate 6, probably dating to the 1860s, has a row of small, blue, open diamonds with terraced triangles as borders woven with the earlier bayeta. Larger stepped open diamonds with thin stripes of green

Figure 22

Beeldléí (blanket),
1870–75.
Handspun wool
and raveled yarn,
140.3 × 189.5 cm. (22.1687)

chief blanket in which small blocks of crimson bayeta had been inserted at the ends and centers of each of the narrow blue stripes (see plate 14). This pattern has come to be known as the Second Phase chief blanket and was the dominant pattern during the 1850s and 1860s. Still another variety that falls into this time range is one in which concentric rectangles take the place of the smaller red blocks at the end and center of the broad black bands. A variant of this form, in which nested rectangles extend out into a field of black and white stripes, is seen in plate 38; the blanket dates to between 1865 and 1875.

By the early 1860s, Navajo weavers began to use some of the terraced triangles that had been used in sarapes in the early decades of the nineteenth century, instead of the rectangles of red. At first these figures were small and confined within the width of the end and center bands. About

1860, at Fort Laramie, Wyoming, Thomas Twiss collected a blanket, transitional between Phase II and III, in which the top and bottom figures extended into the field of black and white stripes (see plate 13).

The pattern termed the Third Phase chief blanket began to be made in the late 1860s, and by 1875 it had become the dominant style of shoulder blanket. It is characterized by a large, terraced diamond in the center of the center band and terraced half-diamonds at the sides and ends, with a quarter-diamond at each corner, all of which extend into the panels of black and white stripes. Diamond centers may have various kinds of embellishment. Characteristic of this pattern is the blanket illustrated in fig. 22, with narrow stripes through the diamond centers. Still another version displays large, simple crosses in the diamonds (see plate 24). An indication that Navajos

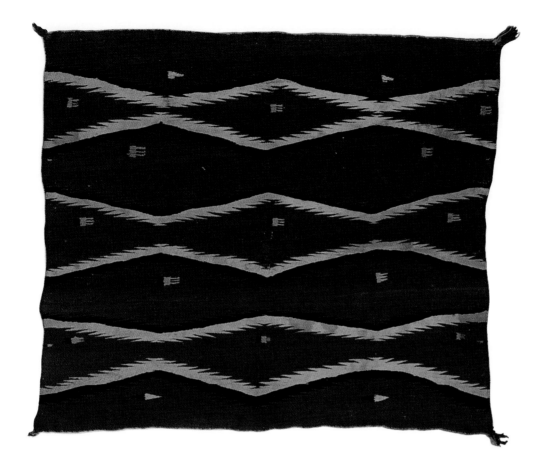

Figure 23

Beeldléí (blanket),
ca. 1870.
Handspun wool
and raveled yarn,
111 × 134 cm. (20.3035)

did not adhere to the so-called classic patterns of the time is the blanket shown in plate 18, which has five diamond figures forming a row across it. Many later chief blankets have diamonds that meet at their crests, and a few chief blankets add pictorial elements. Sometimes men's blankets were made with end and center bands of continuous geometric patterns. A few shoulder blankets were decorated with patterns derived directly from the wearing sarapes of their day. The layout of the blanket shown in fig. 23 consists of three pairs of opposed zigzag stripes enclosing elongated diamond spaces with small comb figures at the centers. Collected in 1870, this piece was woven of handspun yarn and late raveled bayeta.

With some variation, all of the patterns made for men's chief blankets were also woven for women. These shoulder blankets were generally smaller than those for men and usually had narrower stripes of gray or white rather than broad black and white stripes. A classic Second Phase design has twelve red blocks in the blue inner stripes and is further decorated with small zigzag elements in the red blocks (see plate 27). Another blanket has continuous bands of serrate zigzags and triangles at the center and ends (see plate 26). The serrate figures, together with handspun yarns and mixed natural and synthetic dyes, suggest a date of about 1880. A third woman's blanket, with gray and black stripe panels, was woven as a serrate variation of the Third Phase pattern (see plate 30). Some of the red wefts in this blanket consisted of raveled threads which had been rolled into bundles of six to ten, probably to match the weight of the handspun yarns.

Navajos wove many kinds of wearing blankets which were longer than wide. Their greatest achievement in weaving was the finely woven "sarape Navajo," made with the finest of materials and with beautiful patterns. In many sarapes, a slit was left in the center for the head to pass through so the sarape could be used as a poncho. A few archaeological sarape fragments have been found that indicate that by 1800 tapestry techniques were used to produce designs of terraced diamonds, triangles, and other figures. For materials Navajos used fine handspun yarns in natural wool colors, handspun yarn dyed with indigo, and fine lac-dyed crimson yarns of raveled bayeta. The years from about 1800 till the early 1860s are known as the Classic period.

The Classic sarape poncho illustrated in plate 7 is characteristic of blankets woven from about 1840 to 1860. On a crimson ground woven of 100-thread bayeta, the center and ends are decorated with series of terraced figures arranged to form zigzag stripes at the ends, and diamond spaces framed by zigzag stripes through the center panels. Across the center of a more elaborate poncho is a row of small solid white diamonds at the center of larger diamond spaces, with terraced edges flanked by a zone of concentric stepped zigzag stripes (see plate 3). The end panels are composed of vertical zigzags, which, like the horizontal ones, create diamond spaces. This poncho probably dates to between 1850 and 1860.

Another standard layout used by Navajo weavers was a network of contiguous diamonds. In the sarape shown in plate 19, the diamond net, woven in white on a crimson ground of raveled bayeta, encloses diamond figures in blue, which are filled with fine paired lines. At the ends are half- and quarter-diamonds. This piece probably dates to around 1860. While most fine Classic sarapes were woven with a background of red, there are some in which raveled red was used together with indigo-dyed blue handspun yarn

to build the design on a white ground. In the sarape shown in plate 33, the center carries large, flattish, opposed terraced zigzag stripes woven in blue and red. Paired red and blue-and-red stripes are used to mark the center panel. The ends have a three-spot layout of flattish triangles, with small stepped "antennae" on the center figure. Between ends and center are rows of small zigzags.

Toward the end of the Classic period many pieces were carelessly woven, with the designs becoming small and fussy. Backgrounds tended to white, with numerous stripes in natural brown or black wool, or, occasionally, in indigo blue. A blanket characteristic of this style, shown in plate 12, has a white ground with brown-black stripes and diamond figures composed of alternating red and blue bars. Small zigzag elements adorn the center of each diamond. At the ends of the blanket are small, carelessly drawn triangles, while a row of small diamonds lies halfway between. This blanket was collected about 1860.

In the early 1860s the Navajo increased the intensity of their raids for sheep and other things on the Pueblos and Spanish and Anglo settlers. In response, the U.S. Army began a campaign to remove the Navajo from their home country and, by what the Navajo call the Long Walk, to place them on a reservation called Bosque Redondo near Fort Sumner on the Pecos River. It was a bitter experience for the Navajo. With few sheep or other supplies, they had to rely on the army for food, clothing, and materials for weaving.

During this time many new kinds of materials made their appearance in Navajo weaving. Most of these new materials were issued to the Navajo at Bosque Redondo as regular annuities. These included bayeta cloth with thicker, fuzzier yarns—increasingly Z-spun and dyed with cochineal or synthetic dyes—and commercial three-ply early Germantown yarns. These began to replace the fine worsted bayeta dyed with lac. With the new materials came a flood of new colors. The character of the handspun wool changed as well. The old churro sheep were being crossed with merino sheep, making the wool greasier and more difficult to card, spin, and dye.

Group near Bosque Redondo, Fort Sumner, New Mexico, ca. 1870. Photographer unknown. Courtesy U.S. Signal Corps, National Archives. (#111-SC-87976)

These changes in material were matched by changes in the way old Navajo design elements were drawn and used, often making them more elaborate. New elements such as simple and complex crosses and meanders were introduced. From their Spanish-Mexican neighbors Navajos borrowed new design elements and new systems of composition. These had been derived, in simplified form, from the fine Saltillo weaving of northern Mexico by the Spanish colonial weavers of the Rio Grande valley. The Saltillo system introduced the vertical orientation of background elements, the use of serrate figures, center-dominant motifs, and borders. The Navajo accepted these new influences, but soon they combined and integrated the new elements with their old traditions and layout.

Stepped-edge figures came to have serrate edges, and vertical zigzag elements began to appear. Many blankets were still woven using only the old Navajo elements. These blankets have been called Late Classic, but increasingly, and often contemporaneously, the vertical orientation, serrate adaptations and elements, and center-dominant motifs changed the feel of Navajo weaving. The new concepts became integrated in such a way that they were uniquely Navajo. These fabrics with integrated designs are usually termed Transitional.

A sarape that combines Classic design and layout with a wide variety of later materials is shown in plate 20. The design consists of a center panel with opposed zigzag stripes in red and white on a ground of red with narrow compound stripes in blue and green. Rows of terraced diamonds, woven in white on a red ground with narrow blue and green stripes, cross the blanket. White stripes separate the red zones. The materials consist of handspun wool and four kinds of raveled yarns in crimson and green. Another blanket, shown in plate 32, has a white ground crossed by clustered red stripes. The center, mid-center, and end zones have a crimson ground woven of large, soft, late raveled bayeta with terraced zigzag stripes in blue and a greenish blue enclosing diamond and part-diamond spaces. This sarape was collected about 1869. Another sarape collected at the same time combines Late Classic and Transitional features (see plate 31). The layout consists of alternating bands of stepped zigzag stripes elaborated into multicolored checkerboards and bands of chevrons. Five varieties of late raveled yarns are combined with three-ply early Germantown yarns and handspun wool. A third blanket from this period (see plate 22) was collected in 1868 by Gen. William Tecumseh Sherman, who signed the treaty with the Navajo allowing them to return to their homeland. The blanket's rows of terraced zigzag stripes were woven in various colors and combinations of commercial three- and six-ply yarn dyed with synthetic and natural dyes.

Typical of the small sarapes of the early 1870s are two collected about 1871. One of these (see fig. 12) has a white ground and bands of clustered red stripes. The ends have terraced triangles, while the center and mid-center zones have traditional zigzag figures executed in narrow, "broken," alternating stripes of black and white. The zigzag stripes of the center zone enclose diamond spaces, while those of the mid-center form a composite zigzag band. The blanket was woven of handspun, raveled, and three-ply yarns. Another small blanket, shown in plate 28, has a similar layout, with zones of narrow blue stripes on a red ground separated by white bands. The ends have strongly terraced triangles with a row of terraced diamonds across the center. On either side of the center zone are stripes in which white wool is carded together with red-dyed wool to produce combed pink, a color used by many weavers

during the 1870s. Another blanket uses an allover red ground of raveled flannel and raveled and respun flannel (fig. 2). It has very large, open terraced triangles and large open diamonds across the center. Smaller open diamonds mark the mid-center space. A four-ply yarn, faded to light olive on the interior of the terraced figures, marks an early introduction of four-ply Germantown.

A tattered sarape in the museum's collection is an early example of Navajo use of the Saltillo design system (see fig. 4). Two concentric diamonds form a center-dominant motif in white, red, and blue on a solid, dark indigo-blue ground. In the center is a typical, small, open Navajo terraced diamond. Vertically along the center is a row of small red and white concentric diamonds, while at the corners and bracketing the center are triangles in black, red, and brown diagonal stripes, like those sometimes used by Spanish colonial weavers. Across the end is a border of alternating brown and blue stripes, and along the sides is a border of alternating brown triangles and white, somewhat starlike figures. Handspun and three-ply yarns were used. Another sarape in the collection (24.1902) also shows Spanish influence, notably in the use of more than ten weft colors, many of them pastel shades frequently seen in Rio Grande blankets. Handspun white was combined with five raveled and eight three-ply weft yarns, some of which were paired; together with the use of four-ply warps, these yarns suggest a date of about 1875. The warps extend as a fringe and are tied off in a Spanish technique. The decoration consists of terraced zigzags, triangles, and checkerboard diamonds, with a border of green and pink triangles. The initials "JE" in the center suggest that this may have been a commissioned piece.

The blanket shown in plate 17 is a Transitional blanket that epitomizes the mixture of old and new traits in use during the mid 1870s. The design layout is typical Navajo with stepped triangle figures at each end and a center zone of terraced diamonds and half-diamonds. Vertical zigzag stripes reflect Saltillo design form, but the figures have Navajo stepped edges. Small stacked triangles as well show the Navajo adaptation of Saltillo elements. At each end the

Figure 24

Beeldléí (blanket),

ca. 1880.

Handspun wool,

129.2 × 77.5 cm. (17.9694)

inner zigzag triangles display a new element—the comb or square-fringed treatment. The materials are just as diverse as the design, with handspun, three- and four-ply Germantown yarns and two kinds of raveled yarns.

Only handspun yarns with synthetic dyes were used in the Late Classic blanket shown in fig. 24. Large terraced triangles are at the corners, while three rows of smaller, concentric terraced diamonds with crosses in the center make a wide zone across the center of the piece. Compound stripes in red and combed gray fill the area between the figured zones. Another Late Classic piece with a few Transitional elements was made of handspun wool and raveled cloth, three-ply and four-ply yarns, suggesting a date near 1875 (fig. 25). There are terraced triangles across the ends, with simple crosses both in and flanking the central triangle. From each outer cross descends a vertical zigzag, but with stepped edges, which is typical of the early applications of Saltillo design elements. Across the center are double, opposed terraced zigzags in lavender (faded to green), blue, and red with a combed pink central stripe. Combed pink is also used in stripe zones above and below the center. Collected at the same time was another blanket with Late Classic and Transitional elements (see fig. 11). On a ground of pale whitish gold are bands of design in blue, black, and white on a raveled crimson ground. The center and end bands are decorated with broad figured stripes filled with vertical zigzag elements in blue and blue-and-white, the Navajo adaptation of vertical serrate stripes, to make a horizontal band. The mid-center bands have rows of small stepped triangles. This five-zone layout was frequently used during the Late Classic and Transitional phases. One small Late Classic blanket, shown in fig. 26, has a white ground with red, blue, and yellow stripes. At each end and across the center, this piece has bands of red with rows of nested rectangles with simple crosses at their centers. The mid-center bands have rows of small triangles.

The Transitional blanket illustrated in plate 25, with a ground of two shades of raveled red, has terraced triangles at the ends, and a wide zone at the center with

Figure 25

Beeldléí (blanket),
ca. 1875.
Handspun wool,
raveled and commercial yarn,
135.2 × 84.7 cm. (22.7955)

Figure 26

Beeldléí (blanket),
1865–75.
Handspun wool,
raveled and commercial yarn,
132.8 × 78.8 cm. (22.7695)

adaptations of vertical zigzag stripes with stepped edges all drawn in somewhat cursive fashion. Flanking the central zone is a row of small, solid diamonds, while between this band and the end zones is a double row of bars in narrow stripes, offset so as to form a flattish zigzag. A date of about 1870 to 1875 is suggested by the use of handspun, raveled, and three-ply yarns. A very similar, but slightly later blanket, with a red ground of late raveled bayeta, has designs woven in handspun and four-ply Germantown yarns. A small Transitional sarape, with a ground of late raveled bayeta, is laid out in horizontal rows of diamond figures enclosed by crossed zigzags in alternating colors with halved triangles between (fig. 19). Across the center is a wider zone with a row of simple crosses framed by serrate zigzags in pinkish raveled yarn.

One small sarape (see fig. 15) uses a variety of handspun, raveled, and three-ply early Germantown yarns. The design consists of a diamond net woven in several red materials. The diamonds in the center have alternate blue and white stripes, with those at the ends having concentric, terraced diamonds in red and blue. From materials and design, the sarape should date to about 1870 to 1875. Another piece from around the same date has a red ground with zones of pattern in blue and white and in blue, white, and yellow (see plate 37). The center design consists of broken-stripe triangles, which form a zigzag, and stripes of rectangles with square centers woven in small lines. The ends have quarter-diamonds at the corners and diamond figures in the center. A small sarape dating slightly later is woven of raveled red and blue and handspun yarn laid out in a series of decorative bands separated by white stripes (see plate 5). The ends have quarter-diamonds in a white checkerboard on a red ground. Next to each end band is a band with opposed and offset triangles in blue, white, and red. The center zone has a ground of combed pink and is decorated with a row of solid, offset opposed triangles in blue, with a negative zigzag of red between. Flanking the center is a band with a row of white diamonds with red centers.

A small sarape illustrated in plate 34 has five patterned bands separated by compound stripes of red, blue, and green on a white ground. The outer panels have half- and quarter-diamonds over a striped ground of blue and green on red. Across the center is a red zigzag formed by offset opposed triangles in broken stripes. Mid-center bands have red and dark-blue zigzag stripes. The design and the use of handspun and raveled red and green yarns suggest a date of about 1875 to 1885.

Not all finely woven sarapes were decorated with elaborate designs. One small sarape, shown in fig. 27, bears a pattern of compound stripes separated by zones of white. Each stripe band consists of three blue stripes outlined in red with a ground of combed tan between. All yarns were handspun. The sarape may have been collected as early as the 1850s, but probably not until about 1870.

The Navajo wove one pattern decorated in panels of stripes alternating dark brown-black and shades of indigo blue, which they termed the "Mexican pelt," pointing to its introduction from the Spanish weavers. The pattern was used widely by southwestern weavers, and is generally called the Moqui, or Moki, after the Spanish name for the Hopi, who wove similar striped blankets.

The Moki blanket was made in many grades. An elaborate blanket shown in plate 39 has a Moki-striped ground over which is a layout of large serrate diamonds in blue and white on a raveled red base. The central row of two diamonds has stacked terraced triangles with small quarter-diamonds. The outer rows consist of diamonds and half-diamonds filled with vertical zigzags. The weft selvage uses three-ply yarn, which, together with the handspun and raveled yarns, suggests a date of 1870 to 1875.

A less elaborate blanket (see fig. 10) has a Moki-striped ground of brown and blue. At the ends of the blanket and separating the Moki panels are diamond stripes with stepped-edges woven in blue and orange-red with combed pink borders alternating with simple stripes in combed pink. Materials include handspun, two raveled, and two three-ply yarns, a combination that indicates a date of 1865 to 1875. The darkish Moki-pattern blanket shown in plate 29 has a ground of narrow blue and black stripes divided into panels by red stripes with beaded edges. Each panel has a central stripe of red beading, while the center of the blanket has a narrow green stripe with white and red rhombs flanked by beaded lines. This blanket is said to have been woven by a Hopi, but the presence of lazy lines and a Navajo selvage system suggests a Navajo origin instead. In an earlier blanket, illustrated in plate 1, dated about 1865 to 1875, the panels of brown and blue stripes are separated by white stripes with beaded edges in brown. In one fine, soft *diyogí*, the panels of blue and brown stripes have a narrow beaded center line and are separated by white stripes (see plate 16).

The Navajo word "diyogí" means "soft" or "fluffy." Most of the handspun yarns were larger in diameter and somewhat less tightly spun than those used in the finely woven sarapes made with exotic materials. The diyogí, or diyugí, was the everyday blanket of the Navajo. It served to sleep on, to hang over the door of the hogan, and to wrap the baby in; most of all, it served as a blanket to wear every day. Many diyogí were decorated in combinations of stripes, but many had patterns akin to those of the finer sarapes, although usually less elaborate. Because most diyogís were made for use, they were often used until they wore out, and then discarded.

One diyogí (see fig. 14) has a pattern of five broad zones of compound stripes woven in coarse yarns of natural dark brown, combed gray, and indigo blue, separated by white stripes. Another striped diyogí has eight bands of compound stripes in natural dark brown, white, indigo-dyed blue, and light pink, raveled from soft flannel and respun (see plate 40). Both of these blankets date from about 1880.

Figured sarapes in diyogí weave increased in numbers during the late 1870s and 1880s. One sarape diyogí (see fig. 13), collected about 1875, bears three wide zones of decorations all on a ground of combed gray. Each end

Figure 27

Beeldléí (blanket),
1868–70.
Handspun wool,
130.2 × 92.4 cm. (23.2816)

zone has large concentric zigzag stripes in pink and pale yellow, while the center has a more elaborate zigzag in white, dark brown, and pink. Across the outer ends are stripes of orange, yellow, and pink. Another sarape diyogí, illustrated in fig. 28, has a striking design of vertically oriented meanders in brown-black, flanked by dark indigo meanders along the edges. The field between the meanders alternates orange and tomato-red, all in handspun yarns.

Over the centuries, many Navajos were captured by slaving expeditions and held by Spanish masters and, after the Mexican War in 1846, by Americans as well. The practice did not cease until the late 1870s. Both men and women were taken—men as general hands, women to work in the household. For the most part, these people were treated as servants. Among the tasks carried out by the women was weaving. Many Navajo women married into their owners' families. While most Navajo women wove on their own looms, they had access to a suite of synthetic, pastel dyes favored by, and available only to, the weavers of the Rio Grand valley. The products of these Navajos have come to be known as "slave" or "servant" blankets. A slave blanket in the museum's collection, shown in fig. 16, is woven in diyogí weave in an elaborate pattern that features both Spanish dye colors and Spanish layout and design elements. A wide center panel, framed by a red border with an inner zigzag edge, has a pattern of the "Chimayo leaf," done in tapestry weave, and another leaf-and-diamond pattern with lenticular inserts. The border has large quartered crosses and lozenges forming a diamond shape. The design zones are framed by compound stripes in pastel colors.

Another type of blanket usually woven as a diyogí is one termed the wedge weave, a variety of eccentric weaving. In this weave, a wedge or triangular figure is woven on one side. All wefts are then inserted parallel to the diagonal edge of the initial wedge, making stripes of different colors. The technique builds patterns of diagonal stripes, chevrons, or vertical zigzags. Wedge weave, developed in the 1870s, was popular during the last part of the nineteenth century, and with a few exceptions died out about 1900.

The well-woven wedge weave blanket illustrated in plate 11 has a finely drawn allover "lightning" design of vertical zigzags mainly in dark brown-black and white, but with salient wedges in green, golden tan, red, and blue, forming a complete band across the center. The materials, including handspun and four-ply yarns, suggest a date of about 1880. Another, well-woven wedge weave is decorated by an allover vertical zigzag pattern in dark blue, combed gray, and yellow (faded from green) four-ply yarn on a red ground of four-ply Germantown yarn (see plate 42).

Blankets made for wearing are rarely woven today. After Bosque Redondo more and more clothing was sewn of cotton or various other materials. The sewing machine gradually became a household item in Navajo homes. Commercially woven shawls—often Pendleton blankets today—increasingly replaced the sarape and even the diyo-gí. The diyogí survived as a weave, however, as many diyo-gís began to be placed on the floor as rugs. The Navajo rug replaced the sarape. And the fine weaving of the early sarapes returned as weaving to produce wall hangings or tapestries. As it changes to adapt to modern ways, Navajo weaving continues to follow the old Navajo way.

A SELECTION OF TEXTILES
FROM THE COLLECTION

Plate 1

Beeldléí (blanket), 1865–75.
Handspun wool,
153 × 132.7 cm. (1410)

Many people think it's easy to keep the stripes straight in a Navajo blanket, but it's not. The trick is to make sure that your warps are evenly spaced. If they're not, or if the warps are too close together, your weaving will go up faster in those places. The tension of your warps also has to be evenly distributed. I am very interested in Moki blankets; I like to combine contemporary patterns with these older, classic styles.

Marilou Schultz

This blanket reminds me of the dark black night, in the early morning before the skyline begins to turn into day. The stripes are bold, especially the natural white against the blue and black. The beading combines the two colors into one that is both dark and light—the point of conflation and change.

Wesley Thomas

Díí o'oolkidígíí 1

*Beeldléí, 1865–75.
Aghaa' yilá bee yisdízígíí,
153 × 132.7 cm. (1410)*

Diné t'óó ahayói ádeinízin, diyogí t'óó noodǫ́zígíí doo nanitł'agóó k'ézdongo jidootł'óół danízin. Áko nidi doo ákót'ée da. Nanoolzhee'ígíí iiyisíí bóhólníih. Nanoolzhee' nizhónígo t'áá aheełt'éego bita' nidahaz'ą́ą́go éí yá'át'éehgo yitł'ó. Doo Hazhó'óó nanoolzhee'ígíí bita' nidahaz'ą́ą́góó, honíí'eiigo éí doodaii' diłch'ilgo jitł'óogo t'áadoo hodina'í dego dilki' dóó łahgóó adaazts'ǫ́ǫ́d yileeh. Áádóó nanoolzhee' jidiłts'ǫ'go, t'áá ahidaałt'éego nídongo éí nizhóní. Shí éí diyogí iiyisíí shił yá'át'éehígíí dóó shił nilínígíí éí "Moki blanket" wolyé. Haalá shich'ooní Oozéí nilį́. Áádóó díishjį diyogí bee nidaach'ą́ą́hígíí dóó ałk'idą́ą́' diyogísání bee nidaach'ą́ą́hą́ą́ ałhii' sinilgo bee ashtł'óogo ayóo bíneeshdlį́.

Marilou Schultz

Díí beeldléí éí tł'éé' shił nahalin. Ts'ídá níléídę́ę́ nihooshkáá' ha'doodlał ts'ídá áají' haiłkáahgo, abínígo, ákót'é shił nahalin. Danoodǫ́zígíí éí dadítą́ą́go danít'i. Díí łigaigo nít'i'ígíí shił ákót'é. Níléí diłhiłgo dootł'izhígíí dóó łizhinígíí bíighahjį' danít'i'go, ahidahidiilt'éego éí naaki iilchí'ígíí t'áałá'í nahaleeh, t'áá iiyisíí łizhinígíí dóó łigaiígíí. Áko áadi ahidahidiideełgo, jó áko éí łahgo ánáyoodlííł.

Wesley Thomas

Plate 2

Beeldléí (blanket), 1880–90.
Handspun wool and commercial yarn,
108.3 × 142.9 cm. (9603)

This blanket was probably made for wear, but not
everyday wear. It may have been woven for a special
occasion, like a gathering for a squaw dance, or an
event at one of the pueblos. Many Navajo blankets
were traded or sold to the Pueblos around the time
this blanket was made.

D. Y. Begay

Díí o'oolkidígíí 2

*Beeldléí, 1880–90.
Aghaa' yilá bee yisdízígíí dóó aghaa' kingóó
nidahaniihígíí. 108.3 × 142.9 cm. (9603)*

Díí beeldléí éí bee na'adáá shį́į́ biniiyé ályaa nidi doo
t'áá ákwííję́ biniiyée da. T'áadoo le'é bił hoo'aah
daats'í biniiyé ályaa nítéé', ákǫ́ǫ́ bee adoodą́ą́ł
biniiyé. Níléí naalyéhé bá hooghangóó da
adeesdzáago éí doodaii' nidáá'góó da. Áádóó ałdó'
níléí Kiis'áaniitahgóó da adeesdzáago. Éí daats'í
biniiyé ályaa nít'éé'. Jó t'óó ahayói éí díí Diné
bibeeldléí naalyéhé bá hooghangóó nidahaaznii'.
Áádóó ałdó' Kiis'áanii nidayiisii.

D. Y. Begay

90

Plate 3

Bi ní ghá dzí itł'ó ní (sarape poncho), 1850–60.
Handspun wool and raveled yarn,
203.8 × 147.3 cm. (1.1225)

These rugs are really different from the work we do today. The designs are different and the colors are different. They make me think of our great-great-grandmothers. We never knew them, but they did all this work. It's important that we keep up with our weaving and with our Navajo ways. My mother was a weaver all her life, but I just started weaving about twenty years ago. I hope that our kids and our grandkids will continue to weave and to pass it on.

Irene Clark

Díí o'oolkidígíí 3

Bi ní ghá dzi itł'ó ní, 1850–60.
Aghaa' yilá bee yisdizígíí dóó aghaa' náost'ahígíí,
203.8 × 147.3 cm. (1.1225)

Díí diyogí éí t'áá íiyisíí łahgo ádaat'é. Dííshjí̧ atł'óhígíí doo bidaałt'ée da. Bee nidaashch'ą̧ą'ígíí ałdó' łahgo át'é. Áádóó ałdó' bee daashchíí'ígíí ałdó' łahgo ádaat'é. Nihichóoni' nihimásání danilínée éí bee bénáshniih, azhá̧ doo béédahoniilzin da nít'éé' nidi. Jó díí t'áá át'é ałtso binaanish ádayiilaa. Áádóó ałdó' ílį̧ díí t'áá ákót'éego da'iitł'óogo, díí Dinék'ehgo é'él'ínígíí. Shimá éí t'áá níléídę̧ę́' atł'ó. Áádóó t'áá shí éí ániid naadiin naahaiídóó índa ha'íítł'ó. Áádóó ałdó' niha'áłchíní dóó nihitsóóké dóó nihinálíké éí t'áá náásgóó da'itł'óóh dooleeł, éí laanaa nisin. Áko éí kót'éego atł'óhígíí náás dayólée dooleeł.

Irene Clark

Plate 4

Beeldléí (blanket), ca.1885.
Handspun wool,
115.6 × 142.9 cm. (6.305)

Navajo people are so adept and so curious about
everything that they will use a new material or a
new design just to get a kick out of it, to see what
the reaction will be, or to feel how it would be to
use something new. It's a trait that has helped our
people survive.

Kalley Keams

The "eye-dazzling" design of this piece is a window
into the weaver's mind, a glimpse of what she wanted others to see. In the weaver's world, when there
are no borders to contain or control the flow, the
design continues off into infinite space.

Wesley Thomas

Díí o'oolkidígíí 4

Beeldléí, 1885 yéędą́ą́' daats'í.
Aghaa' yilá bee yisdizígíí,
115.6 × 142.9 cm. (6.305)

Diné éí ayóo bił éédahózin. Áádóó ałdó' ayóo baa
ádahwiinít'į́į' t'áá ałtsojį'. Jó éí binahjį' éí díí t'áadoo
le'é bee áhodooníłígíí ániid hanááníídee'ígíí
dayiiłtsą́ągo yee éé' ni'dooch'ąh, t'óó hait'ée dooleeł
nízingo. Áádóó binahjį' hait'éego éí diné
deidínóoł'įįł áádóó ałdó' hait'éego éí bee íhodoolnííł
nízingo. Jó éí binahjį' díí kót'éego t'áadoo le'é bee
ni'jich'ąąh dóó t'áadoo le'é doo hógóó áádóó
t'ááhógo bee jidilnishgo jó kót'éego éí nihidine'é
yee yisdáákai.

Kalley Keams

Bee'dilkǫǫrígíí jinił'į́įgo, bee naashch'ąą'ígíí t'óó
ádayiilaaígíí nihíni'éę nihá dínóol'įįł, tsésǫ' bii'
jidéez'į́į' nahalingo danízingo ádayiilaa nahalin, t'óó.
Diyogí bibąąh ích'ąą'ígíí ádingo éí tł'óógóó doo
ninít'i'góó ch'í'iishch'ąą'.

Wesley Thomas

Plate 5

Beeldléí (blanket), 1875–85.
Handspun wool and raveled yarn,
138.5 × 85.8 cm. (6.1088)

The basic reason for weaving is still the same today
as when this rug was made—to fill a need in the
family. Years ago it was to create blankets for wearing
or for everyday use, while today it's to provide
money for food, tuition for college, or money for
the mortgage. But the basic reason is still the same—
to support your family.

Kalley Keams

Díí o'oolkidígíí 5

*Beeldléí, 1875–85.
Aghaa' yilá bee yisdizígíí dóó aghaa' náost'ahígíí,
138.5 × 85.8 cm. (6.1088)*

Ałk'idą́ą́' biniiyé diyogí ádaal'ínée éí dííshjį́į́di t'ahdii
t'áá ákót'é. Jó éí t'áála' hooghan haz'ánígíí
anáhóót'i'ígíí hólǫ́ǫgo éí biniiyé dah 'iistł'ǫ́ ál'į́.
Ałk'idą́ą́' díí dah 'iistł'ǫ́ ál'inígíí éí biniiyé ádaalyaa
áádóó t'áá choo'į́, t'áá ákwííjį́ biniiyé. Dííshjį́ diyogí
ádaal'ínígíí béeso bee ádoolnííł, ch'iyáán bee
nahidoonih éí biniiyé. Áádóó binahjį' éí ólta'góó da
béeso bá hólǫ́ǫ dooleeł biniiyé. Bik'é íídóoltah éí
doodaii' hooghan da bik'é ni'doolyééł biniiyé. Jó
binahjį' éí níléídę́ę̀' dah 'iistł'ǫ́ ádaal'ínée t'áá ákót'é,
anáhóót'i'ígíí hólǫ́ǫgo biniiyé diyogí ál'į́. Áádóó
ha'áłchíní bee bíká anijílwo'. Ha'áłchíní bee
biza'jiłtso' dóó bee baa áhójilyą́.

Kalley Keams

96

Plate 6

Beeldléí (blanket), ca. 1860.
Handspun wool and raveled yarn,
85 × 132 cm. (9.1910)

One of the first things that comes to mind when I
see an old rug is that I wish I could hear the songs
that were sung while it was being made. These rugs
were empowered by the weavers. Weaving is like
creating a living being, a child. When we take a rug
off the loom we go through an emotional separation, but it was probably even harder for weavers
during the period when this piece was woven.

  This piece was probably made for a Hopi woman.
The wearer may have been right-handed, since the
lower right side shows more wear than any other
area. I can picture the wearer pulling the right side
of her shoulder blanket over to cover her grandchildren as she held them—to shield them from the
cold weather or to hide them from the Mud Clowns
dancing in the village plaza.

Wesley Thomas

Díí o'oolkidigíí 6

Beeldléí, 1860 yę́ę́dą́ą́' daats'í.
Aghaa' yilá bee yisdizigíí
dóó aghaa' náost'ahígíí,
85 × 132 cm. (9.1910)

Ts'ídá áłtsé aląąjį' shíni' nilínígíí éí díí kót'éego
beeldléísání yiistséehgo, sin bił danit'i'ígíí éí jółts'ą́ą́'
laanaa nisin łeh, díí dah 'iistł'ǫ́ álnééh yę́ę́dą́ą́'. Jó éí
binahjį' díí dah 'iistł'ǫ beeldléí ádaalyaa bee éí
dabidziilgo ádaalyaa. Ajitł'óogo hiináago ájiił'įįh,
awéé' be'iina' hólónígi át'éego. Ałtso nijitł'óogo dah
'iistł'ónígíí nahjį' níjoo'a'go, hajiłtsosgo, jó áko
kwe'é jitł'óogo bich'į' dah dzizdáago, bich'į'
yájíłti'go da, éí yę́ę k'ad ałts'ą́ą́jigo dahadiit'ééh
nahalin. Jó áko nidi díí k'ad beeldléísání danilínígíí
íídą́ą́' da'atł'óhí danilínée shį́į́ t'áá íiyisíí bá nidanitł'a
nít'éé'. Jó díí beeldléí éí Oozéí asdzání nilį́įgo daats'í
bá ályaa nít'éé'. Háíshį́į́ nish'nááji yee na'ach'idgo
daats'í bibeeldléí nít'éé', ááji t'áá íiyisíí deezhzhaazh
nít'éé' lá.

Wesley Thomas

98

Plate 7

Bi ní ghá dzí itł'ó ní (sarape poncho), 1825–60.
Handspun wool and raveled yarn,
172.2 × 132.6 cm. (9.1912)

I believe very strongly that we need to educate our
young people about this early period of weaving in
Navajo life. Rugs like this speak volumes. They can
give our children a sense of pride, and the kind of
self-respect they need to face the two worlds we live
in.

Kalley Keams

For all we know, weaving may be the central core in
perpetuating Navajo culture.

Wesley Thomas

Díí o'oolkidígíí 7

Bi ní ghá dzí itł'ó ní, 1825–60.
Aghaa' yilá bee yisdízígíí dóó aghaa' náost'ahígíí,
172.2 × 132.6 cm. (9.1912)

T'áá íiyisíí nitsaago niha'áłchíní ałk'idą́ą́' atł'óhą́ą́ bee
nabi'dinitingo éí yá'át'ééh. Jó díí ałk'idą́ą́ dah 'iistł'ǫ́
ádaalyaa yę́ę, Diné ádayiilaaígíí, díí kót'éego dah
'iistł'ǫ́ níl'ı̨́ı̨go, t'óó ahayóígóó yá'áti'ígíí bił silá. Jó
ákót'éego éí niha'áłchíní deiníł'ı̨́ı̨go binahjı̨' yee
ha'ólníídóó t'áábí yee bidziil dooleeł. Áádóó t'áábí
sizínígíí yee ádiłdanidlı̨́ı̨ dooleeł. Jó éí kǫ́ǫ́ nihikéyah
naakigo iiná bii' siláhígíí, Bilagáana dóó Dinéjí,
hazhó'óó yii'jı̨' dadidoogáął dóó hazhó'óó iiná
íídooliił.

Kalley Keams

Jó nihił bééhózingo díí atł'óhígíí da éí Diné
be'í'ool'ı̨́ı̨łígíí bee náhiidoolnaałgo da át'é.

Wesley Thomas

Plate 8

Biil (two-piece dress), ca. 1860.
Handspun wool and raveled yarn,
126.6 × 82.5 cm. (9.1962)

Díí o'oolkidígíí 8

Biil, 1860 yéédáá' daats'í.
Aghaa' yílá bee yisdizígíí
dóó aghaa' náost'ahígíí,
126.6 × 82.5 cm. (9.1962)

The *biil*, a woman's dress, is a symbol of femaleness. A Navajo family contains not only human members, but also those things that provide nourishment or warmth, which are considered "family" or "mother." Any type of food—a vegetable garden, for example—is considered mother because it nourishes. Since fire provides warmth, it may also be considered mother. My great-grandfather always said that you can prepare the meals with a fire, but without the fire-keeper—the mother—it's not a home.

I have wondered many times why the middle part of a biil is one color—black. Maybe it's so the wearer can add personal adornment, such as a woven sash belt or a silver concha belt. More important, the biil has the same design as a Navajo ceremonial basket. What the relationship is between the basket and the biil, that is the question. In the weaving stories, the biil's mid-section is the area of emergence—the center point of creation. A human is created from the center of a woman's body, and so, too, the center of the biil is also the area of emergence.

Wesley Thomas

Biil éí asdzání bi'éé' át'é dóó asdzání yaa halne. Diné t'áála' hooghan haz'ą́ądóó éí doo t'áála'í diné háájéé'ígíí t'éiyá át'ée da. T'áadoo le'é, t'áá ałtsoní bee atah yá'áhoot'ééh áhósinii dóó binahjį' éí t'áála' haz'ą́ądóó bee baa nitsíhákees. Jó áko amá nilínígíí éí ákót'é. Áádóó ch'iyáán al'ąą ádaat'éhígíí áhót'é dóó akǫ́ǫ́dí dá'ák'ehgóó nidanise' nilínígíí jó éí t'éí nihimá dabidii'ní ałdó' háálá nihits'íís bich'iiyą' át'é. Áádóó éí kǫ' binahjį' hoozdo biniinaa éí ałdó' nihimágo baa nitsíikees. Ałk'idą́ą́' naakidi nácheii nilį̨igo ání, "Díí kǫ'ígíí éí ch'iyáán bee ájiił'įįh. Áádóó kwe'é hooghan yaa áhályánígíí dóó kǫ' yaa áhályánígíí jó éí amá. Éí doo ákwe'é hólǫ́ǫgo éí doo hooghan da.

Díkwíídí shį́į́ éí ha'át'íílá éí biniinaa kojí biil ałníí'gi éí t'áá łizhingo ályaa lá nisin łeh. Éí daats'í bi'éé' il'ínígíí t'áá hait'éego da yoo' da ádaat'éhígíí kwe'é bee naashch'ąą'ígíí hólǫ́ǫ́ dooleeł éí daats'í biniiyé ákót'é nisin. Jó éí áahdishnínígíí éí díí sis łichí'í da éí doodaii' sis łigaii da jó éí daats'í biniiyé át'é? Áádóó ałdó' díí alááh áníłtsogo baa nitsíhákeesígíí éí díí biil bee naashch'ąą'ígíí éí akǫ́ǫ́ ts'aa' bee ályaaígíí t'áá ákót'éego éí bee naashch'ąą', Dinék'ehjí bee nidahagháhígíí k'ehgo. Ako bína'ídíkid nilínígíí éí díí ts'aa'ígíí dóó biil lá hait'éego aheełt'éego baa hane' lá? Ako kojí atł'óójí baa hane'go díí biil ałníí'ii éí hahóóyá. Ákót'éego baa hane'. Áádę́ę́' iiná nilínígíí háát'i. Éí ákwe'é ałníí'ii áádę́ę́' éí ha'iizná. Jó ákót'é. Ako bíla'ashdla'ii, éí áádę́ę́' hazlį́į́'. Ako asdzání éí ałníí'ii akwe'é bits'íís bą̨ahgi bibidgónaa ałníí'. Áádę́ę́' éí awéé' nilínígíí nidahwiileeh. Jó ákót'éego éí biil níl'į.

Wesley Thomas

102

Plate 9

Beeldléí (blanket), 1875–80.
Handspun wool, raveled and commercial yarn,
111.1 × 148.6 cm. (9.1978)

This was a trade piece, woven by a Navajo for a
Hopi person. It was probably intended for special
occasions only, not everyday use. There are seven
stepped diamonds at each end of the blanket, just the
same as in some *biil*. I wonder if the number seven
refers to a significant event in Navajo culture that
made it important to express publicly?

Wesley Thomas

Díí o'oolkidigíí 9

Beeldléí, 1875–80.
Aghaa' yilá bee yisdizígíí dóó aghaa'
náost'ahígíí áádóó kingóó nidahaniihígíí,
111.1 × 148.6 cm. (9.1978)

Díí diyogí beeldléí nilínígíí éí Dinégo áyiilaa. Éí kojí
Oozéí daats'i t'áadoo le'é bił ałnánáályá. Áádóó ałdó'
t'áadoo le'é é'élnéehgo bił hoo'aahgo da, ákwe'é éí
choo'įį shįį éí biniiyé ályaa. Doo t'áá ákwííjį éí
choo'įį da. Jó níléí ałts'ą́ąhjí bee aditł'įhí tsosts'idgo
bee naashch'ąą' t'áá dííshjį biil ádaal'ínígi át'éego
ályaa. Baa nitséskeesgo díídí tsosts'idígíí daats'i éí díí
Dinéjí baa hane' dóó bee í'ool'įįłii t'áá hait'éego
daats'i áájí bídéét'i', tsosts'idígíí ałk'i náhást'ą bee
ályaaígíí. T'óó ákót'éego baa nitséskees.

Wesley Thomas

Plate 10

Biil (two-piece dress), probably 1885–1900.
Handspun wool,
133.7 × 82.6 cm. (9.1992)

I am interested in the history of this *biil*, although I don't think that we will ever find the answers. I know it was collected at Hopi, but was it made for the Hopi people? It's an early dress style, but it may have been made late in the nineteenth century. It seems to show signs of wear. Did a Navajo woman wear it?

D. Y. Begay

This is my favorite *biil*. When I first saw it, I was lost in it. It has a very clean, powerful design. It was either made early in the nineteenth century or later at the request of a Hopi person as a replica of the black manta the Hopi wore.

Wesley Thomas

Díí o'oolkidígíí 10

Biil, 1885–1900.
Aghaa' yilá bee yisdizígíí,
133.7 × 82.6 cm. (9.1992)

Shí beeldléí nát'ą́ą' baa náháne'ígíí ayóo bíneeshdlį́. Azhą́ shį́į́ íiyisíí baa hane'ígíí doo nihił béédahodoozįįł da nidi díí shił bééhózinígíí éí díídí beeldléí Oozéídi nídiiltsooz. Áádóó ałdó' Oozéí diné'é éí daats'í bá ályaa. Jó éé' éí át'é, t'áá ałk'idą́ą' daa'éé'ígíí. Áko díí náhást'éíts'áadahdi neeznádiin bee wólta'ígíí, íídą́ą' daats'í ádaalyaa. Jó bii' oodzá dóó chooz'įįd nahalin. T'áá daats'í Diné asdzání bi'éé' nít'éé'?

D. Y. Begay

Díí biil éí t'áá íiyisíí shił nilį́. T'óó yiiłtsánéedą́ą' t'áá íiyisíí néél'į́į' dóó ayóo éí bąąh chin ádin nahalingo naashch'ąą'. Doo nidi nanitł'agóó níl'į́igo naashch'ąą'. Díí náhást'éíts'áadahdi neeznádiin wólta'ígíí t'óó bee hahóóyáhą́ądą́ą' daats'í ályaa éí doodaii' t'áá ániidóó, Oozéí dine'é daats'í ła' bá áyiilaa. Éí díí kojí Oozéí bi'éé' łizhingo yee hadít'éhígíí, éí daats'í be'elyaa. Jó ákót'é nahalin.

Wesley Thomas

Plate 11

Beeldléí (blanket), ca. 1885.
Handspun wool and commercial yarn,
119.4 × 91.4 cm. (9.9821)

This piece reminds me of a phrase in a prayer from a male version of the Blessing Way ceremony. The phrase begins, "With lightening surrounding me, I will be protected." That is a very loose translation, since I am not in a position to make a direct translation from the ceremony. The literal translation does not belong in the public domain. I'm using this phrase only as a way to describe my thinking about this particular blanket. I believe the wearer was a man who had esoteric knowledge of Navajo religion. Only a man of power could wear this blanket and call it his own. I refer to it as the "Blanket of Protection."

Wesley Thomas

*Beeldléí, 1885 yéédą́ą́' daats'í.
Aghaa' yilá bee yisdizígíí
dóó aghaa' kingóó nidahaniihígíí,
119.4 × 91.4 cm. (9.9821)*

Díí beeldléí nilínígíí éí sodizin ádaalne'go kojí Hózhǫ́ǫ́jí diné bá ál'inígíí éí bee baa nitséskees. Kót'éego éí sodizin bee hahwiit'ééh, "Atsiniltł'ish shináhoodiłgo hózhǫ́ǫgo naasháa doo." Jó ákót'éego éí saadígíí bee yá'áti'. Nidi shí sézį́įdóó ts'ídá áníit'éí át'éego sodizin nít'i'ígíí éí díí sodizin álnéehgo hoogáál góne' jó éí baa hane'ígíí doo bee shá haz'ą́ą da. Éí doo kǫ́ǫ́ t'óó bóhólníihgóó dinétah baa yá'átéi'da. Biniinaa díí kwe'é ch'íní'ánígíí éí t'óó baa nitséskeesgo díí beeldléíígíí t'óó shił ákót'é. Áko shí baa nitsískeesgo éí Diné hastiingo éí bibeeldléí nít'éé' nisin. Áko t'áá iiyisíí daats'í Diné binahagha'ígíí bił bééhózingo. Jó díídí beeldléíígíí ákót'éego diné ééhósinígíí bidziilgo nitsékeesígíí jó éí ákót'éhígíí dabibeeldléí nít'éé'. Áko shí éí kodóó nísh'į́igo díí beeldléí bee ách'ą́ą́h na'adáhígíí át'é.

Wesley Thomas

Plate 12

Diyogí (utility blanket), 1850–60.
Handspun wool and raveled yarn,
121.9 × 84.5 cm. (10.8456)

With Navajo weaving, you have to know where the
raw materials come from—about the sheep, and
what plants they eat. You have to have an understanding of the weaving process. You also have to
have an intimate relationship with your rug, and you
have to love what you do in order to do a good job.

Esther Yazzie

Díí o'oolkidigíí 12

Diyogí, 1850–60.
Aghaa' yilá bee yisdizígíí dóó aghaa' náost'ahígíí,
121.9 × 84.5 cm. (10.8456)

Díí Diné bidiyogí ál'ínígíí binahji' bééhózinígíí éí
aghaa' bee ályaaígíí éí hoł bééhózin dooleeł. Háádéé'
shíí éí kót'éego bee da'atł'ó. Dibéhígíí bééhojósin
áádóó tł'oh yiłchozhígíí da. Jó éí binahji' dah
'iistł'ónígíí bee hahwiilzhíízh dóó yitł'óhígíí baa
ákóznízin. Áádóó ałdó' hadah 'iistł'ónígíí hoł nilíįgo
baa ákoznízin. Áádóó ayóo ájó'níigo ákót'éego éí
nizhónígo hanaanish ájiił'įįh.

Esther Yazzie

110

Plate 13

Beeldléí (blanket), 1850–60.
Handspun wool and raveled yarn,
147 × 198 cm. (10.8457)

My grandmother calls these blankets "leaders' blankets." I can't relate to the term "chief blanket." In the beginning they were probably just common everyday blankets, but then they evolved into a status symbol.

Wesley Thomas

My grandmother calls these blankets "*naat'áanii bii beeldléí*" (leader). Our people have seen enough photographs of them over the years to know that they were worn by respected people like Barboncito and Manuelito. The photographs were probably all posed, but, even so, this is what has been suggested to us.

Kalley Keams

Díí o'oolkidigíí 13

Beeldléí, 1850–60.
Aghaa' yilá bee yisdizígíí dóó aghaa' náost'ahígíí,
147 × 198 cm. (10.8457)

Shimásání éí díí beeldléí naat'áanii bibeeldléí ní. Áko kojí aláąji' "chief blanket" bi'di'níigo ákót'éego shí doo bééhonisin da. Níléídą́ą́' shį́į́ t'áá ákwíįį́ beeldléí shį́į́ át'é. Áádóó wóshdę́ę' náás hodeeshzhiizhdóó éí wónáásdóó naat'áanii ídlį́įgo t'áadoo le'é t'áá ílį́įgo baa nítsíhakeesgo bee níl'į́į shį́į́ silį́į'.

Wesley Thomas

Shimásání éí díí beeldléí "naat'áanii" yilní. Áko nihidine'é t'óó ahayóí akǫ́ǫ́ beda'alyaago naaltsoos yii' deinééł'į́į'. Díkwíí shį́į́ nááhai, ákót'éego. Éí binahji' éí Diné ałk'idą́ą́' binaat'áanii yę́ę t'áá iiyisíí ílį́įgo baa nitsíhákees. Ła' Barboncito wolyé dóó ła' Manuelito. Áádóó ałdó' beda'alyaaígíí éí hazhó'óó hasht'e' nidaháaztą́ągo ádaalyaa, anihi'dilkeed bi'di'níigo daats'í. Jó ákót'é éí nihi'doo'niid.

Kalley Keams

112

Plate 14

Beeldléí (blanket), 1840–50.
Handspun wool and raveled yarn,
128.9 × 181 cm. (11.8280)

These rugs are personal in the sense that we know
they were made by our ancestors—people who
wove in the past. Rugs were the first clothing sent to
us on this earth, along with our jewelry. That is how
we were brought here, on this earth. It is our way of
building an invisible shield that will repel certain
forces away from us, leaving only goodness.

Rita Jishie
(Translated by Esther Yazzie)

Díí o'oolkidígíí 14

Beeldléí, 1840–50.
Aghaa' yilá bee yisdizígíí dóó aghaa' náost'ahígíí,
128.9 × 181 cm. (11.8280)

Díí dah 'iistł'ǫ́ ádaalyaa dóó beeldléí danilį́į́go éí t'áá
íiyisíí áhánígo éí nihídéét'i', háálá nihichóoni'
ádayiilaa. Ałk'idą́ą́' deeztł'ǫ́. Dah 'iistł'ǫ́ nilínígíí éí
áłtsé nihi'éé' silį́í, kwe'é nahoosdzáán bikáá'ji'
nanihi'deelyáago, nihiyo' t'áá bił. Kót'éego éí koji'
nahosdzáán bikáá'ji' nanihi'deedlá. Ákót'eego ałdó'
ach'ą́ą́h naalyéhé nilį́, t'áadoo yit'íní. Ako níláahdę́ę́'
bee ak'iji' na'anish danilínígíí éí níwohji' kóyósin.
Áádóó binahjį' éí yá'ádaat'éhígíí t'éí nihinízin. Jó
ákót'é.

Rita Jishie

114

Plate 15

Beeldléí (blanket), 1840–50.
Handspun wool and raveled yarn,
142 × 191 cm. (11.8281)

If you look closely at this chief blanket, you can see through the wide stripes to a series of white and dark-brown warps. This was probably not done for the sake of design. The warps represent rain. When we see rain coming down from the sky, we see a series of dark and light bands of different colors. The weaver probably incorporated this series of bands for warps so that her rug would maintain good relations with the natural elements.

Harry Walters

It is generally understood among traditional Navajo weavers that darkness is a representation of maleness and light of femaleness. Furthermore, the color combination in this piece includes all the colors important to Navajo society. White is of the east, blue of the south, red of the west, and black of the north. The color combination in this piece draws the colors of the four directions into one entity, creating a sense of wholeness.

Wesley Thomas

Díí o'oolkidígíí 15

Beeldléí, 1840–50.
Aghaa' yilá bee yisdizígíí dóó aghaa' náost'ahígíí,
142 × 191 cm. (11.8281)

Díí hazhó'óó naat'áanii bibeeldléí jiníł'į́įgo díí nitsaago danít'i'ígíí éí biyi'góne' biníkáhoot'į́. Biyi'góne' ch'íhoot'inígíí éí łigai dóó t'áá íiyisíí dinilchíí'go nanoolzhee'ígíí hólǫ́. Díí éí doo bee naashch'ąą'ígíí biniiyé ályaa da sha'shin. Áko nanoolzhee'ígíí éí níłtsą́ yaa halne' nisin. Jó nahałtingo éí níléí yá diłhił biyi'déé' éí tó hólǫ́. Áádóó jiníł'į́įgo, ła' éí t'áá íiyisíí dadiłhił, ła' éí dadinilgaigo, ákót'éego nidahaazt'i'. Áádóó ałdó' łahgo át'éego daalchíí'. Áko díí yiztł'ónígíí éí díí dah 'iistł'ǫ́ níłtsą́ yiih yiyíílá, nanoolzhee'ígíí éí nahalin. Éí binahjį' éí diyogí níłtsą́ ádaat'éhígíí yééhósin. Díí akǫ́ǫ́ iiná bił nidaazláhígíí bii' silá.

Harry Walters

Díí bééhózingo éí Dinéhígíí yaa halne', bee í'ool'įįł nilínígíí dóó atł'óhígíí. Díí t'áadoo le'é łizhingo yistł'ǫ́ǫgo éí t'éí koji Dinéhígíí, hastói idlį́į́jí áájí yaa halne'. Áádóó ałdó' dinilgai éí doodaii' łigaigo éí áájí asdzání yaa halne'. Áko díí hazhó'óó níl'įgo éí bee naashch'ąą'ígíí t'áá áłah ahiih náádláago díí beeldléíígíí bii'jį' áko t'áá át'é bee naashch'ąą'ígíí éí díí koji Diné binahagha'jí t'áá át'é t'áá íiyisíí bídadéét'i'. Díí łigaiígíí éí ha'a'aahdéé' bee bééhózin. Dootł'izhígíí éí shádi'ááh áádóó łichí'ígíí éí e'e'aah. Aádóó łizhinígíí éí náhookǫs. Áko bee yistł'ónígíí t'áá át'é bee naashch'ąą', t'áá díí'déé'go. Éí binahjį' éí t'áá át'é t'ááłá'í nánídlį́.

Wesley Thomas

Plate 16

▬▬
▬▬

Beeldléí (blanket), 1870–80.
Handspun wool and one raveled thread,
183.3 × 138.5 cm. (15.4616)

There is a single raveled crimson thread visible in
this rug. It may be a marker signifying a particular
maker or owner. Weavers do this with their rugs as
women sometimes use identifying marks on their
pots. I call it a weavership mark. The thread is laid in
between the wefts.

D. Y. Begay

Even though the colors in this piece are distinct
from one another, the beading creates a blend. The
beading is transitional between dark and light
wefts—it creates unity.

Wesley Thomas

Díí o'oolkidígíí 16

▬▬
▬▬

*Beeldléí, 1870–80.
Aghaa' yilá bee yisdizígíí dóó aghaa'
náost'ahígíí t'ááła'ígo,
183.3 × 138.5 cm. (15.4616)*

Díí kwe'é t'ááła'í náost'ahígíí t'ááyó dinilchíí'
nahalin, tł'ólígíí. Díí dah 'iistł'ónígíí t'áá bééhóziní
nilį́. T'óó daats'í bee esht'ishígíí át'é. Éí binahjį' éí
ééhózin nilį́, bee esht'ishígíí éí doodaii' ałdó'
ákót'éego daats'í ła' díí shí níigo yee iit'ish, éí daats'í
át'é. Jó da'atł'óhígíí ła' ákódaat'į́. Doo da'atł'óhígí
t'éiyá da, akǫ́ǫ́ sáanii da łeets'aa' da ádeile'ígíí
ákódeił'į́. Áko shídę́ę́'go bee yíníshíigo éí díí dah
'iistł'ǫ́ íɫ'ínígíí yee ádá'iit'ishígíí át'é dishnii łeh. Áko
díí bee ná'ałkadí nahalingo tł'ólígíí éí t'óó ákwe'é
niilyá, nanoolzhee'ígíí bita'gi.

D. Y. Begay

Azhą́ shį́į́ díí bee da'iilchíhí ał'ą̨ą̨ ádaat'éego bee
naashch'ą̨ą̨' nidi yisht'eezhgo yistł'ónígíí yee
áłhídadínéelná. Áko aghaa' daalzhinígíí dóó
dadinilgaiígíí bita' yisht'eezhgo daastł'ǫ́ǫgo éí bee
t'ááła'í nilį́ nádleeh.

Wesley Thomas

118

Plate 17

Beeldléí (blanket), ca. 1875.
Handspun wool, raveled and commercial yarn,
128.3 × 81.9 cm. (15.7719)

Just looking at these old rugs reminds me of when I was a little girl. I was just thinking how hard we all worked at putting out a rug, but when we were young, everything was so good and so easy. Now when I think about it, it makes me sad.

Glennabah Hardy
(Translated by
Marie Hardy-Saltclah)

Weaving has been my mother's whole life, ever since she was a child. She never went to school. She took care of the sheep, sheared the wool, cleaned the wool, carded the wool, spun the wool, and finished the rugs.

Marie Hardy-Saltclah
(Glennabah Hardy's daughter)

Beeldléí, 1875 yę́ędą́ą́' daats'í.
Aghaa' yílá bee yisdízígíí dóó aghaa' náost'ahígíí
áádóó kingóó nidahaniihígíí,
128.3 × 81.9 cm. (15.7719)

Díí beeldléísání níl'ị́ịgo yínáshiilniihígíí éí níléí at'ééké yázhí nishłínéedą́ą́' bénáshniih. Áko baa nitséskeesígíí éí ts'ídá bee naanish ályaaígíí yéigo bina'anishgo éí ályaa díí dah 'iistł'ǫ. Nidi ádaniilts'íísí yę́ędą́ą́' t'áá ałtsojį' éí nizhóní dóó t'áá ałtsojį' doo nanitł'a da. Áko k'ad baa nitséskeesgo éí kodi éí nashiiłná dóó baa atídinishdlį́.

Glennabah Hardy

Shimá éí dah 'iistł'ǫ be'iina' át'é, t'áá níléídę́ę́', t'ah áłchíní nilínéedą́ą́'. Doo éí ííłta' da. Dibé éí yaa áhályą́ą́ nít'ę́ę́' dóó tá'díígizh dóó aghaa'ígíí yizgis. Áádóó ha'nííłchaad dóó aghaa' yizdiz. Áádóó dah 'iistł'ǫ áyiilaa.

Marie Hardy-Saltclah

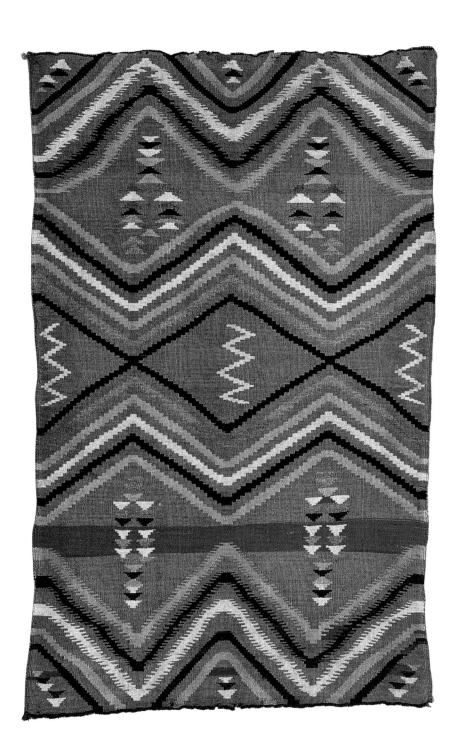

Plate 18

Beeldléí (blanket), 1865–75.
Handspun wool and raveled yarn,
143.5 × 185.5 cm. (19.3022)

I come from a long line of weavers. My mother, my
grandmother, and my aunts were weavers. I can
remember some of the names that these rugs were
called. My mother and my grandmother used to talk
about them. My mother wove large rugs. It was a
family effort. In the summer the loom was so large
that it would go through the roof of the summer
arbor. My mother and aunt would weave the
designs, and I would fill in the spaces. Then in the
fall we would take the rugs to the trading post and
sell them.

Laura Cleveland
(Translated by Harry Walters)

Díí o'oolkidígíí 18

Beeldléí, 1865–75.
Aghaa' yilá bee yisdizígíí dóó aghaa' náost'ahígíí,
143.5 × 185.5 cm. (19.3022)

Shí níléí t'óó ahayói da'atł'ó nilį́įdóó éí bits'ą́ądę́ę́'
she'iina' yit'ih. Shimá lá, áádóó shimásání áádóó
shimáyázhí éí da'atł'óó nít'éé'. Áko ła' béédaashniih
díí dah 'iistł'ǫ bee daójíhígíí. Shimá dóó shimásání
yaa yáłti' nít'éé'. Shimá ts'ídá nitsaago atł'óó nít'éé'.
Áádóó t'áá ałtsoní áká'iijah nít'éé'. Ákwe'é t'áála'
haz'ą́ądóó. Áko shį́įgo éí dah 'iistł'ǫ ayóó'ániłtsogo
ál'įįh. Níléí gódeg hooghan biníkáágóne' íít'i' łeh,
shį́įgo, chaha'oh biyi'. Áko shimá dóó shimáyázhí éí
díí neich'ą́ąhgo yitł'óó nít'éé'. Áádóó shí éí bita'gi
hasht'eesh'į́į́ nít'éé', t'áá nidahaz'ą́ągóó. Áádóó
aak'eedgo éí dah 'iistł'ónígíí naalyéhé bá
hooghangóó nahidoonih biniiyé yiltsos.

Laura Cleveland

Plate 19

Beeldléí (blanket), 1850–60.
Handspun wool and raveled yarn,
175.3 × 130.8 cm. (19.3037)

This design reminds me of the stars, especially the digger story in the Creation stories. It also reminds me of the strings that we played with in the winter when I was a child. Our grandparents would show us different ways to make designs, like stars, with string. It provided entertainment on cold winter nights as the wind howled outside. Nestled next to the fire, we would re-create the world with strings.

Wesley Thomas

Díí o'oolkidígíí 19

Beeldléí, 1850–60.
Aghaa' yilá bee yisdizígíí dóó aghaa' náost'ahígíí,
175.3 × 130.8 cm. (19.3037)

Díí bee naashch'ąą'ígíí éí sǫ' nahalin. Íiyisíí yaa halne'ígíí éí kojí t'óó hodeeyáádą́ą́' baa hane'ígíí háíshį́į́ na'ageedgo baa hane'ę́ę. Áádóó ałdó' haigo éí tł'óól bee nida'iitł'o' nít'éé' áłchíní daniidlínéedą́ą́'. Áko nihimásání da nihicheii da nihinálí da éí nihił nidaanéé nít'éé'. Éí na'atł'o' yee nidanihinitin nít'éé', łahgo ał'ąą át'éego tł'óól bee hála' bee nijich'ąąhígíí. Áko t'áá íiyisíí hodina' ákót'éego ádajiłʼį́įgo haigo, tł'ée'go. Tł'óo'di éí daniyolgo, kǫ' binahjį' éí nidahísíitą́ągo. Éí bee hoozíligo díí tł'óół bee nida'iitł'o' łeh. Jó ákót'éego éí nahosdzáánígíí t'áá át'é baa náháne'. Sǫ' da ádaat'é, t'áá ał'ąą ádaat'éego ádaalne'go ákót'éego bénáshniih.

Wesley Thomas

124

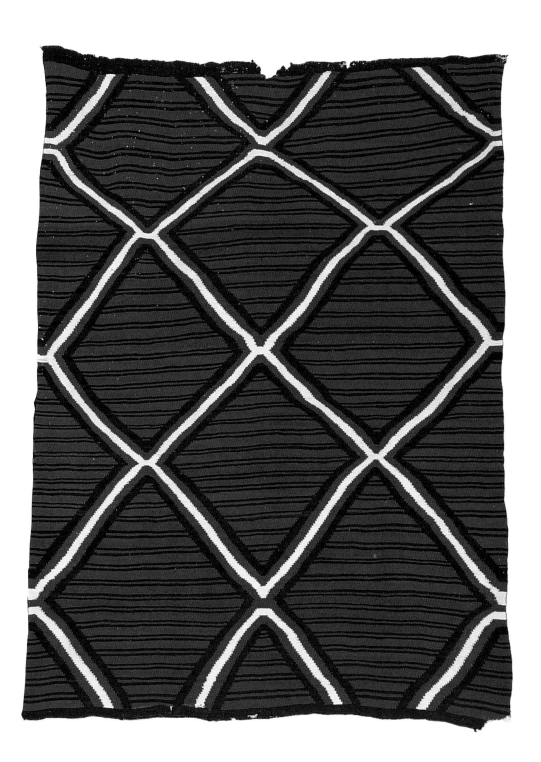

Plate 20

Beeldléí (blanket), 1865–70.
Handspun wool and raveled yarn,
185.4 × 141.7 cm. (19.3039)

Who knows? My great-great-great-grandmother
may have woven this rug or one of the others in this
collection. What amazes me is that they are over one
hundred years old, and they were used. People wore
them as clothing, and yet they still look good. As a
child, I helped my mother prepare the wool for her
weaving. When I was about twelve years old, I set up
a loom, strung the warp, and started weaving. But it
was time to go back to school, and I didn't finish the
rug. In boarding school they told us to forget our
language, forget our traditions.

Inez Yazzie

Díí o'oolkidigíí 20

Beeldléí, 1865–70.
Aghaa' yilá bee yisdizígíí dóó aghaa' náost'ahígíí,
185.4 × 141.7 cm. (19.3039)

Háíshíini' bił bééhózin? Táadi shimásání nánídlįįgo
éí doodaii' táadi binálí nánídlįįgo daats'i beeldléí
áyiilaa díí ła' kǫ́ǫ́ áłah nilínígíí. Áádóó aláah
áníłtsogo nashiiłnánígíí éí díí dah 'iistł'ónígíí éí
neeznádiin nááhai yéę́dą́ą́' ádaalyaa dóó íídą́ą́'
chodaoz'įįd. Diné dabi'éé' nít'éé' áádóó t'ahdii éí
danizhóní yee'. T'ah áłchíní nishłínéedą́ą́' shimá bíká
anáshwo' łeh nít'éé' díí aghaa'ígíí hasht'e yilnéehgo,
bee adootł'óół biniiyé. Naakits'áadah shináahaigo
t'áá shí dah 'iistł'ó ła' biisį'. Áádóó t'áá shí na'níshee'
áádóó a'niitł'ǫ. Ákót'ée nidi ólta'góó nídésdzáago
biniinaa t'áadoo éí áłtso sétł'ǫ́ da dah 'iistł'ǫ. Áádóó
áadi ólta'di éí ádanihijiníí nít'éé', "Nihizaad éí
t'áadoo bee yádaałti'í, baa deidiyohnah dóó kǫ́ǫ́
Diné bee i'ool'įįł nilínígíí bee iiná ál'ínígíí ałdó' baa
deiidiyohnah," nihi'doo'niid.

Inez Yazzie

126

Plate 21

Beeldléí (blanket), 1840–50.
Handspun wool,
137.8 × 180.7 cm. (20.1339)

I wonder how the Brulé Sioux got this piece? Our head men rarely wore blankets like this except in formal photographs. A lot of trading went on, and I'm intrigued by what that tells us—that woven blankets were a source of communication among tribes.

D.Y. Begay

The cross-cultural exchange in this weaving is at least three-fold. The blanket is Navajo-woven. The Brulé Sioux decorated the blanket with quillwork and added two buttons—one probably of German silver and the other of brass. Wear patterns on the center panel suggest that an additional strip may have been added, possibly beaded or quilled, alluding to similarly adorned buffalo robes of the Plains. It's fascinating to see how the "original collectors" of this blanket incorporated it into their aesthetic world.

Kathleen E. Ash-Milby

Díí o'oolkidígíí 21

Beeldléí, 1840–50.
Aghaa' yílá bee yisdizígíí,
137.8 × 180.7 cm. (20.1339)

Baa nitséskeesgo haalá yit'eego Brulé Sioux daalyéhígíí díí beeldléí nídeidiiłtsooz lá? Áko nihinaat'áanii danilínígíí éí doo díí dabibeeldléí da nít'éé'. T'áá hazhó'óó nidabi'dinilkaadgo ako éí dabibeeldléí nít'éé'. Áko t'óó ahayóígóó éí kót'eego naalyéhé ałná dahaas'nil lá. Éí binahjį' éí t'áá íiyisíí bíneeshdlį́igo nísh'į, yaa halne'ígíí. Áko díí beeldléíígíí binahjį' ałch'į' yáda'ati' nít'éé' lá díí bíla' ashdla'ii bitsį' yishtłizhii ał'ąą ádaa'éhígíí bił. Kót'eego binahjį' ałch'į' yáda'ati' nít'éé' lá.

D.Y. Begay

Díí dah 'iistł'ǫ́ beeldléíígíí díkwíidi shį́į́ kót'eego ał'ąą dine'é bílák'ee dahaazna'. Táadi daats'í ałhą́ą́h nániilyá ákót'eego ał'ąą dine'é nihibeeldléí nideijaah nít'éé'. Beeldléíígíí éí Diné éí áyiilaa, áko bił dahnát'áhígíí éí naaki bąąh hólǫ́. Ła' éí Béésh Bich'ahii bibéésh łigaii bee ályaa. Áádóó ła' éí béésh łitsoii bee ályaa. Áádóó ałdó' áadi bee nináánáshch'ąą' nilínígíí éí dahsání bits'os bee naashch'ąą' díí kojí Brulé Sioux danilį́igo yee yikáá' nináádeeshch'ąą' lá. Áádóó ałdó' haashį́į́ níłtsogo éí deezhaazh lá ałníí'gónaa. T'óó baa nítsíhákeesgo ła' bighą́ą́h nínáádeiltsooz nít'éé'nahalin. Áko yoo' daats'í éí doodaii' dahsání bits'os daats'í bee naashch'ąą' nít'éé'. Éí binahjį' níl'į́igo ch'idí ákót'eego nideich'ąąh łeh, Naałání nilínígíí. Áko t'áá íiyisíí éí bóhoneedlį́ díí jiníł'į́igo beeldléí náás níłhę́ęzhígíí. Háishį́į́ néidiiłtsoozígíí éí ádíyiiltsood dóó łahdóó bee'í'ool'į́ł nilínígíí áyiilaa.

Kathleen E. Ash-Milby

Plate 22

Beeldléí (blanket), 1865–68.
Commercial yarn,
198.1 × 151.1 cm. (20.5235)

During the time this blanket was woven, the Dine'é
feared the military men on horseback. They feared
the removal of their families and relatives, they
feared for their sheep and horses, and they mostly
feared losing their birthplace and their identity. My
mother tells me about my great-great-grandmother,
who was captured during the time that Kit Carson
rounded up Navajo women, men, and children. My
great-great-grandmother made the Long Walk from
Canyon de Chelly to Bosque Redondo in New
Mexico. She and another woman escaped from camp
before the others were allowed to return to their
homeland. She traveled at night and hid during the
day. Even though she was eight months pregnant, she
made it back to the Black Mountain region, where
my family still lives today.

D. Y. Begay

Díí o'oolkidígíí 22

Beeldléí, 1865–68.
Aghaa' kingóó nidahaniihígíí,
198.1 × 151.1 cm. (20.5235)

Díí beeldléí álnééhą́ą́dą́ą́' Diné nidanichééh nít'éé'.
Akǫ́ǫ́ siláo łį́į́' yee nidaakaigo béédadzildzid nít'éé'.
Báhádzid nilínígíí éí diné bik'éí dóó t'áábí bił
nidahaz'ánídóó nahjį' kónihi'dit'oolnííł sha'shin
danízingo. Áádóó díí dibé dóó łį́į́' danilínígíí éí ałdó
nihits'ą́ą́' nahjį' kódoolnííł danízingo éí yéédaaldzid
nít'éé'. Áádóó ałdó' nidabi'diishchínáagóó nahjį'
hanihi'dínóolkał sha'shin danízingo nitsídaakees.
Áádóó bee nihéého'dólzin dóó bee Diné
nihi'dó'nínée nihits'ą́ą́' doo ákódoonííł da, nihits'ą́ą́'
dínóotsis, nihits'ą́ą́' nahjį' kódoonííł danízingo
yéédaaldzid nít'éé'. Áádóó shimá shił halne' díí naaki
nánálí naaki amásání nilįįgo kót'éego shił dahoolne'
jó ní. Jó éí aníigo éí naaki amásání nánídlínígíí siláo
danihiizbaa' dóó nihił dadeezdééł. Éí díí Kit Carson
sáanii dóó diné dóó áłchíní ahídeeniiłkaad yę́ędą́ą́'.
Áádóó atah éí Hwééldigóó niséyá. Níléí
Ch'ínílį́įdóó dóó níléí Hwééldigóó ákǫ́ǫ́ Yootó bił
hahoodzo biyi'góne' atah niséyá. Áádóó shí dóó
nááná ła' asdzání éí yóó' anáhi'niilchą́ą́'. Éí t'ahdoo
Diné hooghangóó béé'ilníihgóó. Tł'éé'go éiyá
t'ááni' néiit'ash łeh. Jį́įgo éí naniit'in ní't'éé' ní. Azhą́
shį́į́ yiztsą́ą́ nidi tseebíí nídeezidjį' kót'éego awéé'ígíí
shitsą́ sitįįgo yóó'anááshwod. Éí níléí Dziłíjiindi
nánísdzá. Éí áadi shik'éí dííshjį́įdi nidi t'ahdii ákwe'é
dabighan.

D. Y. Begay

Plate 23

Biil (two-piece dress[one panel]), 1850–60.
Handspun wool and raveled yarn,
132.8 × 83.8 cm. (20.7822)

My hunch is that women empowered *biil* with their protection songs, similar to the way that Ghost Dance shirts are thought to have protective powers. Biil were probably considered immune to bullets and arrows at a time when the people were on the run from U.S. soldiers and other raiders, as well as from hunger or harsh weather. Biil empowered them not only in spirit, but in a physical sense—they shielded and protected Navajo women, the carriers of human life.

Wesley Thomas

Díí o'oolkidígíí 23

Biil, 1850–60.
Aghaa' yilá bee yisdizígíí dóó aghaa' náost'ahígíí,
132.8 × 83.8 cm. (20.7822)

Shí baa nitsískeesgo éí díí asdzání bibiiligíí éí bits'á honíyée'go ádaalyaa. Ach'ą́ą́h sodizin bił shį́į́ nidadeest'ą́. "Ghost Dance" ha'níigo baa hane'ígíí át'éego é'ígíí ádaalyaa, hane'ígíí t'áá ákót'éego shį́į́ ádaalyaa. Díí biilígíí shį́į́ t'áá'aaníí bits'á dahwiníyée'go ádaalyaa dóó doo bidahwidééłnii da. Áko doo k'aa' dóó bee'eldǫǫh bik'a' da doo biníká dadoowoł da. Íídą́ą́' Diné ákót'éego nidanichéhą́ą́dą́ą́' Wáashindoon bisiláo yits'ąą áádóó háíshį́į́ baa tiihnídaakaiígíí dó'. Áádóó dichin da bits'ąą áádóó akǫ́ǫ́ haigo da jó éí da shį́į́ ákódaat'éé nít'éé'. Áko biilígíí éí bits'á dahoníyée'go ályaahígíí éí doo níłch'i k'ehgo t'éiya da t'áá akǫ́ǫ́ ha'at'íishį́į́ bee nahóhonitaahígíí bits'ąą shį́į́ ałdó' kódaalyaa. Biilígíí éí ach'ąąh naalyé nahalingo shį́į́ sáanii yaa ádahalyą́ą́ nít'éé', Diné asdzání dabi'ée'go ako éí be'iináhígíí doo bee tílnéeda. Sáanii éí bilá' ashdla'ii nááś yoolééł.

Wesley Thomas

Plate 24

Beeldléí (blanket), ca. 1875.
Handspun wool and raveled yarn,
160.8 × 188.2 cm. (21.4886)

Portions of the Navajo Creation stories appear in this blanket. The six wide white bands are balanced by the four wide dark bands. The white bands represent the six sacred mountains, and the dark bands represent the four stages of life: birth, growth, maturity, and old age. The crosses are transitional points—new crossings. The zigzags represent life as something that is often confrontational on the way to the next stage.

Wesley Thomas

I look at this blanket for its design. The red meandering crosses inside the indigo blue crosses pose a lot of questions. Research indicates that the meandering crosses may represent snakes, but reptiles—including snakes—are not customarily represented in our weaving. I have asked many weavers about the red crosses and they say, "It's just a design." This weaver was probably overwhelmed with the size of the blanket and the freedom she had to create such a design.

D. Y. Begay

Díí o'oolkidígíí 24

*Beeldléí, 1875 yę́ę́dą́ą́' daats'í.
Aghaa' yílá bee yisdizígíí
dóó aghaa' náost'ahígíí.
160.8 × 188.2 cm. (21.4886)*

Haashı̨́ı̨́ nı́łtsogo díí akǫ́ǫ́ Diné baa hane', "Hajíínéí" wolyéhígíí baa hane'ígíí jó éí díí beeldléíígíí biyi' hóló nahalin. Díí hastą́ą́go łigaigo nít'i'ígíí éí kojí dı̨́ı̨́'go łizhingo danít'i'ígíí éí biłgo aheełt'éego áyósin. Díí łigaigo danít'i'ígíí éí hastą́ą́ dził sinilígíí át'é. Áádóó dı̨́ı̨́' łizhingo nít'i'ígíí éí dı̨́ı̨́'go ałk'éé' haz'ą́ą́go iiná siláhígíí át'é. Áłtsé ho'dichííh áádóó jidínítsééh áádóó hojiyą́ą́h áádóó éí są́ biih náhóót'i'. Ałná da'asdzohígíí éí t'éí tsé'naa nidahwiizt'i'ígíí iina bił siláhígíí át'é. Áádóó ániidí danilı̨́ı̨́go tsé'naa nináádahwiizt'i'. Nidaneeshtł'iizhgo nidaazt'i'ígíí éí iiná át'é. Doo éí t'áá k'éházdónígo iiná siláa da. T'áá ałtsoní éí bee nahóho'dinitaah. Éí bee tsé'naa nidahwiizt'i'.

Wesley Thomas

Díí beeldléí bee naashch'ą́ą́'ígíí éí biniiyé nísh'į́. Díí łichíí'go naanídaazhahígíí dootł'izhgo ałnádasdzohígíí bii' nít'i'ígíí éí na'ídíkidígíí díkwíígóó shı̨́ı̨́ bee hóló. Áko ła' nida'ałkaahii éí ání, díí naanídaazhahgo nidaazt'i'ígíí, tsé'naa nidahaazt'i'ígíí na'ashǫ́'ii beda'alyaago ádaat'ée sha'shin ní. Áko nidi díí na'ashǫ́'ii danilínígíí t'áadoo le'é ni'góó nidaana'ígíí éí doo kojí Diné yaa yádaałti' da dóó kót'éego da'atł'óogo doo yiih dayiiłééh da. Áko díí łichíí'go naanídahaazt'i'ígíí éí díkwíí shı̨́ı̨́ akǫ́ǫ́ da'atł'óhígíí bínabídéełkid. Éí ádaaniigo éí t'óó bee na'ach'ą́ą́hígíí át'é daaní. Díí yiztł'ónígíí nidi shı̨́ı̨́ dah 'iistł'ǫ́ ayóo áníltsooígíí biniinaa t'áábí nízinígi át'éego éí na'azhch'ą́ą́.

D. Y. Begay

Plate 25

Beeldléí (blanket), 1870–75.
Handspun wool, raveled and commercial yarn,
132.1 × 83.8 cm. (22.7957)

Beeldléí, 1870–75.
Aghaa' yilá bee yisdizígíí dóó aghaa' náost'ahígíí
áádóó kingóó nidahaniihígíí,
132.1 × 83.8 cm. (22.7957)

This sarape was collected in Zuni. It may have arrived there through intermarriage or trade. There are two Navajo clans related to the Zuni people. The first clan is called Naasht' ézhí Dine'é, or Zuni People. The second clan is Naaneesht' ézhí Táchii'nii, or Zuni/Red Streak Running into the Water People. When a woman married into the Zuni tribe, her children were born either to the Naasht' ézhí Dine'é or to the Naaneesht' ézhí Táchii'nii. The family would have been influenced by the arts, social structure, and language of the Zuni people.

D. Y. Begay

This is a blanket created to enforce symmetry. The weaver created large zigzags representing the long drawn-out rains and thundering lightning of late summer. The sharp edges indicate the quick and sudden flashes of lightning as they occur in mid and late summer within Dine'tah. The short rows indicate rainbows, as seen in sandpaintings in some versions of the Blessing Way ceremony.

Wesley Thomas

Díí éí beeldléí biníkáhoodzánígíí át'é, t'óó biníkázhnílniihígíí. Naasht'ézhídi éí nídiiltsooz. Díí shį́į́ ałháá' ályéhígíí át'é. Nááná łahjį' Naasht'ézhíjį' da adzizyehgo jó ákót'éego ałháá' ályéhígíí daats'í át'é. Diné ádóone'é naakigo éí Naasht'ézhí yił k'é dahi'di'ní. Áłtséhígíí éí Naasht'ézhí Dine'é. Naakigóne'ígíí éí Naasht'ézhí Táchii'nii. Asdzání ła' Naasht'ézhí dinéhígíí yił sikéego ako ba'áłchínígíí éí Naasht'ézhí Dine'é nilį́į́ dooleeł éí doodaii' Naasht'ézhí Táchii'nii. Jó ákót'éego éí k'é bi'di'ní. Áko áají nida'ach'ą́ą́hígíí éí yits'ą́ą́dóó yídahwiidooł'ááł dóó áají be'í'ool'į́įłígíí ałdó' yíhooł'ááh. Áádóó Naasht'ézhí bizaad ałdó' yíhooł'ááh. Díí t'áá át'é Diné be'í'ool'į́įł yił ałhiihyinił dóó t'ááłá'í náádleeh.

D. Y. Begay

Díí beeldléí bee naashch'ą́ą'ígíí t'áá át'é ahedaałt'éé dóó ahídadínéelnáa dooleeł jó áají t'eiyá baa nitsíhákeesgo yiztł'ǫ́ nahalin. Aztł'ónígíí shį́į́ díí nitsaago nidaneeshtł'iizhígíí níłtsá dóó da'di'nínígíí dóó atsiniltł'ish, shį́įgo bee nahałtinígíí yaa nitsíkeesgo áyiilaa. Áko díí háádahaashchii'jį'ígíí tsxį́įłgo atsiniltł'ish hidilyeed łeh éí át'é. Éí shį́ iíł'níí' dóó shį́ k'adą́ą́ bił ahagháahgo Diné bikéyahgi ákót'ée łeh. Ádaałts'íísígíí éí nááts'íílid át'é. Éí Hózhǫ́ǫ́jí iikááh bił nidaasyáhígíí át'é.

Wesley Thomas

Plate 26

Beeldléí (blanket), ca. 1880.
Handspun wool,
115.5 × 144.5 cm. (22.9191)

Often we see little lines of different colors that
extend to the edge of a Navajo weaving. We call
these "spirit lines." This is done so the rug will not
be perfect. In this weaving, one of the black stripes is
wider than the others. It was probably not a mistake,
but done on purpose so that the weaving would not
be perfect. If a weaver makes a perfect rug, it means
there is no room for improvement.

Harry Walters

This is a beautiful piece that reminds me of the
spring in Dine'tah. Among the rocks and on the
cliffs you find brightly colored flowers full of energy
and life. This weaver had an eye for combining colors and created a wonderfully pleasing blanket. The
zigzags are like mountains in the distance, and the
small upright elements in between seem like pine
trees. It's a lively blanket that's full of energy.

Wesley Thomas

Díí o'oolkidigíí 26

*Beeldléí, 1880 yę́ędą́ą́' daats'í.
Aghaa' yilá bee yisdizígíí,
115.5 × 144.5 cm. (22.9191)*

T'áá ałhą́ą́h, diyogí ałníí'déé' aghaa' áłts'óózígo łahgo
át'éego yiilchíí'go abą́ąhjį' ch'ínít'i' łeh. Éí "nítch'i
hwii' sizíinii" bá ch'íhonít'i'. Biniiyéhígíí ałdó'
binahjį' dah 'iistł'ónígíí doo t'áá íiyisíí hadíłt'éehgo
ál'į́į da. Łahgóó łizhin bee daastł'ónígíí daniteel éí
t'éiyá t'áá ákólnéehgo ákót'é, éí doo asdzihígíí át'ée
da. T'áá shį́į́ ákólnéehgo ákólyaa. Binahjį' dah 'iistł'ǫ́
bee naach'ą́ąhígíí náásgóó bá ahóót'i'.

Harry Walters

Díí éí nizhóní yee'. Dą́ągo Dinétahdi át'é nahalin.
Níléí tsé bą́ąhgóó, tsé yadadii'áagóó, ch'il látah
hózhóní danizhóní yee' ał'ąą át'éego daalchíí' dóó
dadootł'izh łeh. Éí bee hadít'éhígíí dóó be'iina'ígíí
nizhónígo dziiłtséeh łeh. Éígi át'éego díí beeldléí
yiztł'ónígíí bee na'ach'ą́ąhígíí dóó bee iilchí'ígíí
ts'ídá nizhónígo ałhiiyiyíínil lá. Díí
nidaneeshtł'iizhígíí dził haashį́į́ nízáadi jiníł'į̃ nahalin.
Áádóó ádaałts'íísígo dego yadadii'áhígíí éí t'éiyá
nídíshchíí' nidahalin. Díí beeldléí éí ayóo biinéíí'.

Wesley Thomas

138

Plate 27

Beeldléí (blanket), 1865–70.
Handspun wool and raveled yarn,
105.4 × 160 cm. (23.921)

We call small striped blankets like this piece "shoulder blankets" because they wouldn't envelop a woman entirely. Most of them are not large enough to wrap completely around you. To me, a "blanket" would envelop the whole body, not just a part of you.

Kalley Keams

Díí o'oolkidigíí 27

Beeldléí, 1865–1870.
Aghaa' yilá bee yisdizígíí dóó aghaa' náost'ahígíí,
105.4 × 160 cm. (23.921)

Díí beeldléí ádaałts'íísígíí danoodǫǫzgo daastł'ónígíí éí "awos beeldléí" dabidii'ní. Łą'í éí doo ák'ízhdoołti'ígi ádaníłtso da, t'áá bich'į'ígi ádaníłtso. Áko shí beeldléí nísh'įįgo éí t'áá át'é hak'ésti' łeh, doo t'áá łahdóó éí hak'ésti' da łeh.

Kalley Keams

140

Plate 28

Beeldléí (blanket), 1865–70.
Handspun wool, raveled and commercial yarn,
126.4 × 81.6 cm. (23.923)

The terraced half- and quarter-diamonds containing
fine horizontal stripes are typical of sarapes of the
1860s, but they are also reminiscent of the chief
blanket designs of the same period. Like a chief
blanket, when this blanket was worn, these elements
would join at the front of the wearer to create a
complete diamond.

Kathleen E. Ash-Milby

Bee'ééhozinígíí 28

Beeldléí, 1865–70.
Aghaa' yilá bee yisdizigíí dóó aghaa'
náost'ahígíí áádóó kingóó nidahaniihígíí,
126.4 × 81.6 cm. (23.923)

Bee aditł'įhí t'áá ałní'ídóó nahalingo ałkéé' sinilígíí éí
ałts'óózígo danoodǫǫ́zgo bii' danít'i'. Éí kojí beeldléí
biníkázhnílnihígíí éí níléí 1860s yę́ę́dą́ą́' ádaalyaaígíí
ákót'éego nidaashch'ąą' nít'éé'. Áko shí shił
ánoolingo éí díí naat'áanii bibeeldléí nahalingo
naashch'ąą'. Íídą́ą́' ákódaat'éé nít'éé'. Ákó díí
naat'áanii bibeeldléí biih jigháahgo bidáahjį'
naashch'ąą'ígíí nizhónígo t'áá ła' si'ą́ nahalin yileeh,
jó bee aditł'įhí nidahalingo bee naashch'ąą'ígíí da.

Kathleen E. Ash-Milby

Plate 29

Beeldléí (blanket), 1875–85.
Handspun wool and commercial yarn,
177.5 × 124.9 cm. (23.2466)

I cherish old rugs like this one. When I hear grandparents weaving rugs, just the sound of the comb
tapping down the wool gives me a sense of security.
It reminds me of my mom's heartbeat. Sometimes
they say that you lose a lot of things when you are
born. But in Navajo we believe differently. We
believe that some things are always carried with us
in our culture and in our language, and I believe that
includes our weaving.

Edsel Brown

Looking at this blanket, we not only see the object,
but some of us hear it too. This is such a wonderful
experience, which I still find impossible to convey in
words.

Wesley Thomas

Díí o'oolkidígíí 29

Beeldléí, 1875–85.
Aghaa' yílá bee yisdizígíí dóó kingóó nidahaniihigíí,
177.5 × 124.9 cm. (23.2466)

Shí éí díí beeldléí kódaat'éhígíí t'áá át'é shił
yá'ádaat'ééh. Áko kót'éego amásání danilínígíí, análí
danilínígíí da'atł'ó yiits'a'go éí bee ha'íínishnii łeh.
Áko éí shimá bijéí diits'a' nahalingo baa nítsískees
łeh. Áko ła' ádaaníigo éí níléí hodi'chíigo t'óó
ahayóí éí hats'á' ní'dah daaní. Nihí kojí Dinéjí
ádii'níigo éí doo ákót'ée da. Éí łahgo át'é. Áko
deiniidláągo éí díí haashíí níłtsogo ó'ool'įįł nilínígíí
t'ááhó hwe'iina'jí bił deiít'éhígíí éí t'áá náasgóó
deiílyé. Kǫǫ́ nihizaad ádaat'éhígíí da. Áko kǫǫ́
atł'óhígíí ákót'é nisin, nihee'í'ool'įįl bił náasgóó
yidił.

Edsel Brown

Díí beeldléí nísh'įįgo doo éí t'óó naashch'ąą'go
nísh'įį da. Nihí ła' dadiits'a'go át'é. Díí beeldléí
danííl'įįgo t'áá íiyisíí nizhóní yee'go nihił íishjáán
yileeh. Áko saad bee ha'doodzihígíí t'áá bąąh ádin
nahalin. Ts'ídá t'óó nizhónígo t'éiyá nísh'į́.

Wesley Thomas

144

Plate 30

Beeldléí (blanket), ca. 1868.
Handspun wool and raveled threads in bundles,
74.9 × 101.6 cm. (23.2770)

Even after working with rugs for eighteen years, I get a lump in my throat thinking about the conditions under which these blankets were made. How strong the inclination to weave must have been. We work under greatly improved conditions today. I remember my grandmother taking down her rug to move from one sheep camp to another. Often we lived in outcroppings of rocks similar to caves so that we could find grass for the sheep. That's how I learned to weave.

Kalley Keams

We weave in a totally different world today. We transported only the technique of weaving across the two centuries. Today we're on our way into a world of assimilation and acculturation, in danger of losing the essential meaning of weaving as we leave our cultural identity behind.

Wesley Thomas

Díí o'oolkidigíí 30

Beeldléí, 1868 yę́ędą́ą́' daats'í.
Aghaa' yilá bee yisdizígíí dóó aghaa' náost'ahígíí,
74.9 × 101.6 cm. (23.2770)

Azhą́ shį́į́ diyogí binaashnishgo tseebííts'áadah nááhai nidi shidáyi'di éí niná'álts'i', t'óó baa nitsískeesgo. Díí beeldléí ádaalyaa yę́ędą́ą́' iinánée baa nitsíhakeesgo áyóo na'iiłná. Bidziilgo nahonitł'a nidi éí diné da'atł'óó nít'éé'. K'ad éí dííshjį́ t'áá ałtsojį' doo nidahonitł'agóó diyogí ádaal'į́. Bínáshniihgo éí shimásání nááná łahjį' nináánii'nééh biniinaa dah 'iistł'ó nínéidiitį́į́h nít'éé'. Dibé éí bił nida'anéego. Łahda éí níléí tsé binii'jį' anídeii'nééh nít'éé'. Tsé'áángóó ch'il dahólǫ́ǫgo, ákwe'é dibé tł'oh bá hadaniitáah łeh. Éí binahjį' éí atł'óhígíí bíhooł'ą́ą́'.

Kalley Keams

Dííshjį́ łahgo áhoot'éego nihił haz'ą́ą́go da'iitł'ó. T'áá hazhó'ógo atł'óhígíí t'éiyá bił tsé'naa niniidééł díí neeznádiin nináháháahgo wólta' bił hoolzhizhígíí bii'. k'ad éí t'áá ałtsojį' nihee'í'ool'į́įłę́ę t'óó atah níłnii'silį́į́'. Áko éí da'iitł'óhę́ę doo bínídahwiil'aah da. T'óó nihits'ą́ą́' yóó'iideeł, nihee'í'ool'į́įł bee nihéého'dólzinée t'áá bił.

Wesley Thomas

Plate 31

Beeldléí (blanket), 1868–70.
Handspun wool, raveled and commercial yarn,
177.8 × 113.3 cm. (23.2814)

A blanket made of raveled weft, probably from commercial cloth acquired at Fort Union and vicinity—material once used by European-Americans, undone and re-created in another world, the world of the Dine'é. Aesthetically, it's an attractive rug, but too busy at the same time. The arrows indicate comings and goings, a sense of confusion, and a world out of order.

Wesley Thomas

This rug has a more complex pattern than the chief blankets and *biil*. Those are attractive, but I feel this complex pattern has more of a story to tell. I remember my mom had Navajo rugs under the dining room table, and I would race my matchbox cars along the woven zigzag roads.

Kenneth L. Yazzie

Beeldléí, 1868–70.
Aghaa' yilá bee yisdizígíí dóó aghaa'
náost'ahígíí áádóó kingóó nidahaniihígíí,
177.8 × 113.3 cm. (23.2814)

Beeldléí díí naak'a'at'áhí hááheesdǫǫzgo bee ályaa. Éí shı̨́ı̨́ íídą́ą́' naak'a'at'áhí kingóó nidahaniihę́ę daats'í át'é. Bilagáana bi'éé' yee ádeiɫ'inígíí éí náost'ahgo áádóó éí Dinéjigo ákót'éego beeldléí yee ánídayiidlaa. Áko hazhó'óó níl'įįgo éí t'áá íiyisíí nizhóní yee' díí diyogí, baa dzólní. Áko nidi t'óó ahayóí bee iilchíhígíí bee naashch'ą́ą' áádóó naashch'ą́ą'ígíí ałdó' t'óó báhádzidgo naashch'ą́ą' K'aa' bee naashch'ą́ą'ígíí éí ahiihnídahaazt'i' dóó háádahaast'i' biniinaa éí doo hazhó'óó ééhózin da, nahosdzáán bikáá'gi áhoot'éhígi át'éego.

Wesley Thomas

Díí diyogí éí t'áá íiyisíí naat'áanii bibeeldléí dóó biil biláahgi át'éego naashch'ą́ą'. Azhą́ shı̨́ı̨́ éí baa dadzólnii nidi shídę́ę́'go baa nitsískeesgo éí díí diyogí naashch'ą́ą'ígíí nanitɫ'ago naashch'ą́ą' dóó baa hane' shı̨́ı̨́ hólǫ́ nisin. Shimá bínáshniihgo éí diyogí beeldléíígíí bee hólǫ́ǫ́ nít'éé'. Ła' níléí bikáá' adání biyaadi yiskaad nít'éé'. Áko shichidí yázhí bikáá' bee naashnée łeh nít'éé', nidaneeshtł'iizhígóó éí atiin danilį́įgo.

Kenneth L. Yazzie

Plate 32

Beeldléí (blanket), 1868–70.
Handspun wool and raveled yarn,
171.5 × 139.7 cm. (23.2815)

I see these rugs as the weavers' personal expressions.
I see them as a way for a person to become balanced, to deal with what is going on in his or her
life. Even the rugs that were made to be used, even
the wearing blankets, have spiritual meaning. How
can anyone create a piece, any kind of art or craft,
without putting himself or herself into it?

Kalley Keams

This blanket seems to have been woven to fill a
void, maybe in the midst of major changes and con-
flict. I sense suffering and hardship.

Wesley Thomas

Díí o'oolkidígíí 32

Beeldléí, 1868–70.
Aghaa' yilá bee yisdizígíí dóó aghaa' náost'ahígíí,
171.5 × 139.7 cm. (23.2815)

Díí diyogí t'áá háíshį́į́ deiztł'ǫ́ǫ́ shį́į́ t'áábí haashį́į́
yit'éego binitsíkeesígíí bee adaalyaa nisin. Nísh'į̜̀go
éí ła' diné nilínígíí aheełt'éego t'áadoo le'é álnéehgo
bee iiná siláhígíí da éí t'áábí bił haz'áánígíí éí k'ehgo
yiníł'į̜́ nisin. Áádóó akǫ́ǫ́ diyogí beeldléí biniiyé
ádaalyaaígíí nidi ákot'é, biníłch'i dahólǫ́ Haash
yit'éego éí t'áadoo le'é ájílééh dooleeł t'áadoo éí baa
nitsídzískéézgóó. Jó díí diyogí éí nihichóoni'
binitsíkees yiih dayiizlá.

Kalley Keams

Díí beeldléí éí haashį́į́ níłtsogo t'áá bitah nahalinígíí
éí yaa halne' nisin. Nidahonichéhą́ą̀dą́ą̀ daats'í ályaa,
ił dahonoochaał nidi. Haashį́į́ níłtsogo bitahgi éí
ákwe'é yaa halne' nisin. Éí binahjį' t'óó kodóó baa
nitsískeesgo t'áá ałtsoní bee ach'į̀'nahwii'ná éí yaa
halne' nisin.

Wesley Thomas

Plate 33

Beeldléí (blanket), 1860–65.
Handspun wool and raveled yarn,
151.1 × 117 cm. (24.1901)

When this rug was made, time for weaving was probably far more highly valued than it is today. First, the people had to survive—there was constant chaos. Some weavers were on the move, and their looms had to be small so they could be dismantled quickly. The outcome of weaving was also different from what it is today. At that time, most of the rugs were kept in the family for years. Later, rugs became trade items and, finally, at the turn of the century, they assumed monetary value.

Wesley Thomas

I am impressed with the consistency of the twist and size of the weft in this blanket. The weft is very fine and tightly spun, which indicates to me that the spinning was done by a very good spinner. We admire spinners who do quality work.

D. Y. Begay

Díí o'oolkidígíí 33

Beeldléí, 1860–65.
Aghaa' yilá bee yisdízígíí dóó aghaa' náost'ahígíí,
151.1 × 117 cm. (24.1901)

Díí beeldléí ályaa yę́ędą́ą́' shį́į́ t'áá íiyisíí íłį́įgo baa nitsíhákees nít'éé', díishjį́į́di biláahgi át'éego. Áłtsé éí yisdá hodoot'i' hwiinidzin, háálá áłahjį' ił dahonoochaał hóló̜ íídą́ą́'. Ła' da'atł'óhígíí éí áłahjį' naanídeii'néehgo bidah 'iistł'ó ádaałts'íísí nít'éé'. Éí t'áá hooshch'į' nidi'dootį́ł biniiyé. Áádóó atł'óhígi ałdó' łahgo át'éé nít'éé', doo díishjį́į́di daatł'óhígíí nahalin da nít'éé'. Íídą́ą́' diyogí t'áá ákwe'é hooghanígi nízaadgóó nidaagéé nít'éé'. Áádóó wóshdę́ę́' nááás hodeeshzhiizhgo éí diyogí bee aháá' ii'nííł silį́į́'. Áádóó naalyéhé bá hooghandi bił ałná'ii'nííł nít'éé'. T'áá ániidóó éí béeso bee íl'į silį́į́'.

Wesley Thomas

Shí éí díí diyogí aghaa' bee yistł'ónígíí aheełt'éego yizdízígíí dóó áníłtsáázígíí baa jíínishłí. Aghaa' áłts'óózígo dóó ahineestihgo éí bee yistł'ó. Éí binahjį' níl'į́įgo t'áá íiyisíí ayóo adizii éí azdiz sha'shin. Ákót'éego da'adizígíí ayóo nihił da'ílį́įgo binaanish ádeil'į.

D. Y. Begay

Plate 34

Beeldléí (blanket), 1875–85.
Handspun wool and raveled yarn,
110.2 × 77.5 cm. (24.2306)

I have heard stories from my grandmother that this
type of blanket was used to cover doorways or open-
ings of sweathouses. Some photographs show these
blankets used as doors to hogans, Navajo homes. In
this way, a person passes between the outside world
through the combined cosmology of the universe
(the blanket door) and into another world, the
hogan. The hogan itself is composed of the universe:
the roof is father—the sky—and the ground is
mother—the earth. Inside the hogan, the mountains
(pillars) hold up the sky above the earth, and the
humans reside in the middle.

Wesley Thomas

Díí o'oolkidígíí 34

Beeldléí, 1875–85.
Aghaa' yílá bee yisdizígíí dóó aghaa' náost'ahígíí,
110.2 × 77.5 cm. (24.2306)

Shimásání áníigo éí díí dáádiníbaal ádaat'éé nít'éé.
Táchééh da bidádadiníbaal nít'éé' ní. Ła' naaltsoos
dabikáá' díí beeldléí dádadiníbaalgo ałk'idą́ą́'
dahooghanée adahaaskidgo. Kót'éego éí diné
ch'égháahgo beeldléí dádiníbaalígíí yii'góne'
ch'égháah dóó áádóó tł'óo'ji' yádiłhił bił
hahodít'éeji' ch'égháah. Áádóó nááná la' hooghan
yiih náánádááh, éí nahosdzáán lá. Díí hooghan
dijoolí nilínígíí éí t'áá ałtsoní yá bił hadít'éhígíí át'é.
Hooghan dijoolí bikáádę́ę́'ígíí éí yá, nihitaa' át'é.
Áádóó ni'ji', łeeshtah éí nihimá át'é, jó éí
nahosdzáán. Áádóó hooghan dijoolígóne' tsin
á'adaaz'áhígíí éí dziłígíí yá dego yótą'ígíí ádaat'é.
Áádóó diné éí ałníí'ii kééhat'į.

Wesley Thomas

154

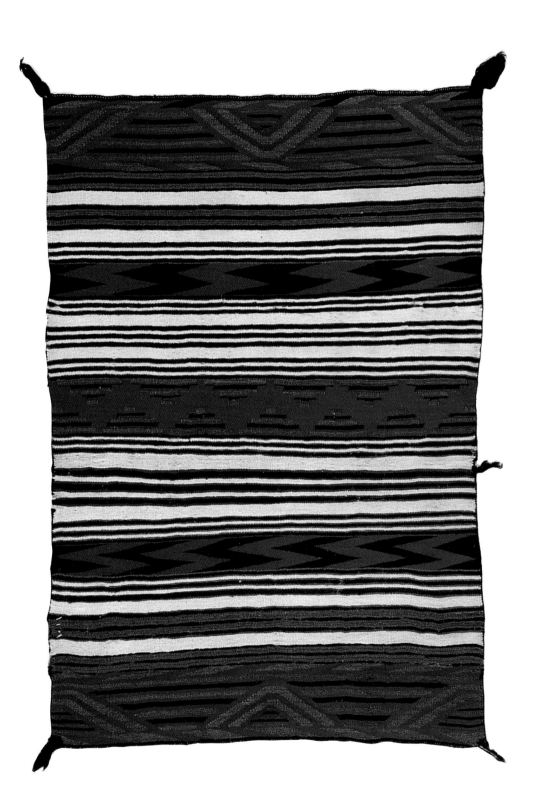

Plate 35

Beeldléí (blanket), 1875–80.
Handspun wool and raveled yarn,
176 × 204.4 cm. (24.2373)

Max Hanley, Sr., my *nálí* (grandpa), born in the 1800s,
relates what he wore as a child herding sheep near his
mother's hogan in an oral history compiled by the
Navajo Community College:

> In those days there were hardly any fabrics for clothes.
> From flour sacks I would ask that shirts be made for me.
> The crisscross design of wheat would be on the back.
> These I really liked, and I wore them while herding
> sheep. Other sacks were made into jeans, with slits up the
> sides. These I wore during the summer while herding. It
> was during the winter that heavier blue jeans usually
> were better. They were bought for me. Also, when I was
> very cold, I wore something warm as underwear. There
> were no coats. Instead, blankets were used. Lambskins or
> sheepskins were sewed together, just the right size for
> me, and I wore the garment under the blanket, which
> was really warm. That way I herded sheep.[1]

I think my nálí would especially love the design of the
man on the horse in the center of this blanket. In fact, he
would probably use it as a conversation piece. I can imagine him saying to other Navajos, "That's me on my donkey," which would most likely lead to him making a donkey noise, or singing the Navajo donkey song, a particular
favorite of his. This colorful, warm and strong blanket—
full of beauty and power—reminds me of him.

Andrea R. Hanley

Díí o'oolkidígíí 35

Beeldléí, 1875–80.
Aghaa' yilá bee yisdizígíí dóó aghaa' náost'ahígíí,
176 × 204.4 cm. (24.2373)

Max Hanley, Sr., shinálí tseebíí ts'áadahdi neeznádiin bii'
yihaháą̄dą́ą́' bi'dizhchí. Íídą́ą́' yaa halne'go éí áłchíní
nilį́igo bimá baghan binaagóó na'niłkaadgo bi'é'ę̄ę̄ yaa
nát'į̄. Éí Navajo Community Collegedi ahíídzo díí nát'ą́ą'
náhane' ła' yaa halne'ígíí:

> "Íídą́ą́' éí naak'a'at'ą̄hí ádaadin nít'éé' éé' biniiyé . Ak̄ó̄ó̄
> ak'áán bizis bee shi'éé' ádaołééh dishnii łeh nít'éé. Tł'oh
> naadą́ą̄' ahidinílnáago nidaashch'ą̄'ígíí éí shine'dę́ę̄' łeh.
> Díí éí t'áá íiyisíí shił yá'át'ééh nít'éé' dóó na'nishkaadgo
> she'éé' nít'éé. Áádóó nááná ła' azis éí shitł'aają̄'éé'
> ádaalyaa éí booshk'iizhją́ éí t'áá haashį́ı̄ níłtsogo t'áá
> náost'ah, díí shi'éé' nít'éé' na'nishkaadgo. Haigo éí
> tł'ają̄'éé' dootł'izhí ditánígíí éí yá'át'ééh nít'éé'. Éí shá
> nahaaznii'. Áádóó ayóo yishdlóohgo éí ayaadi'éé' bee
> dahoozdooígíí bii'sétį̄į̄ łeh. Íídą́ą́' éétsoh ádaadin. Nidi
> beeldléí chodeiiniil'į̄į̄ nít'éé'. Dibéyázhí bikágí éí doodaii'
> dibé bikágí ahídadiilkadgo, t'áá sheeníłtsóhígo beeldléí
> biyaadi bii' sétį̄į̄ nít'éé'. Éí ayóo bee deesdoigo akót'éego
> bee na'nishkaad nít'éé'."

Áko íínisingo éí díí hastiin łį́į' yikáá' dahsidáago
naashch'ą̄'ígíí shį̄į̄ shinálí ayóo bił yá'át'éeh dooleeł
nít'éé. Díí yiyiiłtsą́ą̄go ha'át'íish da didooniił nít'éé. T'óó
kóníigo baa nitsískees, "Díí shí télii bikáá' dah sédá,"
áádóó téliiyeel'į̄į̄ dooleeł éí doodaii' télii biyiin da yee
hodootał, éí ayóo bił nizhóní nít'éé'. Díí beeldléí
nizhónígo deilchii'go bee naashch'ą̄' dóó sido dóó
dits'id. Áádóó nizhóní dóó bidziil áko shinálí bee
bínáshniih.

Andrea R. Hanley

Plate 36

Diyogí (utility blanket), 1870–75.
Handspun wool and commercial yarn,
173.5 × 126.7 cm. (24.6899)

The interplay between the glowing blue and red,
and the gradation of color in the natural gray stripes,
give this piece an added vibrancy. Its thick, heavy
quality reminds me of a rug my great-grandmother
made that my family still uses as a blanket on especially cold nights.

Kathleen E. Ash-Milby

Díí o'oolkidígíí 36

Diyogí, 1870–75.
Aghaa' yílá bee yisdizígíí dóó
aghaa' kingóó nidahaniihígíí,
173.5 × 126.7 cm. (24.6899)

Shí éí díí shił yá'át'ééh háálá bee naashch'ąą'ígíí ayóo
ahedaałt'é. Dootł'izhígíí éí ayóo bits'á' dinílííd
nahalin dóó díí bee iilchíí'ígíí ałkéé'honí'ą́ago
danoodǫ́ǫ́z éí yee hiináago íyósin. Áádóó díí
dootł'izhígíí dóó łichíí'ígíí dóó aghaa' bee yistł'ónígíí
nizhónígo ahił nidaalnishgo ałhii'sinil. Áádóó ditą́ago
nizhónígo t'áá aghaa'ígíí bee ályaa. Binahjį'
bínáshniihígíí éí naakidi shimásání nánídlį́įgo beeldléí
áyiilaa yę́ę. Éí t'ahdii nideeltsoos dóó tł'éé'go ayóo
deesk'aazgo éí choo'į.

Kathleen E. Ash-Milby

Plate 37

Beeldléí (blanket), 1870–75.
Handspun wool and commercial yarn,
120.7 × 90.4 cm. (24.7839)

These box designs remind me of trains I first saw on
the reservation. The train tracks run south of where
we live, and I remember being scared of the noisy
metal boxes. The sound was ear-piercing. The squares
in the middle portion of this blanket look like a
train without the wheels. The black and white lines
in the background are the hills as the train moves
along the southern portion of Dine' Bikeyah
(Navajoland).

Wesley Thomas

The composition expresses innovation and possible
Spanish influence. My parents often speak of our kin
who were born to the Mexican Clan. They say that
our kin went to live with the Mexican people and
learned their ways. I often wonder if the women
were influenced by the Spanish Saltillo blankets. The
vibrant colors in this piece are surely an example.
The fine meandering design in blue and white with
serrated edges is similar to some Saltillo patterns.

D. Y. Begay

Beeldléí, 1870–75.
Aghaa' yílá bee yisdizígíí dóó aghaa'
kingóó nidahaniihígíí,
120.7 × 90.4 cm. (24.7839)

Díí tsits'aa' nahalingo bee naashch'ąą'ígíí
kǫ'na'ałbąąsii ts'ídá áłtsé Diné bikéyah bikáá'
yiiłtsánéedą́ą́' bee bínáshniih. Kǫ'na'ałbąąsii bitiin éí
nihighanídóó shádi'ááhjí nít'i'. Kǫ' na'ałbąąsii
yilwołgo ayóó'ííts'a'go áyóo binásdzid nít'éé. Áko
díí beeldléí ałnii'gi dadik'ą́ągo sinilígíí kǫ'na'ałbąąsii
bijáád t'áágééd nahalin. Áádóó łizhin dóó łigaigo
danít'i'ígíí éí kǫ'na'ałbąąsii deiílk'idgóó yilwołgo át'é
nahalin. Éí Diné bikéyah bikáá' shádi'ááhjígo
ákóhoot'éego bitiin.

Wesley Thomas

Díí bee naashch'ąą'ígíí t'óó bínahonitaahgo dóó
Naakaii k'ehjí ályaa nahalin. Shimá dóó shizhe'é
nihik'éí Naakaii Dine'é danilínígíí yaa yáłti' łeh. Éí
Naakaiitahdi kéédahatįį nít'éé' ako éí yits'ą́ą́dóó
Naakaiijí iiná yídahooł'ą́ą' níigo. Áko łahda baa
nitséskees díí sáanii daats'í Naakaii yee da'atł'óhígíí
dóó bibeeldléí át'éhígíí daats'í yits'ą́ą́dóó
nida'ach'ąąh daazlį́į' nisin łeh. Áko bee iilchíhígíí
ayóo bits'á' diníííídígíí bee ííshjáán nahalin.
Áłts'óózígo dootł'izh dóó łigai doolzhah dóó
nooltł'iizhgo naashch'ąą'ígíí Naakaii bina'ach'ąąh
be'elyaa nahalin.

D. Y. Begay

Plate 38

Beeldléi (blanket), 1870–75.
Handspun wool, raveled and commercial yarn,
153.2 × 185.4 cm. (24.7840)

This is a later chief blanket. I like it because it has a
simple and symmetrical pattern, yet it has not only
stripes but an unusual box design. When I went to
state fairs or the Shiprock fair as a youngster, and my
brother and I would see a chief blanket, my mother
would tell us that when these blankets were worn,
the patterns at the edges would meet and make a
whole design.

Kenneth L. Yazzie

I find most chief blankets from this period very creative and very well woven. Large rugs are challeng-
ing and laborious to weave; they demand great mental as well as physical effort. Size was probably not
important to weavers one hundred years ago because
they had to accommodate the family's need for
warm blankets during the winter.

D. Y. Begay

Díí o'oolkidígíí 38

Beeldléi, 1870–75.
Aghaa' yílá bee yisdizígíí dóó aghaa'
náost'ahígíí áádóó kingóó nidahaniihígíí,
153.2 × 185.4 cm. (24.7840)

Díí t'áá ániidídóó naat'áanii bibeeldléi át'é. Doo éí
t'áá íiyisíí naashch'ąą'da áko shił yá'át'ééh, azhą shįį
t'óó noodǫǫz dóó dik'ąągo naashch'ąą' nidi
ahídadínéelná. Na'ahóóhaigóó naasháahgo éí
doodaii' Toohdi na'ahóóhai alééhgo akǫǫ
naasháahgo, ánii naasháádą́ą́', shik'is bił, łahda
naat'áanii bibeeldléi yiistsééh. Áko shimá ánii łeh, díí
beeldléi bee nida'aldeehgo, bidáahgi ahíjiiłtso'go bee
naashch'ąą'ígíí t'ááłá'í yileeh.

Kenneth L. Yazzie

Díí naat'áanii bibeeldléi kwe'é nahalzhiizhgo
ádaalyaaígíí t'áá íiyisíí nidaashch'ąą' dóó nizhónígo
daastł'ǫǫ nít'éé'. Dah 'iistł'ǫ ayóó'áníłtsogo éí ayóo
bina'anish áádóó háni' dóó hats'íís yaa nát'į́.
Áníłtsooígíí éí doo t'áá íiyisíí yaa nitsídaakees da
nít'éé' neeznádiin nááhaiídą́ą́' da'atł'óhą́ą. Háálá t'óó
ha'áłchíní t'éí bá ájit'į́į doo, beeldléi haigo bee
hoozdo doo biniiyé.

D. Y. Begay

162

Plate 39

Beeldléí (blanket), 1870–75.
Handspun wool, raveled and commercial yarn,
187.4 × 134.4 cm. (24.7841)

This is a blanket of stars. It seems like the stars in the circle are about to start spinning. There are small stars within large stars and huge stars. It's the construction of the universe on a textile. The black area is the universe beyond the identified stars. The Egyptians built their pyramids according to the location of the stars, but Navajo weavers placed the stars on their looms.

Wesley Thomas

Díí o'oolkidigíí 39

Beeldléí, 1870–75.
Aghaa' yilá bee yisdizígíí dóó aghaa'
náost'ahígíí áádóó kingóó nidahaniihígíí,
187.4 × 134.4 cm. (24.7841)

Díí beeldléí éí sǫ' be'alyaa. Díí názbąsígíí biyi'góne' éí sǫ' t'óó ahééhéjeeh doo nahalin. Sǫ' danitsaaígíí bii'góne' sǫ' ła' ánáádaałts'íísígo naaz'nil. Yádiłhił be'elyaago yistł'ǫ. Łizhiníigi éí sǫ' bilááhgóó yádiłhił át'é. "Egyptian" éí sǫ' yik'ehgo da'aztł'in. Diné éí sǫ' bidiyogí yiih deiz'nil.

Wesley Thomas

Plate 40

Diyogí (utility blanket), 1875–85.
Handspun wool, raveled and recarded yarn,
193 × 130.4 cm. (24.7843)

It's very interesting, the different approaches that
people take toward Navajo weavings. Often the first
thing that non-weavers see is the color combination,
design, or texture of a rug. But weavers take the
process of weaving into consideration. For instance,
non-weavers may see striped blankets such as this
piece as plain, but, from a weaver's point of view, a
straight line is very difficult to weave, especially on a
large loom.

Wesley Thomas

Díí o'oolkidigíí 40

Diyogí, 1875–85.
Aghaa' yilá bee yisdizígíí dóó aghaa'
náost'ahígíí áádóó háánoolchaadígíí,
193 × 130.4 cm. (24.7843)

T'áá íiyisíí bóhoneedlį́ díí diné da'atł'óhígíí díkwíí
shį́į ał'ąą át'éego yee da'atł'óhígíí. Doo da'atł'óhígíí
diyogí yiníł'į́igo, ts'ídá áłtsé yaa ákoniizį́įhígíí éí bee
da'iilchí'ígíí dóó bee naashch'ąą'ígíí dóó
bízhdílnihgo át'éhígíí. Da'atł'óhígíí éí, haalá yit'éego
yistł'ǫ́ nízingo deiníł'į́į łeh. Áádóó ałdó' doo
da'atł'óhígíí beeldléí t'óó noodǫ́ǫzgo ályaago, doo
nidi la' naashch'ąą' da danízin łeh. Nidi da'atł'óhígíí
yiníł'į́igo t'óó k'éhézdónigo noodǫ́zígíí nidi ayóo
nanitł'ago yitł'ó danízin łeh.

Wesley Thomas

166

Plate 41

Biil (two-piece dress [one panel]), 1880–1900.
Handspun wool and raveled yarn,
124.8 × 88.9 cm. (24.7844)

Worn sashed at the waist and loosely draped across bare shoulders, *biil* are among the most intimate of Navajo wearing blankets. There is an emotional resonance that remains with the dresses today. My grandma wanted to weave a biil for me but passed away before starting it. She left one of her upright looms to me, and I hope someday to weave a biil myself.

Kathleen E. Ash-Milby

Biil identify a woman. When a woman wears a biil she is declaring respect for her people and her culture. Biil are still woven and worn today. Many young girls and women wear them during special occasions such as puberty ceremonies, parades, and beauty pageants. Sometimes I see the female *yei* dancers in the healing ceremony wearing biil adorned with jewelry and a sash belt. We believe that Spider Woman gave us the gift of weaving so that we could make our own clothing and never be cold.

D. Y. Begay

Díí o'oolkidígíí 41

Biil 1880–1900.
Aghaa' yilá bee yisdizígíí dóó aghaa' náost'ahígíí,
124.8 × 88.9 cm. (24.7844)

Díí biil bii'dziztįįgo haníí'gónaa sis bee ałch'į' be'estł'ǫǫ łeh. Hawos t'áá łichíí'go biil t'éí bitis haazt'i' łeh. Biil éí ákót'éego Diné yee nidaakai nít'éé'. Ako k'ad biil t'ahdii haashįį níłtsogo háni' nayiiłná. Shimásání ła' biil ákót'éego nádeeshtł'óół shił nii nít'éé' t'áadoo ájiléhé t'áá bich'į'dóó ájídin. Áko bikáá' atł'óhí éí ła' shaazhnítą dóó hahgo da biil ła' ádádeeshtł'óół laanaa nisin.

Kathleen E. Ash-Milby

Biil éí binahjį' asdzání bééhózin. Asdzání biil yii' sitįįgo éí bidine'é dóó be'i'ool'įįl bił ílįį łeh. Díishjį éí biil t'ahdii daatł'ó dóó t'ahdii chodaao'į. T'óó ahayói at'ééké dóó sáanii dabi'éé' t'áadoo le'é baani'diildahgo. Áádóó kinaaldá da biniiyé dóó kintah ha'diinéehgo da. At'ééké nizhónii nabíhonitaahgo atah nídaakahgo kót'éego dabi'éé' łeh. Łahda éí sáanii ye'ii bicheii bee da'azhizhgóó ákót'éego yee da'alzhizh łeh. Biyo' dahólǫǫgo áádóó sis łichí'í binídaazt'i'go. Áko deiniidlá nilínígíí éí Na'ashjé'ii Asdzáán kót'éego atł'óhígíí niheinílá. Éí binahjį' éí t'áá nihí'éé' ádeiil'į áko doo deiidlóóhgóó ahool'áah doo.

D. Y. Begay

168

Plate 42

Beeldléí (blanket), 1880–90.
Handspun wool and commercial yarn,
152.4 × 143.5 cm. (25.3708)

Díí o'oolkidígíí 42

Beeldléí, 1880–90.
Aghaa' yilá bee yisdizígíí dóó aghaa'
kingóó nidahaniihígíí,
152.4 × 143.5 cm. (25.3708)

We explore and learn by experimenting. Our great-great-grandmothers must have had the same curiosity as we do today. I have always been fascinated by wedge weave blankets. My inquiries led me to experiment with the technique. To begin a wedge weave, you build up a section of weft on one side. You wrap the weft two or three times around the first warp or selvage cord. Next you go over, then under, the second warp, and back to the selvage cord. In the next opening you go to the third warp and so on until the area is built up to a sharp or shallow angle. You must change colors often to create a zigzag pattern. When you reach the opposite selvage cord, you repeat the process. During the weaving process the warps will remain perpendicular to the wefts. Upon completion of the weaving, and when you remove the rug from the loom, the changing angles will pull the warps out of line and create a scalloped edge.

Weavers have many different ideas about the technique. Sometimes the weave is called the "dancing selvage" or "pulled warps." Wedge weaves allow you to create a distortion which, ironically, is what we discourage today. We tell our daughters and students to keep the edges of a rug straight and to maintain the correct tension throughout their weaving.

D. Y. Begay

Nideiilkaah dóó nabídaniitaahgo bits'ą́ą́dóó ídahwiil'aah. Díkwíidi shį́į́ nihimásání dóó nihinálí nánídlį́igo t'áá ákót'eego na'ídanitaahgo dííshjį́ ádeiit'íinígi át'eego shį́į́ áda'al'į́į́ nít'éé'. Díí éí ayóo bíneeshdlį́, dilkǫǫhígíí, bibąąhjí t'ááyó naanídahazhahgo yistł'ónígíí. Áko shí díí bína'ídíshkidgo éí ła' nabínítą́ą́. Díigi át'eego booshk'iizhjí adahaazts'ǫ́ǫ́dgo yitł'óhígíí łahjí éí áłtsé ha'jitł'óóh áádóó nááżhdíłts'ǫ'. Nanoolzhee'ígíí abąąh nááťi'í bik'izhdídiz naaki éí doodaii' táadi da. Áádóó inda bikáá' dóó biyaagóne' ajiłt'ih nanoolzhee' abąąh nááťi'í bíighahgi nít'i'ígíí. Áádóó abąąh nááťi'í bik'ínááżhdídiz. Áádóó tá'ígóne' nanoolzhee' nít'i'ígíí t'áá ákónááajiłt'įįh. Ákót'eego dego hááʼáago jitł'óóh. Aghaa' al'ąą át'eego deilchíígo bee ajitł'óhígíí éí t'áá al'ąą ánijoodliiłgo jó áko éí naneeshtł'iizhgo naashch'ąą' yileeh. Nanoolzhee' ałtso bitah hazhdiigháahgo, náťą́ą́' t'áá ákót'eego jitł'óohgo hanáázhdiidááh. Jitł'óogo, nanoolzhee' dóó aghaa' bee jitł'óhígíí, t'áá ahidiníłná sinil łeh. Ałtso ajitł'óohgo, áádóó dahiistł'ǫ́ nizht'iiłtsosgo dóó níjoo'a'go díí nizhdiłgeesgo jitł'óhą́ą bibąąhgóó doolghas yileeh.

Áko díí da'atł'óhígíí éí t'óó ahayóí al'ąą át'eego díí bee atł'ó danízin. Łahda da'atł'óhígíí díí bee atł'óhígíí bízhi' ádeile' łeh, "abąąh alzhizh" éí doodaii' "nanoolzhee' deests'ǫ́ǫ́d." Bii' dilkǫǫhí éí łahgóó doolghasgo ál'į́. Áko k'ad éí t'áadoo bibąąh nooltł'iizhgo da'ohtł'óhí nihidi'ní. Nihich'é'éké dóó ídahooł'aahígíí hazhó'óó bibąąh k'éhézdongo da'ohtł'ó dabidii'ní. Áádóó nanoolzhee' áłahjį' t'áá aheełt'eego nídongo da'ohtł'ó dabidii'ní.

D. Y. Begay

NOTES ON SELECTED COLLECTORS

Eulalie H. Bonar

The collectors of the nineteenth-century Navajo blankets now among the holdings of the National Museum of the American Indian (NMAI) are an integral part of the history of the textiles. The brief biographical sketches that follow, focusing on collectors' experiences out West, were drawn up largely in response to Navajo people involved in creating this book and exhibition who wanted to know how the blankets ended up in New York. Perhaps, too, information about the collectors will enhance non-Navajo readers' and museum-goers' understanding of the blankets as something more than art objects to be hung in a gallery or illustrated in a book.[1]

The NMAI Navajo blanket collection was assembled under the stewardship of George Gustav Heye (1874–1957), founder of the Museum of the American Indian–Heye Foundation (MAI). The first Indian item Heye acquired, and the beginning of his collecting obsession, was a Navajo deerskin shirt that he purchased in 1897. Many others shared Heye's instinct to collect, though seldom on the same scale. Among the collectors of the Navajo weavings Heye acquired for his museum, now NMAI, were army officers, explorers on surveying expeditions, natural historians, traders and dealers, ethnologists and archaeologists, western artists, and private collectors. In some cases the blankets represent only a portion of larger collections these individuals gathered.

Popular fascination with the Southwest and with the Native peoples of the region grew throughout the 1800s, fueled by Mexico's independence in 1821, the opening of the Santa Fe Trail, the end of the Civil War, and the construction of the transcontinental railroad that reached New Mexico and Arizona in the early 1880s. Scholars are examining the historical implications of this fascination. Curtis Hinsley, for example, identifies a deliberate process of nation-building as central to the Southwest's hold on the public imagination;[2] others cite the conviction of scientists that Native cultures would soon disappear.[3] There was also an aesthetic element at work. Navajo textiles were seen as colorful and beautiful objects to be enjoyed in private homes, or exotic keepsakes to remind people of brief visits or long service out West. The collectors below provide a crucial link between the blankets in their Native, nineteenth-century context and in the museum's collections today.

EMILY OTIS BARNES (b. Evanston, Illinois, 1906).[4] Barnes's father, Joseph Edward Otis (1867–1960), was a banker in Chicago and an avid collector of American Indian art. He was a director of the Santa Fe Railroad and made inspection trips of the railway line at least twice a year. As a child, Barnes accompanied him on many of these journeys, which lasted about a month. The train carried them west from Chicago on the southern route to New Mexico and Arizona, up the California coast, east across western and central Canada, and back to Chicago. Every director had his own railway car, and there were frequent stops at trading posts along the way. Otis continued to collect into the 1920s, after he left the railroad's board.

Barnes, a Santa Fe resident and former president of the board of directors of the Wheelwright Museum of the American Indian, lived in New York City from 1963 to 1971. When she left to return to New Mexico, she presented MAI with two Navajo textiles, including a finely woven Navajo wedge weave blanket (25.3708–plate 42) collected by her father.[5]

EUGENE BEAUHARNAIS BEAUMONT (b. Wilkes-Barre, Pennsylvania, 1837–1926).[6] Beaumont, a graduate of West Point, served in the Civil War, winning a Medal of Honor for gallantry. In 1866 he was placed in command of A Troop, Fourth Cavalry, at San Antonio, Texas. He fought in numerous battles, including an 1873 attack on the Kickapoo villages in Mexico, and commanded the advance battalion in the 1874 Palo Duro Cañon battle against the Comanches. In 1879 he joined Mackenzie's expedition against the Uncompaghre Utes. From 1881 to 1883 Beaumont was stationed at Fort Wingate, New Mexico, and, in 1884, at Fort Bayard, New Mexico. From June 1884 to December 1888 he commanded Fort Bowie, in Arizona. He was acting inspector general of the Department of Texas when he retired in 1892.

A Navajo sarape (23.3105–fig. 22) collected by Beaumont was purchased by the museum in 1963 from his granddaughter, Margaret R. Elliot. Museum records state that the blanket belonged to a member of Naiche's band at the time of surrender to Colonel Beaumont in 1873. Naiche, a Chiricahua leader, would have been very young at that time, and it's more likely that Beaumont collected the blanket at the surrender of Naiche and Geronimo near Fort Bowie in 1886. The Margaret R. Elliot Collection of documents on federal government policy and American Indians in the first half of the twentieth century is at the Huntington Free Library, Bronx, New York.

SUMNER HOMER BODFISH (b. Chicopee, Massachusetts, 1844–94).[7] Bodfish enlisted in the Union army during the Civil War and saw action in North Carolina, as well as in the Boston draft riots. President Lincoln appointed him to West Point, from which he was graduated in 1868. He served in the Sixth Cavalry at Fort Tyler, Texas, later becoming regimental adjutant and provost marshall. He resigned from the army in 1871 to work as a hydraulic engineer in Langley, Georgia, and then Washington, D.C. In 1878 he returned to the West with John Wesley Powell's U.S. Geographical and Geological Survey of the Rocky Mountain Region, mapping in Arizona. After the U.S. Geological Survey (U.S.G.S.) was established in 1879, Bodfish was appointed topographer in the Colorado Division; from 1879 to 1881 he led a party that surveyed the Grand Canyon district, including the Kaibab Plateau. From 1882 to 1888 he mapped in California, Washington, D.C., and Massachusetts, before returning to the West to make detailed surveys of reservoir sites in the Arkansas River basin and other parts of Colorado for the U.S.G.S. Irrigation Survey.

The chief blanket and small sarape collected by Bodfish (22.8875; 22.8877) were purchased by the museum from his niece, Elizabeth Howell Wilkins (1872–1965), and accessioned in 1960.

EDWARD BOREIN (b. San Leandro, California, 1872–1945).[8] Borein was a cowboy artist, traveling on horseback across the West and into Canada and sketching the settlers and Indians he met. Later he would create pen-and-ink drawings from his sketches and sell them to western magazines and newspapers. In 1903, returning from a cattle drive in Mexico, he visited Laguna, Acoma, and Taos Pueblos in New Mexico, and the Hopi villages of Oraibi and Walpi in Arizona. His drawing, *The Child of the Rainbow,* depicts a group of Navajo men on horseback; it was published as an illustration in *The Craftsman.* Borein later reprinted it as an etching, with the new title, *Navajos.* Another Borein etching with Navajo people as the subject is called *Navajo Visitors at Oraibi.* In 1907, Borein set up a studio on 42nd Street in New York.

Now at NMAI, Borein's collection includes three Navajo *biil,* or two-piece dresses (20.7807; 20.7808; 20.7820–fig. 20; 20.7821; 20.7822–plate 23; 20.7823), and a biil sewed from four biil borders (20.7806).

DOUGLAS DHER GRAHAM.[9] Graham arrived in Zuni on 3 September 1879 and opened a trading store south of the pueblo.[10] Known in Zuni as Tsibon K'winna (Blackbeard), Graham also served as unofficial agent, teacher, and government farmer. In 1881 he was instrumental in the initial planning for Blackrock Dam, which was constructed in 1906; in 1882 and again later he was temporary caretaker for the government school. His trading business thrived, and toward the late 1880s he operated out of the same house where Frank Hamilton Cushing, the young Smithsonian ethnologist, had lived.[11] In 1903 Graham was appointed the first superintendent of the Zuni Indian agency, a post he held until 1906.[12]

The chief blankets (22.7949; 22.7950–fig. 6) and sarapes (22.7951; 22.7953; 22.7954; 22.7955–fig. 25; 22.7956–fig. 11; 22.7957–plate 25) collected by Graham were presented to the museum by his nieces, Evelyn B. Lent, G. B. Oman, Beatrice A. B. Young, and Mary F. B. Van Houten; they were accessioned in 1959. All of the blankets show signs of much wear. They may have been traded into Zuni by Navajos, or Graham may have collected them directly from Navajos; in his 1903 Report to the Commissioner of Indian Affairs, Graham estimated that there were five hundred Navajos living on the border of the Zuni reservation.[13]

WILLIAM NICHOLSON GRIER (b. Pennsylvania 1813–85).[14] Grier spent most of his career as a cavalryman in the West. He was graduated from West Point in 1835 and was posted to Fort Gibson in Indian Territory, now Oklahoma. He went to New Mexico in 1846, in preparation for the Mexican War, and remained there until 1856. He was probably the first U.S. officer to lead troops in armed confrontation with the Navajos, near Isleta Pueblo late in 1846.[15] His service in New Mexico included campaigning in patrols and skirmishes against Navajos, Utes, and Apaches. He fought during the Civil War in the Army of the Potomac and was brevetted brigadier general in 1865. After the war, he was posted to New Mexico again for two years at Fort Union. He retired in December 1870.

Grier collected three Navajo sarapes (23.2814–plate 31; 23.2815–plate 32; 23.2816–fig. 27), possibly while stationed at Fort Union between 1868 and 1870. The Grier Collection was presented to the museum by Robert C. Campbell, Grier's grandson. The textiles were accessioned in 1964.

THEA KOWNE PAGE HEYE (1888–1935).[16] Thea Heye was the second wife of George Gustav Heye (1874–1957), founder, director, and chairman of the board of trustees of MAI. They were married in 1915 and spent their honeymoon excavating the Nacoochee mound site in White County, Georgia, a joint project with the Smithsonian's Bureau of American Ethnology (BAE). Thea Heye was a spirited supporter of her husband's passion for all things Indian and financed many MAI expeditions. She kept an "Indian garden," complete with maize, beans, and squash, at the museum's Research Branch in the Bronx. She

Ganado wearing chief blanket, Rodman Wanamaker expeditions, 1908–17. (N36113)

traveled with her husband on buying trips across the country and to Europe, and after visiting the Southwest began a warm correspondence with Nina Hotina, Lorenzo Chavez Natusey, Tom Kawaya, and others from Zuni Pueblo; they call her "Theasitsa" in some of their letters.[17] In 1933 she was elected to the museum's board of trustees.

Thea Heye is listed as donor of thousands of objects in NMAI's collections; in addition, she interested other donors in contributing to the museum. One item presented by Heye was a Navajo chief blanket (9.1290), accessioned in 1919.

JOSEPH KEPPLER (1872–1956).[18] Keppler, a political cartoonist and part-owner of the magazine *Puck*, lived in Woodland Valley,

New York. The protégé of Harriet Converse, Keppler was adopted into the Wolf Clan of the Seneca in 1898 and given the Indian name Gyantwaka. His advocacy on behalf of the Iroquois included participation in drafting state and national legislation, but he also provided many individuals and their families with monetary gifts and other aid. His deep interest in American Indian art led him to help market the works of many artists, including the Seneca painter Jesse Cornplanter; in return, these artists helped Keppler expand his collections and those of MAI. In 1937 Keppler was awarded the first Seneca Silver Star award. Keppler's collection was considered one of the finest of its kind, and photographs of his "Indian room" still prompt viewers' amazement today.

An MAI trustee, Keppler made numerous gifts to the museum. The Navajo material includes blankets accessioned in 1906 (9603–plate 2; 9608; 9612] and 1917 (6.302–fig. 21; 6.304; 6.305–plate 4; 6.1086; 6.1088–plate 5), as well as woven saddle blankets and garters, and shell and turquoise jewelry. The Joseph Keppler Iroquois Papers are at the Huntington Free Library.

DANIEL WALTER LORD.[19] Lord accompanied the Hemenway Southwestern Archaeological Expedition for a year, arriving at Camp Hemenway in Arizona on 28 April 1888, and remaining until mid May, 1889.[20] The expedition, sponsored by Mary Hemenway of Boston, was the first major scientific project to investigate pre-Contact sites in the Southwest. Lord was a friend of Sylvester Baxter, the Boston journalist who popularized the expedition back East, and of Frank Hamilton Cushing, director of the expedition.[21] Between 1888 and 1890 the expedition was at Zuni, excavating in the ancestral village of Halona and at Heshotauthla, another Zuni site; correspondence suggests that Lord was in charge of the camp at Heshotauthla while Cushing was at Camp Cibola.[22]

The Navajo textiles collected by Lord include a Pueblo-style manta (11.9315), a sarape (11.9323), fragments of two wedge weave blankets (11.9324; 11.9327) and a Moki blanket (11.9326). They were presented to the museum by Lord's sister, Mary Patterson Lord, and accessioned in 1923.

SAMUEL KIRKLAND LOTHROP (b. Milton, Massachusetts, 1892–1965).[23] Lothrop, an archaeologist whose interests led him primarily to investigate pre-Contact sites in Central and South America, attended Harvard University, where he studied under the anthropologist Alfred M. Tozzer; he did his first archaeology work with Alfred Kidder. Lothrop was associated with the Carnegie Institute of Washington, MAI, and, from 1930 until his retirement in 1957, the Peabody Museum of Harvard. He went to the Southwest in 1923 to excavate at the ancestral Zuni village of Kechibawa for Lewis Clark of the University Museum at Cambridge, England, in conjunction with Frederick Webb Hodge of MAI; probably during that expedition Lothrop collected a Navajo Moki-pattern sarape (15.4616–plate 16), accessioned by the museum in 1927.

NELSON APPLETON MILES (b. Westminster, Massachusetts, 1839–1925).[24] Miles, a first lieutenant at the beginning of the Civil War who rose rapidly to the rank of colonel, was for fifteen years a regimental commander in the Indian wars. His service included the 1876–77 campaign against the Sioux in the northern Plains, including the pursuit of the Hunkpapa Sioux leader Sitting Bull to the Canadian border, and the assault against the Nez Perce in the Bear Paw Mountains of Montana. Miles became a brigadier general in 1880 and in 1886 succeeded George Crook as commander of the Department of Arizona. Although Crook was responsible for the cessation of the Apache wars, Miles accepted credit for Geronimo's surrender. He commanded the field operations that led to Wounded Knee. As a lieutenant general during the Spanish-American War, he led the campaign against Puerto Rico. He retired in 1903.

Miles's daughter and son, Mrs. Samuel K. Reber and Maj. Sherman Miles, gave their father's collection of Indian material to the museum, including a Navajo chief blanket (22.1687–fig. 22) and a Moki-pattern sarape (22.1688–fig. 10), accessioned in 1953.

GEORGE HUBBARD PEPPER (b. Tottenville, New York, 1873–1924).[25] Pepper was an anthropologist with a special interest in Navajo weaving. Between 1896 and 1900 he was field director of explorations at Pueblo Bonito, Chaco Canyon, New Mexico, conducted by the Hyde Exploring Expedition, sponsored by Fred and Talbot Hyde under the auspices of the American Museum of Natural History. Pepper began his study of Navajo textiles here, including his experiments with native dyes. The Hyde Expedition maintained curio stores in New York and Phoenix, as well as a string of trading posts in the Southwest, and Richard Wetherill operated a thriving trade in Navajo blankets for the Hyde brothers out of the Chaco store. Pepper, like the trader J. Lorenzo Hubbell, promoted a return to the older blanket styles and presynthetic colors. In 1904 Pepper became a consultant for George Heye and in 1910 joined MAI full-time. He participated in archaeological work in Mexico and, with Marshall Saville, in Ecuador. In addition, he wrote for *The*

Papoose, published monthly by the Hyde Expedition, and lectured widely on southwestern archaeology and on his fieldwork among Navajo and Pueblo peoples.

The large collection of southwestern material assembled by Pepper and acquired by the museum includes a number of *biil* (4.4674; 9.1930; 9.1960–fig. 5; 9.1962; 9.1989–fig. 3; 9.1992–plate 10), mantas (9.1910–plate 6; 9.1977; 9.1978–plate 9); chief blankets (9.1945; 9.1946), sarapes (9.1912–plate 7; 9.1942; 9.1990–fig. 4], a woman's shoulder blanket (9.1979), and one Moki fragment (9.1915). The weavings were accessioned in 1919, except for a biil (4.4674) accessioned in 1914. Pepper probably obtained many of the textiles through the Chaco trading post, kept open by Wetherill after the Hyde Expedition ceased operations in 1901.

JOHN WESLEY POWELL (b. Mount Morris, New York, 1834–1902).[26] A geologist, ethnologist, and explorer, Powell conducted a series of geographical surveys of the Rocky Mountains and the canyons of the Green and Colorado Rivers, becoming especially well known for his travels through Grand Canyon. In his book, *Exploration of the Colorado River of the West and Its Tributaries* (1875), he described setting off on 24 May 1869 from Green River City in four boats equipped with provisions and clothing for ten months. "Begun originally as an exploration," he wrote, "the work was finally developed into a survey, embracing the geography, geology, ethnography, and natural history of the country." Powell published the first classification of American Indian languages and was the first director of the U.S. Bureau of Ethnology, established in 1879 (renamed the Bureau of American Ethnology [BAE] in 1894). In 1881 he became director of the U.S.G.S., a post he held until his retirement in 1894.

According to museum records, Powell collected a Navajo woman's shoulder blanket (23.2770–plate 30) during the 1869 expedition; it was acquired by William Randolph Hearst and purchased by the museum in 1963 at a Parke-Bernet auction. Powell gave a Navajo sarape (15.7719–plate 17) to his sister, Mrs. A. H. Thompson, about 1873, after his return from his second Grand Canyon expedition; it was presented to the museum in 1927 by Mrs. Walter W. Davis of Great Neck, New York, who had received it as a gift from Mrs. Thompson in 1903.

WILLIAM TECUMSEH SHERMAN (b. Lancaster, Ohio, 1820–91).[27] Sherman, a graduate of West Point, served in the Second Seminole War in 1840–42. He resigned from the army in 1853. In 1861, however, he was commissioned colonel of the Thirteenth Infantry and soon became one of the most famous

Group in Chaco Canyon, Arizona, 1899. Photo by George H. Pepper. (N33106)

Civil War commanders, best known, if not notorious, for the Union army's march from Atlanta, Georgia, to the sea. In 1868 he was one of three generals named to the U.S. Peace Commission, created to resolve the Indian problem through negotiations that would end in the concentration of Indian peoples on reservations.[28] In May 1868 Sherman went to New Mexico to negotiate with Barboncito and other Navajo leaders for the release of the Navajo people from Bosque Redondo. On 1 June 1868, he and the Navajo leaders signed a treaty permitting the Navajo to return to a portion of their homeland, now a reservation. In 1868 General Grant was elected president and in 1869 Sherman succeeded him as commanding general of the army. Sherman retired in 1884.

A Navajo sarape (20.5235–plate 22) collected by Sherman, possibly in 1868, was one of the items presented to the museum by his granddaughter, Eleanor Sherman Fitch, in 1942.

DECOST SMITH (b. Skaneateles, New York, 1864–1939).[29] Smith, a painter of western scenes, grew up near the Onondaga Indian Reservation and was initiated into the Onondaga tribe. He first went west in 1884, his interest apparently kindled by the paintings of George de Forest Brush (1855–1941). Following visits to the Rosebud and Lower Brulé agencies, Smith spent the winter in Dakota Territory at Fort Yates and Standing Rock. In 1893 he began traveling with the artist E. W. Deming and together they wrote and illustrated articles for *Outlook* magazine; "Sketching among the Sioux" was published in October 1893, and "Sketching among the Crow Indians" in May 1894. Smith also worked as an illustrator for national magazines such as *Century*. His autobiography, *Indian Experiences*, was published posthumously.

Smith's bequest to the museum included a finely woven chief blanket (20.1339–plate 21) collected from the Brulé Sioux in South Dakota and accessioned in 1939. It is decorated with two metal disks from which hang hide thongs wrapped with quillwork and tipped with red horsehair—traditional Sioux ornamentation.

MATILDA COXE STEVENSON (1849–1915).[30] Stevenson was the first woman anthropologist to work in the Southwest. Between 1872 and 1878 she accompanied her husband, James Stevenson, on geological surveys in the West. In 1879 she was his assistant on the first ethnographic and collecting expedition sent to Zuni Pueblo by John Wesley Powell, director of the Bureau of Ethnology. In subsequent years the Stevensons continued their research and collecting at Zuni and, to a lesser extent, among the Rio Grande pueblos, and the Hopi and Navajo people. After her husband's death in 1888, Stevenson continued to work in the Southwest, gathering data for her BAE monograph, *The Zuni Indians* (1904), and a comparative study of Pueblo religion. Recognized as a dedicated scientist, Stevenson also drew criticism for her insensitive field methods. She and her husband collected more than 33,000 Pueblo objects for the Smithsonian, primarily pottery but also stone tools, clothing, basketry, and other items,[31] which they obtained directly from the Indian towns, from archaeological ruins, and by working with traders such as Thomas Keam at Hopi.

A small Navajo sarape, much worn (5.9806), is one of approximately sixty southwestern objects collected by Stevenson now in NMAI's collections. It was accessioned in 1917.

THOMAS S. TWISS (b. New York 1802–71).[32] From 1826 to 1828, Twiss was assistant professor of natural and experimental philosophy at West Point, his alma mater. He resigned from the army with the rank of major in 1829 and began teaching at South Carolina College. In 1847 he became superintendent of the Nesbitt Manufacturing Company's Iron Works, and, in 1850, resident and consulting engineer for the Buffalo and New York Railroad. In 1855 he was appointed U.S. Indian agent for the Upper Platte, and in 1857 he moved the agency from Rawhide

Butte Creek, east of Fort Laramie, to Deer Creek, on the Platte River. His district included Cheyennes, Arapahos, Oglalas, and Brulés, as well as visiting bands of Crows, Pawnee, and Ponca.[33] Twiss was required to distribute blankets, food, and other goods provided by the government, but the Indians complained that frequently they did not receive their fair share. Twiss encouraged the establishment of more military posts in the region and the introduction of agriculture and missions as ways to resolve unrest. His schemes were impractical and expensive, and he quarreled with the military and other traders. In 1861, when President Lincoln took office, Twiss was not reassigned to his post. In 1862 the Deer Creek agency was moved back to Fort Laramie. Twiss married an Oglala girl named Wanikiyewin, whom he called Mary, and today many of his descendants are enrolled Sioux members; most of them live on the Pine Ridge Reservation.[34]

The Thomas S. Twiss Collection was presented to the museum by Harmon W. Hendricks, who purchased it in 1918 and 1919 from Daisy Barnett of New York.[35] The collection includes two Navajo chief blankets (8.8038; 10.8457–plate 13) accessioned in 1918 and 1921, and a small sarape *diyogí* (10.8456–plate 12) accessioned in 1921.

SAMUEL WASHINGTON WOODHOUSE (1821–1904).[36] Woodhouse, a Philadelphia physician and an avid ornithologist, was appointed surgeon and naturalist of two expeditions in 1849 and 1850 to survey the Creek-Cherokee boundary in Indian Territory. In 1851 he participated in a reconnaissance of southwestern territory under the command of Capt. Lorenzo Sitgreaves of the Corps of Topographical Engineers, again as surgeon-naturalist. The region had recently been acquired by the United States from Mexico and was little known. As Sitgreaves wrote in his 1853 *Report of an Expedition Down the Zuni and Colorado Rivers*, his instructions were to explore the Zuni River from Zuni Pueblo to its junction with the Colorado River, "determining its course and character, particularly in reference to its navigable properties, and to the character of its adjacent land and productions," and then to follow the Colorado to its junction with the Gulf of California.[37] The party marched from Santa Fe on 15 August and reached Zuni on 1 September, where it was detained until 24 September. Appended to Sitgreaves's report is one by Woodhouse in which he describes the plants and animals he observed on his travels, making special note of previously unrecorded species.

Woodhouse was probably at Zuni when he collected two chief blankets (11.8280–plate 14; 11.8281–plate 15). The museum purchased the blankets from S. W. Woodhouse, Jr., and they were accessioned in 1923.

WILLIAM WALLACE WOTHERSPOON (1850–1921).[38]

Wotherspoon served in the U.S. Navy from 1870 to 1873, then joined the army as a second lieutenant in the infantry. For the next ten years he was stationed in the West, campaigning in Idaho and Arizona before his regiment was assigned to the Department of the East. In 1893 he was detailed to take charge of Apache prisoners of war who had been sent to Mt. Vernon Barracks, near Mobile, Alabama. From 1899 to 1904, he campaigned in the Philippine Insurrection. When he returned he moved into the army general staff. He was appointed director and then president of the Army War College in Pennsylvania, where he remained for seven years, with a brief interruption to serve as chief of staff of the so-called Army of Pacification in Cuba. His career was capped by appointment as army chief of staff in 1914; he retired that same year.

In a 1972 letter to the museum, Wotherspoon's son, Rear Admr. Alexander Wotherspoon, retired, remembered that his father had purchased the Navajo blankets now in the NMAI collections during the Indian wars.[39] The blankets include sarapes (24.7838; 24.7839–plate 37), a chief blanket (24.7840– plate 38), a Moki sarape (24.7841–plate 39), two *diyogí* sarapes (24.7842–fig. 14; 24.7843–plate 40), and a *biil* (24.7844–plate 41). They were purchased by the museum and accessioned in 1973.

ADDITIONAL COLLECTORS

Collectors of the museum's nineteenth-century Navajo blankets who are not discussed above are listed here. According to museum records, Maj. Gen. Alfred E. Bates collected one-half of a *biil* (23.2212–fig. 1); Capt. H. G. Brady collected a sarape *diyogí* (20.5489) about 1870; Lt. William H. Chase collected a woman's shoulder blanket (20.3005) in 1870; Col. Joseph T. Clarke collected a woman's shoulder blanket (22.9191–plate 26) between 1880 and 1890; and Capt. C. N. B. Macauley collected a sarape *diyogí* (20.5584–fig. 13) about 1875. Rachel Eleanor Griffin McNett collected a woman's shoulder blanket (23.921–plate 27) and two small sarapes (23.922–fig. 12; 23.923–plate 28) between 1870 and 1871 at Fort Defiance.

The Joseph J. Asch Collection includes a small sarape (19.7319) and one-half of a biil (19.7320). The Matthew M. Cushing Collection includes a chief blanket (21.4886–plate 24). The William M. Fitzhugh Collection includes a fancy manta

Colorado (Ute), wearing chief blanket, 1870–80. Gift of W. H. Jackson. (P4512; N35283)

(19.3014), a Pueblo manta with sewed ends cut from a Navajo manta (19.3019), a chief blanket (19.3022–plate 18), a wedge weave blanket (19.3023), a Moki-pattern diyogí (19.3031), and two sarapes (19.3037–plate 19; 19.3039–plate 20). A bequest to the museum from the Katherine Harvey Collection included a Moki-pattern sarape (23.2466–plate 29). The David C. Vernon Collection includes a small sarape (24.2306–plate 34) originally purchased in 1897 and exchanged from Jackson Hole Preserve. The W. C. Wyman Collection includes a small sarape (17.9694–fig. 24) and a chief blanket (17.9699).

B. Altman and Company presented a manta dress (20.4092) to the museum. Susan D. Bliss donated a small sarape (22.9196) and a sarape diyogí (22.9297), collected in 1900. Charles and Ruth de Young Elkus presented a "slave" blanket (23.1277–fig. 16) collected by the Santa Fe dealer Frank Applegate before 1900. Faith Dennis donated a diyogí (24.6899–plate 36). The Mattatuck Historical Society in Waterbury, Connecticut, donated a sarape (24.1901–plate 33) originally purchased from Hubbell's Trading Post in 1892, along with a sarape (24.1902) bought from Fred Harvey's curio store in Winslow, Arizona, in 1903. John F. Meigs presented a Moki-pattern sarape (20.9123) collected in 1875. Mrs. Robert Montgomery donated a pictorial chief blanket (24.2373–plate 35) collected in 1910. Harriet Roeder presented a chief blanket (22.7688) and three small sarapes (22.7693; 22.7695–fig. 26; 22.7701). Mrs. Russell Sage donated one small sarape (4.8802–fig. 19). Ellen Thomas donated a chief blanket (23.796) and a Moki-pattern sarape (23.797).

Museum purchases include a small wedge weave blanket (9.9821–plate 11) recorded as having been collected by Frank Hamilton Cushing. A diyogí (23.9495) was purchased from Mrs. Benjamin Hawkins. A small pictorial manta (23.2772) from the William Randolph Hearst Collection was purchased at Parke-Bernet. Two small diyogí (16.2826; 16.2845) were purchased from the collector and dealer John L. Nelson. A small manta (23.2797) collected between 1870 and 1890 was purchased from C. W. Walton. Additional purchases include two biil (11.8066; 21.7908; 21.7909), a woman's manta (13.5080), and a small sarape (21.3286–fig. 15); the collectors of these blankets are unknown.

One sarape (16.3740) and one diyogí (16.3750) were collected by John L. Nelson. A Moki-pattern sarape (1410–plate 1), small sarape (1.209), and poncho sarape (1.1225–plate 3) were collected by F. M. Covert, a dealer who maintained a curio store on Fifth Avenue in New York in the first decade of the twentieth century.

CATALOGUE OF
THE COLLECTION

The National Museum of the American Indian holds an unusually large and comprehensive collection of more than 120 nineteenth-century Navajo wearing blankets. Identification of these textiles as wearing blankets was based on an analysis of structure, materials, and dye content. Perhaps most important is the fact that they were made as blankets—in other words, they are soft, and draped when worn. What actually happened to the blankets after they came off the loom was not a consideration. Any one of them could have been sold to a U.S. Army officer, traded into one of the pueblos, or worn by a member of the weaver's family. Toward the close of the century, the probability increased that the blankets were being made for a commercial non-Indian market.

Analysis of the textiles began with Joe Ben Wheat's research in the Southwest collections in the early 1970s. In 1990 the museum hosted a workshop to extend the survey and to analyze additional selected blankets. The invited participants included D. Y. Begay, Ann Lane Hedlund, and Joe Ben Wheat. It was this session that determined the nature, range, and variety of the textiles selected for documentation here. New information has been added periodically.

The catalogue of the collection is meant to serve as a guide; the information is neither comprehensive nor final. We hope that further research, such as study to determine contemporary Navajo terminology, will augment the data currently available.

CATEGORIES OF BLANKETS

Due to the substantial breadth of the collection, it was necessary to group the textiles by type. We had hoped to use names and categories of textiles most relevant and useful to a Navajo audience, but we also recognized that most institutions, as well as the literature on Navajo weaving, organize Navajo blankets according to non-Navajo terms. Furthermore, as recent research indicates, Navajo terms for each blanket "type" are rarely agreed upon across the Navajo community. Weavers, for example, often characterize woven textiles according to technique or design elements specific to a particular textile. Perhaps the only exceptions are *biil*, the Navajo word for two-piece dress, and *diyogí*, which, at the turn-of-the-century, meant "soft" or "fluffy," and referred to everyday utility blankets. Even the term diyogí presents a problem today, however, because many Navajo people use the term only in reference to contemporary rugs.

The categories of textiles used here are: women's shoulder blankets, women's mantas, biil (two-piece dresses), chief blankets, sarapes, diyogí (utility blankets), Moki-pattern blankets, wedge weave blankets, "slave" or "servant" blankets, and pictorial blankets. The term "child's blanket" was eliminated and the term "small sarape" used instead; research suggests that many of these blankets were probably not made for children, but rather for sale. All textiles are referred to as *beeldléí* (blankets) in the book's captions, with the exception of biil, diyogí, and *bi ni ghá dzi itłʼó ní* (sarape poncho). Within each category, textiles are listed in chronological order according to NMAI catalogue number. The catalogue numbers indicate the order of accession only and does not refer to the object type or date of manufacture.

CONTENT AND STRUCTURE

An analysis sheet developed by Wheat was completed for each textile and used as the basis for the catalogue entries. Information from these sheets includes identification of weave, fiber, and dye sources, yarn construction, corner and selvage configuration, and other details. Kathleen E. Ash-Milby summarized and augmented the information for this list, modeling the entries on the format established in the literature on Navajo weaving to date.[1] A few of the textiles were on exhibit at the museum's former location at Audubon Terrace in Manhattan and were not accessible for detailed analysis. For this reason, a small number of the entries are incomplete.

DESCRIPTION AND DATE

The approximate date of manufacture given for each textile is based on collection information, where available, and on Wheat's analysis. The word "about" indicates a two- to three-year possible range either before or after the date given.

COLLECTION INFORMATION

Collection information includes the original collector, if known, and the donor. If the date of collection is known, it is provided. See "Notes on Selected Collectors," this volume, for additional information on the collectors.

WEAVE (WOVEN STRUCTURE)

Several terms are used to describe the types of weave represented in this collection. Technically, a woven fabric is composed of interlaced elements, warps and wefts.[2] *Warps* are the parallel foundation elements that run lengthwise through a fabric. The wefts are elements that pass over and under the warps at right angles to them. All of the textiles in this collection are *weft-faced weave*, meaning the wefts conceal the warps. In *plain weave*, each weft passes over one warp, then under one warp, in regular succession. *Tapestry weave* designates a patterned weave in which different colored, discontinuous wefts form a solid block of design, usually in a weft-faced plain weave. In *twill weave*, the weft passes over and under multiple warps, each pass progressing in a diagonal direction. For instance, in the most common twill weave, wefts go over two warps and under two warps. This technique gives the fabric a diagonal ribbed texture and—depending on the number of warps passed and the direction—results in specific geometric patterns. Twill weaves represented in this collection include *diagonal, diamond,* and *herringbone* patterns.

In *wedge weave*, also known as eccentric weave, the wefts deviate from their normal right-angled relation to the warps and force the warps out of their vertical position, often causing scalloped edges to form along the sides of the blanket; panels of wedge weave may alternate with panels of plain weave in some textiles.

DIMENSIONS AND WEFT COUNT

Measurements were taken at the widest points, with the height measured along the warp and the width along the weft. Dimensions do not incorporate corner tassels.

The average number of wefts per inch (2.54 cm) is given as the first number, following "warp" and "weft" in the analysis. For example, "Warp: 8" and "Weft: 44" indicates eight warps per inch and forty-four wefts per inch. Often the count varies within one textile, depending on its materials.

FIBER ANALYSIS

The most commonly identified fiber in the nineteenth-century Navajo blankets is *handspun wool*, typically single-ply with a z twist. *Raveled yarn* indicates commercial cloth, usually chosen for its color, raveled by the weaver and reused as yarn. Unless otherwise noted, as in those instances when they were retwisted, these threads were laid parallel to each other. The term *commercial yarn* identifies commercially processed multi-ply yarn.

Terms used to identify fiber can carry additional meaning for Navajo weavers. For instance, weavers often distinguish between *wool* and *yarn*. To a weaver, yarn implies a commercially processed multi-ply wool, whereas wool refers to single-ply handspun wool. We have tried to stay as true to these definitions as possible, although we do refer to an individual strand of wool as a "yarn."

The second part of the fiber analysis indicates *ply*, *twist*, and *spin*. If no number is given, the structure is *single-ply*; that is, a single strand of spun fiber. The direction of the spin, *z* or *s*, is in lower case. If multiple plies are present, the direction of their final twist together follows in uppercase. For instance, "z" alone indicates the structure is single-ply, z-spun. "4z-S" indicates a 4-ply yarn, each ply is z-spun, and the four plies are twisted together in an s direction.

COLOR AND DYE SOURCES

The third element is the color and dye source; the dye source precedes the color description. For instance, the description may read, "indigo blue and cochineal crimson." The term *natural* is used to indicate the color is the fiber's natural color; no dye was used. *Native* refers to dyes composed of natural elements, including vegetal dyes. *Reinforced brown-black* refers to natural dark brown wool that has been overdyed with native or synthetic dye to create dark brown or black. All commercial dyes, including early anilines, are referred to as *synthetic*.

Cochineal and *lac* dyes were initially identified by color and appearance; later, some were identified by spectrophotometric analysis. If the identification of the dye is questionable, a question mark follows its description.

SELVAGE CORDS

Selvage cords are described in the same manner as warps and wefts. For example, "2 2z-S" indicates two twined cords, each of 2-ply, z-spun strands twisted together in an s direction.

CORNERS

Corner information includes descriptions of the tassels, if they are still present. *Self tassels* are composed only of the warp and weft selvage cords. *Augmented tassels* are supplemented with additional yarns.

Please see Wheat, "Navajo Blankets," this volume, for an historical treatment of structural details and content.

For further reading on textile analysis and terminology see:

Emery, Irene. *The Primary Structures of Fabrics*. Washington, D.C.: The Textile Museum, 1966.

Hedlund, Ann Lane. *Beyond the Loom: Keys to Understanding Early Southwestern Weaving*. Boulder: Johnson Publishing Company, 1990.

Kent, Kate Peck. *Navajo Weaving: Three Centuries of Change*. Santa Fe, New Mexico: School of American Research, 1985.

WOMEN'S SHOULDER BLANKETS

9608 Banded with "diamond stripes," about 1880. Joseph Keppler Collection, accessioned 1906. 45¾" × 57¼" (116.2 × 145.4 cm). Tapestry weave. Warps: 9½, handspun wool, z, natural white and brown. Wefts: 38–41, handspun wool, z, natural white, reinforced black, synthetic orange-red. Selvage cords: handspun wool, 2 3z-S, synthetic orange-red. Corners: self tassels.

6.305 Sarape pattern with serrate diamond network, about 1885. Joseph Keppler Collection, accessioned 1917. 45½" × 56¼" (115.6 × 142.9 cm). Tapestry weave. Warps: 8½, handspun wool, z, natural white. Wefts: 25, handspun wool, z, natural white, indigo blue, indigo over native (?) green, synthetic red. Selvage cords: handspun wool, 2 3z-S, synthetic pink-red. Corners: augmented tassels.

9.1979 Banded, 1880–1900. Collected by George H. Pepper, accessioned 1919. 47⅝" × 61" (121 × 155 cm). Weft-faced plain weave. Warps: 7, handspun wool, z, natural white. Wefts: 16, handspun wool, z, natural black and combed gray, synthetic orange-red. Selvage cords: handspun wool, 2 2z, synthetic orange-red. Corners: self-augmented tassels.

20.3035 Serrate zigzags, about 1870. Collected 1870 by Lt. William H. Chase, presented by Mrs. Randall Chase, accessioned 1940. 43¾" × 52¾" (111 × 134 cm). Tapestry weave. Warps: 8, handspun wool, z, natural white. Wefts: 34, handspun wool, z, natural white, indigo blue, native green; raveled and respun (?) yarn, synthetic tomato-red. Selvage cords: warp, handspun wool, 2 2z-S, native yellow and faded blue; weft, handspun wool, 2 2z-S, synthetic red. Corners: heavy, augmented tassels.

22.9191 Banded with serrate zigzags, about 1880. Collected 1880–90 by Col. Joseph T. Clarke, purchased from his daughter, Mrs. Llewellyn W. Oliver, accessioned 1961. 45½" × 56⅞" (115.5 × 144.5 cm). Tapestry weave. Warps: 7, handspun wool, z, natural brown. Wefts: 32, handspun wool, z, natural gray and brown-black, indigo blue, synthetic tomato-red and bright green, native or synthetic yellow and yellow-green. Selvage cords: warp, handspun wool, 2 3z-S, synthetic tomato-red; weft, handspun wool, 2 3z-S, synthetic red (faded to pink). Corners: augmented tassels.

23.921 Modified Second Phase chief pattern, 1865–70. Collected 1870–71 by Rachel Eleanor Griffin McNett at Fort Defiance, Arizona, gift of her daughter, Mrs. Harvé Reed Stuart, accessioned 1961. 41½" × 63" (105.4 × 160 cm). Tapestry weave. Warps: 10, handspun wool, z, natural white. Wefts: 32, handspun wool, z, natural white and brown-black, indigo blue; raveled yarn, z, cochineal crimson. Selvage cords: warp, handspun wool, 2 3z-S, indigo blue; weft, handspun wool, 2 3z-S, natural brown, indigo blue. Corners: augmented tassels.

23.2770 Modified Third Phase chief pattern, about 1868. Collected 1869 on the Powell Expedition, William Randolph Hearst Collection, purchased at Parke-Bernet Auction 2201 (22 May 1963), accessioned 1963. 29½" × 40" (74.9 × 101.6 cm). Tapestry weave. Warps: 7½, handspun wool, z, natural white. Wefts: 52–56, handspun wool, z, natural white and combed grey, native black and yellow, indigo blue; 34, raveled threads used in bundles, 6-10z-Z, cochineal rose. Selvage cords: handspun wool, 2 2z-S, indigo blue. No corner information.

WOMEN'S MANTAS

9603 Fancy manta, banded, 1880–90. Joseph Keppler Collection, accessioned 1906. 42⅝" × 56¼" (108.3 × 142.9 cm). Diagonal twill tapestry weave. Warps: 18, handspun wool, z, natural white. Wefts: 26, handspun wool, z, synthetic orange, orange-yellow and yellow, indigo blue; commercial yarn, 4z-S, synthetic red. Selvage cords: commercial 4-ply yarn, 2 3s-Z, synthetic blue (faded). Corners: augmented tassels.

9612 Fancy manta with terraced triangles, 1860–80. Joseph Keppler Collection, accessioned 1906. 41½" × 55⅞" (105.5 × 141.8 cm). Diagonal twill tapestry weave. Warps: 16, handspun wool, z, natural brown. Wefts: 20, handspun wool, z, natural brown, indigo blue; raveled yarn, 3s, cochineal crimson and light crimson. Selvage cords: handspun wool, 2 3z-S, indigo blue. Corners: augmented tassels.

6.302 Fancy manta with Spider Woman's crosses, about 1875. Joseph Keppler Collection, accessioned 1917. 43" × 57¼" (109.2 × 145.4 cm). Diagonal twill tapestry weave. Warps: 16, handspun wool, z, natural brown. Wefts: 28, handspun wool, z, native brown-black, indigo blue, synthetic (?) dull crimson (possibly respun); commercial yarn, 4z-S, synthetic (?) scarlet, 3z-S, cochineal

crimson, 4z-S, synthetic purple. Selvage cords: handspun wool, 3 3z-S, indigo blue. Corners: augmented tassels.

9.1910 Fancy manta with terraced diamonds, about 1860. Collected by George H. Pepper at Hopi, Arizona, accessioned 1919. 33½" × 52" (85 × 132 cm). Diagonal twill tapestry weave. Warps: 9, handspun wool, z, indigo light blue. Wefts: 26, handspun wool, z, natural brown and indigo blue; raveled yarn, 3-5s, cochineal red and synthetic (?) orange. Selvage cords: handspun wool, 2 3z-S, indigo blue. Corners: augmented tassels.

9.1977 Small manta with crosses, about 1875. Navajo or Hopi. Collected by George H. Pepper, accessioned 1919. 28" × 39⅜" (71 × 100 cm). Diagonal twill tapestry weave. Warps: 11, handspun wool, z, natural white. Wefts: 24, handspun wool, z, natural white, indigo blue; 40, commercial yarn, 3z-S, synthetic scarlet and yellow-green. Selvage cords: handspun wool, 2 3z-S, indigo blue. Corners: none intact, traces of augmented tassels.

9.1978 Fancy manta with terraced diamonds, 1875–80. Collected by George H. Pepper, accessioned 1919. 43¾" × 58½" (111.1 × 148.6 cm). Diagonal twill tapestry weave. Warps: 14, handspun wool, z, natural brown. Wefts: 18, handspun wool, z, native brown-black, indigo blue, synthetic green; raveled yarn, 2s, synthetic red, 3s, synthetic orange-red; commercial yarn, 4z-S, synthetic purple, 3z-S, synthetic red. Selvage cords: handspun wool, 3 3z-S, indigo blue. Corners: augmented tassels.

11.9315 Fragment of Pueblo-style "maiden's shawl," about 1880. Collected by Daniel W. Lord between 1888–89 on the Hemenway Expedition in Arizona and New Mexico, presented by Mary Patterson Lord, accessioned 1923. 38¼" × 46½" (97 × 118 cm). Weaves: diagonal twill tapestry (center), herringbone twill (mid-center), and diamond twill (ends). Warps: 16, handspun wool, z, natural white. Wefts: 40–44, handspun wool, z, natural white, indigo blue; raveled yarn, 4s, synthetic red. Selvage cords: handspun wool, 3 2z-S, indigo blue. Corners: augmented tassels.

13.5080 Fancy manta with terraced zigzags, 1860–75. Purchase, accessioned 1924. 42½" × 54" (108 × 137 cm). Weaves: diagonal twill tapestry (center), diamond twill (ends). Warps: 16, handspun wool, z, natural brown. Wefts: 64, handspun wool, z, natural brown, indigo blue; raveled yarn, 3s, cochineal (?) crimson. Selvage cords: warp, handspun wool, 3 3z-S; weft, handspun wool, 2 3z-S. No corner information.

19.3014 Fancy manta with crosses, 1875–80. William M. Fitzhugh Collection, accessioned 1936. 44" × 51½" (111.8 × 130.8 cm).

Diagonal twill tapestry weave. Warps: 14, handspun wool, z, natural brown. Wefts: 26, handspun wool, z, natural brown, indigo blue, synthetic green; raveled yarn, z, synthetic (?) dull crimson, 4s, synthetic crimson; commercial yarn, 3s-Z, cochineal (?) rose, 3z-S, maroon (unknown dye). Selvage cords: warp, handspun wool, 2 3z-S, indigo blue; weft, handspun wool, 2 3z-S, synthetic (?) carded yellow. Corners: augmented tassels.

19.3019 Manta ends cut and sewed onto Acoma embroidered manta, 1850–60 (Acoma) and about 1880 (Navajo). William M. Fitzhugh Collection, accessioned 1936. Overall: 49¼" × 53⅜" (125.2 × 135.5 cm); Navajo strips only: 4½" × 53⅜" (11.5 × 135.5 cm) and 5" × 53⅜" (12.5 × 135.5 cm). Herringbone twill tapestry weave. Warps: 20, handspun wool, z, natural black; commercial yarn (added), 7z-S, synthetic green. Wefts: 14, handspun wool, z, natural black. Binding: commercial yarn, 4z-S, synthetic crimson. Corners: augmented tassels.

20.4092 Fancy manta with Spider Woman's crosses, 1880–90. Presented by B. Altman and Company, accessioned 1941. 48" × 55" (122 × 140 cm). Weaves: diagonal twill tapestry (center), diamond twill tapestry (ends). Warps: 14, commercial yarn, 4z-S, synthetic purple. Wefts: 48, commercial yarn, 4z-S, synthetic black, red, purple, and green. Selvage cords: commercial 4-ply yarn, 2 4z-S. No corner information.

23.2797 Small manta with zigzags, 1875–90. Purchased from C. W. Walton, collected by his great-uncle, 1870–90, accessioned 1963. 20" × 29⅛" (51 × 74 cm). Tapestry weave. Warps: 7, commercial yarn, 4z-S, natural tan. Wefts: 25, handspun wool, z, natural white, synthetic orange-red, purple, and yellow; 32–38, handspun wool, z, synthetic (?) steel gray; commercial yarn, 4z-S, synthetic green (faded); raveled yarn bundles, 6-8s, synthetic crimson. Selvage cords: handspun wool, 2 2z-S, native yellow-green. Corners: none intact, augmented tassels.

BIIL (TWO-PIECE DRESSES)

4.4674 One panel, terraced diamonds and triangles, 1896 or later. Collected by George H. Pepper, accessioned 1915. 54" × 32⅝" (137 × 83 cm). Tapestry weave. Warps: 15, handspun wool, z, natural white. Wefts: 48–52, handspun wool, z, indigo (?) blue, synthetic black; raveled yarn, 2s, synthetic (?) red. Selvage cords: warp, handspun wool, 3 3z-S, indigo blue; weft, handspun wool, 2 3z-S, indigo blue. Corners: loose with augmented tassels.

9.1930 Zigzags with crosses at each apex, 1890–1900. Collected by George H. Pepper, accessioned 1919. 46⅞" × 65" (119 × 165

cm). Tapestry weave. Warps: 13, handspun wool, z, natural white. Wefts: 49, handspun wool, z, natural and reinforced brown-black, indigo blue; 66-72, raveled yarn, 2s, cochineal (?) crimson. Selvage cords: handspun wool, 2 3z-S, indigo blue. Corners: augmented tassels.

9.1960 Banded with terraced triangles, about 1860. Collected by George H. Pepper, accessioned 1919. 42" × 25½" (106.7 × 64.8 cm). Tapestry weave. Warps: 14, handspun wool, z, natural white and brown. Tapestry weave. Wefts: 58–60, handspun wool, z, natural brown, indigo blue and light blue; raveled yarn, 2s, lac and cochineal crimson and speckled crimson. Selvage cords: handspun wool, 3 3z-S, indigo blue. Corners: none present.

9.1962 Terraced diamonds, about 1860. Collected by George H. Pepper, accessioned 1919. 49⅞" × 32½" (126.6 × 82.5 cm). Tapestry weave. Warps: 11, handspun wool, z, natural white. Wefts: 72, handspun wool, z, reinforced brown-black, indigo blue; 88, raveled yarn, 2s, lac (?) crimson. Selvage cords: handspun wool, 2 3z-S, indigo blue. Corners: tight augmented tassels.

9.1989 One-piece (?) manta dress, severely damaged, banded ends, 1775–1850 (?). Collected by George H. Pepper at Oraibi, Hopi, Arizona, accessioned 1919. 48¾" × 33⅛" (123.9 × 84.3 cm). Weft-faced plain weave. Warps: 9, handspun wool, z, natural white. Wefts: 60, handspun wool, z, natural brown, indigo blue; 80, raveled yarn, 2z, crimson (dye unknown). Selvage cords: handspun wool, 2 3z-S, indigo blue. Corners: none intact, traces of augmented tassels.

9.1992 Banded, 1885–1900. Collected by George H. Pepper at Hopi, Arizona, accessioned 1919. 52⅝" × 32½" (133.7 × 82.6 cm). Weft-faced plain weave. Warps: 7–9½, handspun wool, z, natural white. Wefts: 49½, handspun wool, z, natural brown, indigo blue. Selvage cords: handspun wool, 2 3z-S, indigo blue. Corners: augmented tassels.

11.8066 Zigzags with crosses at each apex, 1880–1900. Purchase, accessioned 1923. 45⅝" × 59½" (116 × 151 cm). Tapestry weave. Warps: 14, handspun wool, z, natural white. Wefts: 52-60, handspun wool, z, reinforced black, indigo blue; raveled yarn, 2s, cochineal crimson. Selvage cords: handspun wool, 2 2z-S, indigo blue. Corners: augmented tassels.

19.7320 One panel, terraced diamonds, 1850–60. Joseph J. Asch Collection, presented in his memory by Mrs. Asch, accessioned 1937. 46⅞" × 34¼" (119 × 87 cm). Tapestry weave. Warps: 14, handspun wool, z, natural white. Wefts: 66, handspun wool, z, natural black, indigo blue; 108, raveled yarn, 2s, lac (?) crimson and dark crimson. Selvage cords: handspun wool, 2 3s, indigo blue. Corners: self-augmented tassels.

20.7806 Four shortened ends of used two-piece dress sewed together, banded, 1870–75. Edward Borein Collection, accessioned 1945. 41⅜" × 31½" (105 × 80 cm). Tapestry weave. Warps: 12-13, handspun wool, z, natural white. Wefts: 60, handspun wool, z, natural brown-black, indigo blue, native black; raveled yarn, 2s, cochineal crimson, 2-5s, cochineal scarlet and dark crimson. Selvage cords: handspun wool, 2 3z-S, indigo blue. Corners: augmented tassels.

20.7807, 20.7808 Banded, about 1870. Edward Borein Collection, accessioned 1945. **20.7807:** 45" × 31½" (114.3 × 80 cm). **20.7808:** 43¾" × 31⅛" (111.1 × 79 cm). Weft-faced plain weave. Warps: 13, handspun wool, z, natural white. Wefts: 58, handspun wool, z, reinforced black, indigo blue; 88, raveled yarn, 2z, cochineal (?) crimson. Selvage cords: handspun wool, 2 3z-S, reinforced black. Corners: augmented tassels.

20.7820, 20.7821 Terraced diamonds, 1850–60. Edward Borein Collection, accessioned 1945. **20.7820:** 51¾" × 34⅜" (131.5 × 86.8 cm). **20.7821:** 52¾" × 32¼" (134 × 82 cm). Tapestry weave. Warps: 11, handspun wool, z, natural white. Wefts: 88, handspun wool, z, natural brown, indigo blue; 108, raveled yarn, 2s, lac (?) plum-crimson. Selvage cords: handspun wool, 2 2z-S, indigo blue. Corners: augmented tassels.

20.7822, 20.7823 Terraced diamonds and triangles, 1850–60. Edward Borein Collection, accessioned 1945. **20.7822:** 52¼" × 33" (132.8 × 83.8 cm). **20.7823:** 52½" × 33½" (133.4 × 85.1 cm). Tapestry weave. Warps: 16, handspun wool, z, natural white. Wefts: 72, handspun wool, z, reinforced black, indigo blue; 104, raveled yarn, 2s, cochineal (?) and lac (?) crimson. Selvage cords: handspun wool, 2 3z-S, indigo blue. Corners: augmented tassels.

21.7908, 21.7909 Terraced diamonds, 1860–80. Purchase, accessioned 1951. **21.7908:** 46½" × 31⅞" (118 × 81 cm). **21.7909:** 47" × 34" (120.8 × 86.4 cm). Tapestry weave. Warps: 12, handspun wool, z, natural white. Wefts: 64–72, handspun wool, z, reinforced brown-black, indigo blue; raveled yarn, 2s, cochineal crimson. Selvage cords: handspun wool, 2 2z-S, indigo blue. Corners: augmented tassels.

23.2212 One panel, paired and terraced zigzags, about 1870. Collected by Maj. Gen. Alfred E. Bates, gift of Mrs. Frederick H. Brooke, accessioned 1962. 48" × 34½" (121.9 × 87.6 cm). Tapestry weave. Warps: 9, handspun wool, z, natural white. Wefts: 60,

handspun wool, z, reinforced black, indigo blue; 88, raveled yarn, 4s, cochineal (?) crimson, 3s, cochineal (?) crimson. Selvage cords: handspun wool, 2 3z-S, indigo blue. No corner information.

24.7844 One panel, zigzags with crosses at each apex, 1880–1900. Collected by Gen. William Wallace Wotherspoon, purchased by Admr. Alexander Wotherspoon, accessioned 1973. 49⅛" × 35" (124.8 × 88.9 cm). Tapestry weave. Warps: 15, handspun wool, z, indigo pale blue. Wefts: 48, handspun wool, z, native brown-black, indigo blue; 72, raveled yarn, 2s, cochineal (?) crimson. Selvage cords: handspun wool, 2 3z-S, indigo blue. Corners: augmented tassels.

CHIEF BLANKETS

8.8038 First Phase, 1840–50. Collected about 1860 by Thomas S. Twiss at Ft. Laramie, Wyoming, presented by Harmon W. Hendricks, accessioned 1918. 54⅜" × 66½" (138 × 169 cm). Weft-faced plain weave. Warps: 12, handspun wool, z, natural white. Wefts: 60, handspun wool, z, natural white and brown, indigo blue; 40, raveled yarn, 2s, lac crimson. Selvage cords: warp, handspun wool, 2 3z-S, indigo blue; weft, handspun wool, 2 2z-S, indigo blue. Corners: augmented tassels.

9.1290 Second Phase variant, 1875–85. Presented by Thea Heye, accessioned 1919. 62¾" × 72½" (159.4 × 184.2 cm). Tapestry weave. Warps: 8, handspun wool, z, natural white and brown-black. Wefts: 44, handspun wool, z, natural white, reinforced brown-black, indigo blue, native (?) yellow; 34, raveled yarn, 2z, cochineal crimson. Selvage cords: warp, handspun wool, 2 3z-S, indigo blue; weft, handspun wool, 2 2z-S, indigo blue. Corners: augmented tassels.

9.1945 Second Phase, about 1860. Collected by George H. Pepper, accessioned 1919. 55¼" × 69¾" (140.4 × 177.1 cm). Tapestry weave. Warps: 15, handspun wool, z, natural white. Wefts: 68-76, handspun wool, z, natural white, reinforced brown-black, indigo blue; raveled yarn, 2s, lac (?) crimson, s, lac (?) crimson. Selvage cords: warp, handspun wool, traces only of 2 3z-S, indigo blue; weft, handspun wool, 2 3z-S, indigo blue. Corners: traces of augmented tassels.

10.8457 Early Third Phase, 1850–60. Collected by Thomas S. Twiss about 1860, presented by Harmon W. Hendricks, accessioned 1921. 57⅞" × 78" (147 × 198 cm). Tapestry weave. Warps: 11-12, handspun wool, z, natural white. Wefts: 52-56, handspun wool, z, natural white and brown, indigo blue; raveled yarn, 3s, lac crimson. Selvage cords: warp, handspun wool, 2 3z-S, indigo blue;

weft, handspun wool, 2 2z-S, indigo blue. Corners: augmented tassels.

11.8280 First Phase, 1840–50. Collected 1851 by Samuel W. Woodhouse, surgeon and naturalist of the Topographical Engineer Corps accompanying the Sitgreaves Expedition, purchased from Samuel W. Woodhouse, Jr., accessioned 1923. 50¾" × 71¼" (128.9 × 181 cm). Weft-faced plain weave. Warps: 14, handspun wool, z, natural white and brown. Wefts: 64–72, handspun wool, z, natural white and brown, indigo blue; raveled yarn, s, lac crimson, 2-3s, lac crimson. Selvage cords: handspun wool, 2 3z-S, indigo blue. Corners: slight augmentation with braided tassels.

11.8281 Early Second Phase, 1840–50. Collected 1851 by Samuel W. Woodhouse, surgeon and naturalist of the Topographical Engineer Corps accompanying the Sitgreaves Expedition, purchased from Samuel W. Woodhouse, Jr., accessioned 1923. 56" × 75¼" (142 × 191 cm). Tapestry weave. Warps: 9–11, handspun wool, z, natural white and brown. Wefts: 60, handspun wool, z, natural brown and white, indigo blue; raveled yarn, 3z, lac crimson, lac and cochineal crimson. Selvage cords: warp, handspun wool, 2 2z-S, indigo blue; weft, handspun wool, 2 3z-S, natural white. Corners: augmented tassels, braided with selvage cords.

17.9699 Third Phase, about 1875. W. C. Wyman Collection, accessioned 1931. 53½" × 70" (136 × 177.8 cm). Tapestry weave. Warps: 9–11, handspun wool, z, natural white; commercial yarn, 3z-S, synthetic gray. Wefts: 44–52, handspun wool, z, natural white and brown-black, indigo blue; raveled yarn, z, cochineal (?) crimson. Selvage cords: warp, handspun wool, 2 3z-S, indigo blue; weft (traces only), handspun wool, 2 2z-S, indigo blue. Corners: traces of augmented tassels.

19.3022 Third Phase variant, 1865–75. William M. Fitzhugh Collection, accessioned 1936. 56½" × 73" (143.5 × 185.5 cm). Tapestry weave. Warps: 8, handspun wool, z, natural white. Wefts: 60, handspun wool, z, natural white, indigo blue, native black; raveled yarn, z, cochineal crimson, 3s, cochineal crimson. Selvage cords: handspun wool, 2 3z-S, indigo blue. Corners: slightly augmented tassels.

20.1339 First Phase with two large buttons, one of brass lined with lead, the other of German silver (?), to which are attached porcupine quill-wrapped hide cords with tin tinklers and red horsehair, 1840–50. Collected from the Brulé Sioux in South Dakota by artist DeCost Smith, bequest of DeCost Smith, accessioned 1939. 54⅜" × 71⅜" (137.8 × 180.7 cm). Weft-faced plain weave. Warps: 13, handspun wool, z, natural white. Wefts: 60,

handspun wool, z, natural white and brown, indigo blue. Selvage cords: handspun wool, 2 3z-S, indigo blue. Corners: augmented with braided tassels.

21.4886 Third Phase variant, about 1875. Matthew M. Cushing Collection, presented by Nellie I. F. Cushing, accessioned 1950. 63⅜" × 74⅛" (160.8 × 188.2 cm). Tapestry weave. Warps: 12, handspun wool, z, natural white. Wefts: 48–49, handspun wool, z, natural white and brown, native brown-black, indigo blue; raveled yarn, z, cochineal crimson. Selvage cords: handspun wool, 2 3z-S, indigo blue. Corners: augmented tassels.

22.1687 Third Phase, 1870–75. Gen. Nelson A. Miles Collection, presented by Gen. Sherman Miles for himself and in memory of Mrs. Samuel Reber, accessioned 1953. 55¼" × 74¾" (140.3 × 189.5 cm). Tapestry weave. Warps: 9, handspun wool, z, natural white. Wefts: 40–48, handspun wool, z, natural white, indigo blue, native brown-black; raveled yarn, 4s, cochineal crimson, z, cochineal dull crimson. Selvage cords: warp, missing; weft, handspun wool, 2 3z-S, indigo blue. Corners: none intact.

22.7688 Second Phase variant, about 1880. Presented by Harriet Roeder in memory of her mother, Harriet K. Roeder, accessioned 1959. 56⅛" × 71⅜" (142.8 × 181.2 cm). Tapestry weave. Warps: 7, handspun wool, z, natural white. Wefts: 38, handspun wool, z, natural white and brown-black, indigo blue, synthetic yellow and tomato-red. Selvage cords: handspun wool, 2 3z-S, synthetic tomato-red. Corners: self-augmented tassels.

22.7949 Second Phase, about 1860. Collected at Zuni, New Mexico, by Douglas D. Graham, first U. S. Indian Agent at Zuni, and presented by his nieces, Evelyn B. Lent, Mrs. G. B. Oman, Beatrice A. B. Young, and Mary F. B. Van Houten, accessioned 1959. 54⅛" × 71⅛" (137.4 × 180.7 cm). Tapestry weave. Warps: 13, handspun wool, z, natural white and combed gray. Wefts: 70, handspun wool, z, natural white and brown, indigo blue; 84, raveled yarn, 3s, lac purple-red. Selvage cords: handspun wool, 2 3z-S, indigo blue. Corners: none intact.

22.7950 Third Phase, 1870–75. Collected at Zuni, New Mexico, by Douglas D. Graham, first U.S. Indian Agent at Zuni, presented by his nieces, Evelyn B. Lent, Mrs. G. B. Oman, Beatrice A. B. Young, and Mary F. B. Van Houten, accessioned 1959. 49¼" × 71⅝" (125 × 181.9 cm). Tapestry weave. Warps: 10, handspun wool, z, natural white and brown. Wefts: 54, handspun wool, z, natural white and brown, indigo blue; 72, raveled yarn, 3s, lac crimson. Selvage cords: handspun wool, 2 3z-S, indigo blue. Corners: none intact.

22.8875 Second Phase, about 1870. Collected by Sumner H. Bodfish as a member of the U.S. Geographical Survey, purchased from his niece, Elizabeth H. Wilkins, accessioned 1960. 54" × 75" (137.2 × 190.5 cm). Tapestry weave. Warps: 16, handspun wool, z, natural white. Wefts: 62, handspun wool, z, natural white, reinforced brown, indigo blue; raveled yarn, 2z, crimson and pale green (unknown dyes). Selvage cords: handspun wool, 2 3z. Corners: traces of self-augmented tassels.

23.796 Third Phase, about 1875. Gift of Ellen Thomas, accessioned 1961. 48⅞" × 67" (124 × 170 cm). Tapestry weave. Warps: 12, handspun wool, z, natural white. Wefts: 48, handspun wool, z, natural white and brown-black, indigo blue; raveled yarn, s, cochineal (?) crimson. Selvage cords: warp, fragmentary handspun wool, indigo blue; weft, missing. No corner information.

24.7840 Second-Third Phase variant, 1870–75. Collected by Gen. William Wallace Wotherspoon, purchased by Admr. Alexander Wotherspoon, accessioned 1973. 60⅜" × 73" (153.2 × 185.4 cm). Tapestry weave. Warps: 12, handspun wool, z, natural white. Wefts: 72, handspun wool, z, natural white and brown-black (some reinforced), indigo blue; 80, raveled yarn, 3z-S, cochineal crimson; 64, commercial yarn, 3z-S, cochineal crimson. Selvage cords: handspun wool, 2 3z-S, indigo blue. Corners: augmented tassels.

SARAPES

9609 Vertical meander pattern, 1880–85. Joseph Keppler Collection, accessioned 1906. 66½" × 51½" (169 × 130.8 cm). Tapestry weave. Warps: 8, handspun wool, z, native (?) orange. Wefts: 29, handspun wool, z, indigo blue, native (?) orange and native brown-black, synthetic tomato-red. Selvage cords: warp, handspun wool, 2 3z-S, native black; weft, handspun wool, 2 2z-S, synthetic tomato-red. Corners: self tassels.

1.209 Banded with zigzags, 1865–75. Collected by F. M. Covert, accessioned 1906. 54" × 30" (137.2 × 76.2 cm). Tapestry weave. Warps: 16, handspun wool, z, natural white, brown and combed gray. Wefts: 36, handspun wool, z, natural white, indigo blue; 64, raveled yarn, 2z, dark and medium crimson (unknown dye). Selvage cords: handspun wool, 2 3z-S, indigo blue. Corners: augmented tassels.

1.1225 Poncho sarape, terraced pattern, 1850–60. Collected by F. M. Covert, accessioned 1906. 80¼" × 58" (203.8 × 147.3 cm). Tapestry weave. Warps: 14, handspun wool, z, natural white. Wefts: 68, handspun wool, z, natural white, indigo blue; 72, raveled 2-ply

yarn, loosely twisted, 2s-S, lac crimson. Selvage cords: handspun wool, 2 3z-S, indigo blue. Poncho slit selvage: handspun wool, 2z-S, indigo blue. Corners: augmented tassels.

4.8802 Small sarape, serrate zigzags with crosses, 1870–80. Gift of Mrs. Russell Sage, accessioned 1916. 55½" × 33" (141 × 83.8 cm). Tapestry weave. Warps: 10½, handspun wool, z, indigo (?) blue. Wefts: 64, handspun wool, z, natural white, indigo blue, synthetic green and yellow, combed pink (cochineal [?] crimson and natural white); 80, raveled yarn, 2z, cochineal [?] crimson and faded combed pink (cochineal [?] crimson and natural white). Selvage cords: 2 3z. Corners: augmented tassels.

5.9806 Small sarape or saddle blanket, compound bands with vertical zigzags, 1875–85. Collected by Matilda Coxe Stevenson, accessioned 1917. 42⅛" × 29½" (107 × 75 cm). Tapestry weave. Warps: 8½, handspun wool, z, natural brown-black. Wefts: 38, handspun wool, z, natural white and combed gray, indigo blue, native (?) yellow and dark yellow-green, synthetic red. Selvage cords: warp, handspun wool, 2 3z-S, synthetic red; weft, handspun wool, 2 2z-S, synthetic red. Corners: no tassels present.

6.304 Small sarape, zigzag pattern, about 1880. Joseph Keppler Collection, accessioned 1917. 46" × 30⅜" (117 × 77 cm). Tapestry weave. Warps: 8½, handspun wool, z, natural white. Wefts: 48, handspun wool, z, natural white, indigo blue, synthetic yellow, blue-green (unknown dye); raveled yarn, z, synthetic coral. Selvage cords: warp, none; weft, commercial 4-ply yarn, 2 3s-Z, synthetic red. Corners: missing.

6.1086 Small sarape or double saddle blanket with "diamond stripe" pattern, 1875–80. Joseph Keppler Collection, accessioned 1917. 46" × 30¾" (117 × 78 cm). Tapestry weave. Warps: 7½, commercial yarn, 4z-S, synthetic purple. Wefts: 40, handspun wool, z, indigo blue, native yellow-green, synthetic rose-red; commercial yarn, 4z-S, synthetic blue (faded) and yellow-green. Selvage cords: warp, commercial 3-ply yarn, 2 5z, cochineal crimson; weft, commercial 3-ply wool, 2 3z, cochineal crimson. Corners: augmented tassels.

6.1088 Small sarape, banded with diamonds and terraced zigzags and triangles, 1875–85. Joseph Keppler Collection, accessioned 1917. 54½" × 34¾" (138.5 × 85.8 cm). Tapestry weave. Warps: 10–12, handspun wool, z, natural brown. Wefts: 60–63, handspun wool, z, natural white, carded pink (natural white and synthetic red) with one blue thread; raveled yarn, s, cochineal (?) crimson, 3-4z, indigo blue. Selvage cords: handspun wool, 2 2z-S, indigo blue. Corners: damaged with traces of augmented tassels.

9.1912 Poncho sarape, terraced pattern, 1825–60. Collected by George H. Pepper, accessioned 1919. 67¾" × 52¼" (172.2 × 132.6 cm). Tapestry weave. Warps: 14, tightly handspun wool, z, natural white, indigo pale blue. Wefts: 68, handspun wool, z, natural white, indigo blue, native blue-green; 76, raveled yarn, 2s, lac and cochineal crimson. Selvage cords: handspun wool, 2 3z-S, indigo blue. Poncho slit selvage: handspun wool, 2 3z. Corners: missing.

9.1942 Compound bands, about 1880. Collected by George H. Pepper at Hopi, Arizona, accessioned 1919. 66½" × 47¾" (169 × 121 cm). Weft-faced plain weave. Warps: 9, handspun wool, z, natural white. Wefts: 50, handspun wool, z, natural white, brown, and combed tan. Selvage cords: handspun wool, 2 3z-S, natural white. Corners: none intact, augmented tassels.

9.1990 Stacked serrate diamonds, 1860–70. Collected by George H. Pepper, accessioned 1919. 60" × 46" (152.4 × 116.8 cm). Tapestry weave. Warps: 14, handspun wool, z, natural white, brown, and combed brown. Wefts: 60–64, handspun wool, z, natural white, indigo blue; commercial yarn, 3z-S, cochineal (?) crimson. Selvage cords: none present. Corners: missing.

11.9323 Concentric vertical zigzags, about 1880. Collected by Daniel W. Lord between 1888 and 1889 on the Hemenway Expedition in Arizona and New Mexico, presented by Mary Patterson Lord, accessioned 1923. 72½" × 55⅛" (184 × 140 cm). Tapestry weave. Warps: 13, handspun wool, z, natural white. Wefts: 48–52, commercial yarn, 4z-S, natural white, synthetic yellow, dark blue, and green; raveled yarn, z, synthetic red. Selvage cords: handspun wool, 2 3z-S, synthetic red. Corners: augmented tassels.

15.7719 Small sarape or saddle blanket, terraced and serrate zigzags, about 1875. Collected by Maj. John Wesley Powell and presented to his sister, Mrs. A. H. Thompson, upon his return from the Grand Canyon Expedition, given to Mrs. Walter W. Davis about 1900, presented by Mrs. Walter W. Davis, accessioned 1927. 50½" × 32¼" (128.3 × 81.9 cm). Tapestry weave. Warps: 12, handspun wool, z, natural brown. Wefts: 50–56, handspun wool, z, natural white and combed gray, indigo blue; raveled yarn, s, maroon (unknown dye); commercial yarn, 4z-S, synthetic red, red (faded to orange) and yellow-green. Selvage cords: commercial 4-ply yarn, 2 3s-Z, synthetic green (faded to blue). Corners: none intact, augmented tassels.

16.3740 Small sarape, compound bands, 1860–70. Collected by John L. Nelson, Clancy Collection, accessioned 1929. 48¾" × 31⅞" (124 × 81 cm). Tapestry weave. Warps: 12, handspun wool, z, natural white. Wefts: 66–80, handspun wool, z, natural white, indigo blue; raveled yarn, 2z, cochineal (?) crimson and synthetic yellow-green, z, cochineal (?) crimson. Selvage cords: warp, handspun wool, 2 3z-S, indigo blue; weft, handspun wool, 2 2z-S, indigo blue. Corners: augmented tassels.

17.9694 Small sarape or double saddle blanket, compound bands with terraced triangles, about 1880. W. C. Wyman Collection, accessioned 1931. 50⅞" × 30½" (129.2 × 77.5 cm). Tapestry weave. Warps: 9, handspun wool, z, natural white. Wefts: 36, handspun wool, z, natural white and combed gray, native yellow, synthetic black, and scarlet. Selvage cords: handspun wool, 2 2z-S, native (?) gold. Corners: traces of augmented tassels.

19.3036 Small sarape, paired vertical zigzags, 1885–90. William M. Fitzhugh Collection, accessioned 1936. 46" × 30¾" (117 × 78 cm). Tapestry weave. Warps: 11, handspun wool, z, natural white. Wefts: 36, handspun wool, z, natural white, indigo blue, native (?) yellow; 60, raveled yarn, red (unknown dye). Selvage cords: commercial 4-ply yarn, 2 2z-S, synthetic red. No corner information.

19.3037 Diamond network, 1850–60. William M. Fitzhugh Collection, accessioned 1936. 69" × 51½" (175.3 × 130.8 cm). Tapestry weave. Warps: 14, handspun wool, z, natural white. Wefts: 74, handspun wool, z, natural white, indigo blue; 88, raveled yarn, 2s-Z, lac and cochineal rose-crimson; 2z-S, lac crimson. Selvage cords: warp, handspun wool, 2 3z-S, indigo blue; weft, handspun wool, 2 2z-S, indigo blue. Corners: none intact.

19.3039 Compound bands with terraced zigzags, 1865–70. William M. Fitzhugh Collection, accessioned 1936. 73" × 53¾" (185.4 × 141.7 cm). Tapestry weave. Warps: 14, handspun wool, z, natural white. Wefts: 68, handspun wool, z, natural white, indigo blue, green (unknown dye); 44, raveled yarn, z, cochineal (?) crimson; 64, raveled yarn, 2s, cochineal (?) crimson and native (?) green, 2z, cochineal (?) crimson. Selvage cords: warp, handspun wool, 3 3z-S, indigo blue; weft, handspun wool, 2 3z-S, indigo blue. Corners: braided corners with augmented tassels.

19.7319 Small sarape, terraced pattern, 1865–75. Dr. Joseph J. Asch Collection, presented in his memory by Mrs. Asch, accessioned 1937. 50" × 32½" (127 × 82.5 cm). Tapestry weave. Warps: 11, handspun wool, z, natural (?) white. Wefts: 60, handspun wool, z, blue and carded pink (unknown dyes); commercial yarn, 3s-Z, orange-red, 3z-S, crimson and brown-red (unknown dyes). Selvage cords: handspun wool, 2 3z-S, indigo blue. Corners: augmented tassels.

20.5235 Large zigzag pattern, 1865–68. Collected by General William Tecumseh Sherman, presented by his granddaughter, Eleanor Sherman Fitch, accessioned 1942. 78" × 59½" (198.1 × 151.1 cm). Tapestry weave. Warps: 16, commercial yarn, 3z-S, native gold-yellow. Wefts: 88, commercial yarn, 3z-S, cochineal crimson, indigo blue, native orange; 52, 6z-S, natural white, synthetic (?) blue-green, gold, maroon, beige, and brown (unknown dye). Selvage cords: commercial 3-ply yarn, 2 3s-Z, indigo blue. No corner information.

21.3286 Small sarape, diamond network, about 1870. Purchase, accessioned 1949. 47" × 32½" (119.4 × 82.6 cm). Tapestry weave. Warps: 10, handspun wool, z, natural white. Wefts: 44–52, handspun wool, z, natural white, indigo blue; raveled yarn, 2z and 5-6s, cochineal (?) crimson; commercial yarn, 3z-S, cochineal (?) crimson. Selvage cords: warp, missing; weft, handspun wool, 2 3z-S, indigo blue. Corners: none intact.

22.7693 Small sarape, serrate pattern, about 1885. Presented by Harriet Roeder in memory of her mother, Harriet K. Roeder, accessioned 1959. 52⅜" × 32⅜" (133 × 83 cm). Tapestry weave. Warps: 14, handspun wool, z, natural white. Wefts: 56, handspun wool, z, natural white, indigo blue, native (?) yellow; 68, raveled yarn, 2z, cochineal (?) crimson, synthetic yellow, pale green, and dark crimson. Selvage cords: handspun wool, 2 3z-S, synthetic red. Corners: missing.

22.7695 Small sarape, compound bands with crosses nested in squares, 1865–75. Presented by Harriet Roeder in memory of her mother, Harriet K. Roeder, accessioned 1959. 52¼" × 31" (132.8 × 78.8 cm). Tapestry weave. Warps: 13, handspun wool, z, natural white. Wefts: 60, handspun wool, z, natural white, indigo blue; raveled yarn, 2-3s, cochineal (?) crimson; commercial yarn, 3z-S, synthetic yellow and red, cochineal (?) crimson. Selvage cords: warp, missing; weft, commercial yarn, 3z-S, synthetic red. No corner information.

22.7701 Small sarape, banded with terraced triangles, 1880–85. Presented by Harriet Roeder in memory of her mother, Harriet K. Roeder, accessioned 1959. 47⅞" × 34¾" (121.5 × 88.2 cm). Tapestry weave. Warps: 11, handspun wool, z, natural white. Wefts: 40, handspun wool, z, natural white and combed gray, indigo blue, synthetic orange. Selvage cords: warp (replaced), handspun wool, z, synthetic red; weft, handspun wool, 2 3z-S, synthetic red. No corner information.

22.7951 Diamond network, about 1875. Collected at Zuni, New Mexico, by Douglas D. Graham, first U. S. Indian Agent at Zuni,

presented by his nieces, Evelyn B. Lent, Mrs. G. B. Oman, Beatrice A. B. Young, and Mary F. B. Van Houten, accessioned 1959. 74" × 55½" (188 × 141 cm). Tapestry weave. Warps: 9½, handspun wool, z, natural white. Wefts: 40, handspun wool, z, natural white, indigo blue, and green; raveled yarn, 2-3z, synthetic red; 32, raveled yarn, z, synthetic red; 56, commercial yarn, 3z-S. Selvage cords: handspun wool, 2 3z-S, indigo blue. Corners: augmented tassels.

22.7954 Small sarape, terraced zigzags and diamonds, 1875–80. Collected at Zuni, New Mexico, by Douglas D. Graham, first U. S. Indian Agent at Zuni, presented by his nieces, Evelyn B. Lent, Mrs. G. B. Oman, Beatrice A. B. Young, and Mary F. B. Van Houten, accessioned 1959. 49½" × 33½" (126.2 × 85.1 cm). Tapestry weave. Warps: 12, handspun wool, z, natural white. Wefts: 56, handspun wool, z, natural white, indigo blue, native (?) green-yellow; raveled yarn, 3s, synthetic scarlet; commercial yarn, 4z-S, synthetic scarlet, lavender, green, and orange. Selvage cords: warp, handspun wool, 2 3z-S, indigo blue; weft, commercial 4-ply yarn, 2 3s-Z, synthetic green. Corners: none intact.

22.7955 Small sarape, banded with terraced zigzags and crosses, about 1875. Collected at Zuni, New Mexico, by Douglas D. Graham, first U. S. Indian Agent at Zuni, presented by his nieces, Evelyn B. Lent, Mrs. G. B. Oman, Beatrice A. B. Young, and Mary F. B. Van Houten, accessioned 1959. 53¼" × 38⅜" (135.2 × 84.7 cm). Tapestry weave. Warps: 11–12, handspun wool, z, natural white. Wefts: 60, handspun wool, z, natural white, indigo blue, combed pink (natural white and synthetic red); 44, raveled yarn, z, synthetic red-orange; 64–66, raveled yarn, 3s, synthetic crimson and dark crimson; 64, commercial yarn, 3z-S, cochineal crimson, 4z-S, synthetic lavender (faded to blue-green). Selvage cords: warp, handspun wool, 2 3z-S, indigo blue; weft, handspun wool, 2 2z-S, indigo blue. Corners: traces of augmented tassels.

22.7956 Small sarape, compound bands with vertical zigzags, 1875–80. Navajo or Zuni. Collected at Zuni, New Mexico, by Douglas D. Graham, first U. S. Indian Agent at Zuni, presented by his nieces, Evelyn B. Lent, Mrs. G. B. Oman, Beatrice A. B. Young, and Mary F. B. Van Houten, accessioned 1959. 49½" × 31¼" (125.8 × 79.4 cm). Tapestry weave. Warps: 12, handspun wool, z, natural brown. Wefts: 52–64, handspun wool, z, natural white, indigo blue, native gold; 72, raveled yarn, 3z, synthetic crimson, 3s, synthetic scarlet. Selvage cords: warp, handspun wool, 2 3z-S, indigo blue; weft, handspun wool, 2 2z-S, indigo blue. Corners: traces of augmented tassels.

22.7957 Small sarape, vertical terraced zigzags, 1870–75. Collected at Zuni, New Mexico, by Douglas D. Graham, first U. S.

Indian Agent at Zuni, presented by his nieces, Evelyn B. Lent, Mrs. G. B. Oman, Beatrice A. B. Young, and Mary F. B. Van Houten, accessioned 1959. 52" × 33" (132.1 × 83.8 cm). Tapestry weave. Warps: 12–13, commercial yarn, 3z-S, green-gold and 3s-Z, blue (unknown dyes). Wefts: 52, handspun wool, z, natural white, indigo blue; 64, raveled yarn, 3s, cochineal crimson, 2z, cochineal light crimson. Selvage cords: commercial 3-ply yarn, 2 3s-Z, cochineal crimson. Corners: traces of augmented tassels.

22.8877 Small sarape, banded with "diamond stripes," 1868–71. Collected by Sumner H. Bodfish as a member of the U. S. Geographical Survey, purchased from his niece, Elizabeth H. Wilkins, accessioned 1960. 52" × 34¼" (132 × 87 cm). Tapestry weave. Warps: 10, handspun wool, z, natural white. Wefts: 62–72, handspun wool, z, natural white, indigo blue; raveled yarn, 2s, cochineal (?) crimson; commercial yarn, 3s-Z, synthetic (fuschine) magenta (faded to lavender) and light magenta. Selvage cords: commercial yarn, 2 3s-Z, synthetic (fuschine) tan. No corner information.

22.9196 Small sarape, banded with terraced triangles, about 1875. Gift of Susan D. Bliss, accessioned 1961. 52¾" × 33" (134 × 84 cm). Tapestry weave. Warps: 9, handspun wool, z, natural white. Wefts: 44, handspun wool, z, natural white, indigo blue, indigo over native yellow-green; raveled and respun yarn, z, synthetic red; 56, commercial yarn, 4z-S, synthetic coral and pink, 3z-S, synthetic yellow. Selvage cords: handspun wool, 2 3z-S, indigo blue. Corners: augmented tassels.

23.922 Small sarape, compound bands with zigzags, 1865–70. Collected 1870–71 by Rachel Eleanor Griffin McNett at Fort Defiance, Arizona, gift of her daughter, Mrs. Harvé Reed Stuart, accessioned 1961. 44⅜" × 29¼" (110.9 × 72.6 cm). Tapestry weave. Warps: 10, handspun wool, z, natural white. Wefts: 80, handspun wool, z, natural white, indigo blue, combed cochineal red; 60, raveled yarn, z, synthetic red; 36, raveled yarn, 3s, red (unknown dye); 36, commercial yarn, 3z-S, cochineal crimson. Selvage cords: warp, handspun wool, 2 3z-S, indigo blue; weft, handspun wool, 2 2z-S, indigo blue. Corners: augmented tassels.

23.923 Small sarape, compound bands and terraced diamonds, 1865–70. Collected 1870–71 by Rachel Eleanor Griffin McNett at Fort Defiance, Arizona, gift of her daughter, Mrs. Harvé Reed Stuart, accessioned 1961. 49¾" × 32⅛" (126.4 × 81.6 cm). Tapestry weave. Warps: 12, handspun wool, z, indigo blue. Wefts: 52, handspun wool, z, natural white, indigo blue (indigo blue-green over native yellow), carded pink (natural and cochineal); 56, raveled yarn, 3s, cochineal crimson; 64, commercial yarn, 3z-S,

cochineal crimson, yellow (unidentified dye). Selvage cords: handspun wool, 2 3z-S, indigo blue. Corners: augmented tassels.

23.2814 Compound bands with terraced zigzags and chevrons, 1868–70. Collected 1868–70 by Gen. William Nicholson Grier at Fort Union, New Mexico, presented in his memory by his grandson, Robert C. Campbell, accessioned 1963. 70" × 44⅝" (177.8 × 113.3 cm). Tapestry weave. Warps: 13, handspun wool, z, natural white. Wefts: 40, handspun wool, natural white; 48, commercial yarn, 3z-S, cochineal scarlet, pale orange (unknown dye); 6z-S, green-gold (unknown dye); 40–44, raveled yarn, 3-5z, bright blue (unknown dye), 2-3s, olive brown (unknown dye), 2s, lac crimson, z, gray (unknown dye). Selvage cords: warp, commercial 3-ply yarn, 2 2s-Z, maroon; weft, commercial 3-ply yarn, 2 2s-Z, pale orange; both unknown dyes. Corners: augmented tassels.

23.2815 Compound bands with terraced zigzags, 1868–70. Collected 1868–70 by Gen. William Nicholson Grier at Fort Union, New Mexico, presented in his memory by his grandson, Robert C. Campbell, accessioned 1963. 67½" × 55" (171.5 × 139.7 cm). Tapestry weave. Warps: 12, handspun wool, z, natural white (except for three or four natural brown). Wefts: 44–52, handspun wool, z, natural white, indigo blue; raveled yarn, s, lac crimson. Selvage cords: warp, handspun wool, 2 3z-S, indigo blue; weft, handspun wool, 2 3z-S, natural white and indigo blue. Corners: augmented tassels.

23.2816 Small sarape, compound bands, 1860–70. Collected in 1868–70 by Gen. William Nicholson Grier at Fort Union, New Mexico, presented in his memory by his grandson, Robert C. Campbell, accessioned 1963. 51¼" × 36⅜" (130.2 × 92.4 cm). Tapestry weave. Warps: 10, handspun wool, z, natural white. Wefts: 51, handspun wool, z, natural white and combed tan, indigo medium and dark blue, cochineal red combed with natural white. Selvage cords: warp, handspun wool, 2 3z-S, indigo blue; weft, handspun wool, 2 3z-S, one indigo blue, one natural white. Corners: none intact.

23.3105 Small sarape, large terraced diamonds and half-diamonds, about 1875. Collected by Col. Eugene B. Beaumont, purchased in 1963 from his granddaughter, Margaret R. Elliott, accessioned 1963. 52⅝" × 34" (133.7 × 86.3 cm). Tapestry weave. Warps: 9, handspun wool, z, native yellow. Wefts: 50, handspun wool, z, indigo blue; raveled and respun yarn, z, synthetic orange-scarlet; raveled yarn, z, synthetic scarlet; commercial yarn, 4z-S, synthetic green (faded). Selvage cords: handspun wool, 2 3z-S, indigo blue. Corners: augmented tassels.

24.1901 Terraced and rounded zigzags, 1860–65. Originally purchased in 1892 at Hubbell's Trading Post, Ganado, Arizona, gift of the Mattatuck Historical Society, Waterbury, Connecticut, accessioned 1968. 59½" × 46⅛" (151.1 × 117 cm). Tapestry weave. Warps: 10, handspun wool, z, natural white and combed gray. Wefts: 60–62, handspun wool, z, natural white, indigo blue; raveled yarn, 3s, lac crimson. Selvage cords: handspun wool, 2 3z-S, indigo blue. Corners: traces of augmented tassels.

24.1902 Terraced concentric diamonds and zigzags, center rectangle with initials "JE," about 1875. Originally purchased at Fred Harvey's Winslow, Arizona curio store in 1903 (a Fred Harvey tag is attached), gift of the Mattatuck Historical Society, Waterbury, Connecticut, accessioned 1968. 81⅛" × 50⅞" (206 × 129.3 cm). Tapestry weave. Warps: 10, commercial cotton string, 4z-S, natural white. Wefts: 54, handspun wool, z, natural white, synthetic pale green; 72, raveled yarn, 2s, synthetic (?) crimson, 2-3z, synthetic khaki, z, synthetic crimson; commercial yarn, 3z-S, synthetic pale, medium, and dull green, light tan, gray, pink-tan, and olive; raveled yarn, 3-4s, synthetic scarlet. Selvage cords: warp, commercial 3-ply yarn, 2 2z-S, synthetic pale green; weft, 2 2-ply, synthetic red. Corners: no tassels.

24.2306 Small sarape, compound bands with zigzags, 1875–85. Originally purchased in 1897, David C. Vernon Collection, exchanged from Jackson Hole Preserve, accessioned 1968. 43¾" × 30½" (110.2 × 77.5 cm). Tapestry weave. Warps: 13, handspun wool, z, natural white. Wefts: 50–60, handspun wool, z, natural white, indigo blue, synthetic pink (recarded?) and moss-green; 72, raveled yarn, 2z, synthetic green, synthetic (?) crimson. Selvage cords: handspun wool, 2 3z-S, indigo blue. Corners: augmented tassels.

24.7838 Small sarape, banded with terraced diamonds, lozenges, and triangles, 1875–85. Collected by Gen. William Wallace Wotherspoon, purchased by Admr. Alexander Wotherspoon, accessioned 1973. 48" × 33" (122 × 84 cm). Tapestry weave. Warps: 11½, handspun wool, z, natural white. Wefts: 44, handspun wool, z, natural white, indigo blue; 56, commercial yarn, 4z-S, synthetic maroon and lavender. Selvage cords: handspun wool, 2 3z-S, indigo blue. Corners: augmented tassels.

24.7839 Small sarape, banded with zigzags and rectangles, 1870–75. Collected by Gen. William Wallace Wotherspoon, purchased by Admr. Alexander Wotherspoon, accessioned 1973. 47½" × 35⅝" (120.7 × 90.4 cm). Tapestry weave. Warps: 10, commercial yarn, 3s-Z, synthetic lavender. Wefts: 44, handspun wool,

z, natural white, indigo blue, native (?) yellow; 60, commercial yarn, 3z-S, cochineal red. Selvage cords: warp, commercial 3-ply yarn, 2 5s, cochineal red; weft, commercial 3-ply yarn, 2 2s-S, synthetic lavender. Corners: augmented tassels.

DIYOGÍ (UTILITY BLANKETS)

10.8456 Small blanket, banded with zigzags, 1850–60. Collected by Thomas S. Twiss about 1860, presented by Harmon W. Hendricks, accessioned 1921. 48" × 33¼" (121.9 × 84.5 cm). Tapestry weave. Warps: 9, handspun wool, z, natural white. Wefts: 32, handspun wool, z, natural white and brown, carded indigo blue and natural white; 48, raveled yarn, 3-6z, lac and cochineal crimson (faded), 3z, lac crimson. Selvage cords: handspun wool, 2 2z-S, natural white. Corners: augmented tassels.

16.2826 Meander pattern, about 1885. Collected by and purchased from John L. Nelson, accessioned 1928. 78¾" × 45⅜" (200 × 115 cm). Tapestry weave. Warps: 6, handspun wool, z, natural white. Wefts: 24, handspun wool, z, natural white and brown, synthetic yellow and tomato-red. Selvage cords: missing. No corner information.

16.2845 Compound bands with vertical zigzag pattern, 1875–85. Collected by and purchased from John L. Nelson, accessioned 1928. 81⅞" × 54⅜" (208 × 138 cm). Tapestry weave. Warps: 5½, handspun wool, z, natural white and combed gray. Wefts: 19, handspun wool, z, natural white, synthetic yellow, orange, and lavender (faded from red). Selvage cords: warp, handspun wool, 2 3z-S, natural brown, synthetic orange; weft, handspun wool, 2 2z-S, natural white and synthetic orange. No corner information.

16.3750 Compound bands with checkerboard and "diamond stripe" pattern, about 1880. Collected by John L. Nelson, accessioned 1929. 74¼" × 52⅜" (188.7 × 132.5 cm). Tapestry weave. Warps: 10, handspun wool, z, natural white and brown. Wefts: 28, handspun wool, z, natural combed gray, indigo dark and medium blue, synthetic red and dark pink, synthetic (?) yellow and green. Selvage cords: warp, handspun wool, 2 3z-S, indigo blue and synthetic red; weft, handspun wool, 2 3z-S, synthetic red. Corners: traces of augmented tassels.

20.5489 Zigzags composed of large lozenges, about 1870. Collected about 1870, presented by Capt. H. G. Brady, accessioned 1942. 70¼" × 42¾" (178.5 × 108.4 cm). Tapestry weave. Warps: 5½, handspun wool, z, natural white. Wefts: 14, handspun wool, z, natural brown, indigo or native dark blue-green, native yellow and yellow-green, synthetic blue and orange; carded and respun flannel, z, synthetic tomato-red. Selvage cords: raveled and carded handspun yarn, 2 3z-S, synthetic orange-red. Corners: none intact.

20.5584 Large terraced zigzag pattern, about 1870. Collected about 1875 by Capt. C. N. B. Macauley, presented by G. H. Macauley, accessioned 1942. 68⅛" × 49⅞" (173 × 126.7 cm). Tapestry weave. Warps: 9, handspun wool, z, natural white and brown. Wefts: 20–22, handspun wool, z, natural white, brown, and combed gray, native pink, orange, and yellow, 2z, native pale green. Selvage cords: handspun wool, 2 3z-S, native (?) tomato-red. Corners: augmented tassels.

22.7953 Terraced zigzags and serrate diamonds, 1875–80. Collected at Zuni, New Mexico, by Douglas D. Graham, first U. S. Indian Agent at Zuni, presented by his nieces, Evelyn B. Lent, Mrs. G. B. Oman, Beatrice A. B. Young, and Mary F. B. Van Houten, accessioned 1959. 65⅜" × 44⅛" (165.7 × 112.3 cm). Tapestry weave. Warps: 9, handspun wool, z, natural white and brown. Wefts: 34, handspun wool, z, natural white and combed tan, indigo blue, native gold, synthetic red. Selvage cords: warp, handspun wool, 2 3z-S, indigo blue and synthetic red; weft, handspun wool, 2 2z-S, indigo blue. Corners: traces of augmented tassels.

22.9297 Compound bands with "diamond stripes," about 1880. Collected in 1900 by Susan D. Bliss, accessioned 1961. 78⅜" × 57½" (199 × 146 cm). Tapestry weave. Warps: 7, handspun wool, z, natural white. Wefts: 16, handspun wool, z, natural white and brown-black, indigo blue, synthetic yellow and tomato-red. Selvage cords: warp, 3 (one handspun wool, 2z-S, natural white, and two commercial yarns, 4z-S, synthetic orange); weft, handspun wool, 2 3z-S, synthetic orange. Corners: self-augmented tassels.

23.9495 Compound bands, 1885–1900. Purchased from Mrs. Benjamin Hawkins, accessioned 1967. 71¼" × 46⅞" (181 × 119 cm). Weft-faced plain weave. Warps: 7½, handspun wool, z, natural white. Wefts: 20, handspun wool, z, synthetic orange, red, and yellow. Selvage cords: warp, handspun wool, 2 3z, synthetic orange; weft, handspun wool, 2 2z, synthetic orange. Corners: augmented tassels.

24.6899 Compound bands, 1870–75. Presented by Faith Dennis, accessioned 1972. 68⅜" × 49¾" (173.5 × 126.7 cm). Weft-faced plain weave. Warps: 8, handspun wool, z, natural white and brown-black. Wefts: 26, handspun wool, z, natural white, brown-

black and combed gray, indigo blue, synthetic purple; commercial yarn, 3z-S, cochineal (?) crimson. Selvage cords: warp (twisted together): handspun wool, 3z-S, indigo blue and commercial 3-ply yarn, 4s-S, cochineal (?) crimson; weft, handspun wool, 2 3z-S, indigo blue. Corners: augmented tassels.

24.7842 Compound bands, 1875–85. Collected by Gen. William Wallace Wotherspoon, purchased by Admr. Alexander Wotherspoon, accessioned 1973. 67⅜" × 45⅞" (171 × 116.5 cm). Weft-faced plain weave. Warps: 6½, handspun wool, z, natural white. Wefts: 26, handspun wool, z, natural white, brown, and combed gray. Selvage cords: warp, handspun wool, 2 3z-S, natural white; weft, handspun wool, 2 2z-S, natural white. Corners: self-augmented tassels.

24.7843 Compound bands, 1875–85. Collected by Gen. William Wallace Wotherspoon, purchased by Admr. Alexander Wotherspoon, accessioned 1973. 76" × 51⅜" (193 × 130.4 cm). Weft-faced plain weave. Warps: 6½, handspun wool, z, natural white. Wefts: 16, handspun wool, z, natural white and brown, indigo blue; raveled and recarded yarn, 4z, synthetic pink. Selvage cords: warp, handspun wool, 2 3z-S, indigo blue and dark blue; weft, handspun wool, 2 2z-S, natural white. Corners: augmented tassels.

MOKI-PATTERN BLANKETS

1410 Compound bands with "beading," 1865–75. Collected by F. M. Covert, accessioned 1904. 60¼" × 52¼" (153 × 132.7 cm). Weft-faced plain weave. Warps: 12½, handspun wool, z, natural white. Wefts: 48, handspun wool, z, natural white and brown-black, indigo blue. Selvage cords: warp, none present; weft, handspun wool, 2 2z-S, indigo blue. Corners: none present.

9.1915 Fragment, compound bands, 1875–85. Collected by George H. Pepper, accessioned 1919. 52⅜" × 39" (133 × 99 cm). Weft-faced plain weave. Warps: 9½, handspun wool, z, natural white and a few combed gray. Wefts: 36–44, handspun wool, z, reinforced dark-brown, indigo blue, native (?) yellow; commercial yarn, 4z-S, synthetic orange. Selvage cords: none present. Corners: augmented tassels, two present.

9.1946 Compound bands, about 1890. Collected by George H. Pepper at Hopi, Arizona, accessioned 1919. 64⅛" × 48" (163 × 122 cm). Weft-faced plain weave. Warps: 10, handspun wool, z, natural white. Wefts: 40, handspun wool, z, natural white and reinforced brown-black, indigo blue, synthetic orange-red and yellow.

Selvage cords: handspun wool, 2 3z-S, synthetic orange-red. Corners: none intact.

11.9326 Fragment, compound bands, 1880–85. Collected by Daniel W. Lord between 1888 and 1889 on the Hemenway Expedition in Arizona and New Mexico, presented by Mary Patterson Lord, accessioned 1923. 16½" × 50¾" (42 × 129 cm). Weft-faced plain weave. Warps: 6½, handspun wool, z, natural brown. Wefts: 22, handspun wool, z, natural white and brown, indigo blue, synthetic red. Selvage cords: warp, handspun wool, 2 3z-S, indigo blue; weft, handspun wool, 2 2z-S, synthetic red and red-brown. Corners: missing.

15.4616 Compound bands with "beading," 1870–80. S. K. Lothrop Collection, accessioned 1927. 72¼" × 54½" (183.3 × 138.5 cm). Weft-faced plain weave. Warps: 9½, handspun wool, z, natural white and brown. Wefts: 32, handspun wool, z, natural white and brown, indigo blue; 1 thread raveled yarn, z, cochineal crimson. Selvage cords: warp, handspun wool, 2 3z-S, natural white and indigo blue; weft, handspun wool, 2 3z-S, indigo blue. Corners: augmented tassels.

19.3031 Compound bands with "beading," 1875–85. According to NMAI catalogue information, this blanket belonged to Sitting Bull and was collected at his death by James McLaughlin, Indian Agent, purchased from estate of T. S. Lowe by William M. Fitzhugh, accessioned 1936. 65⅜" × 56¼" (166 × 143 cm). Weft-faced plain weave. Warps: 8, handspun wool, z, natural white and brown-black. Wefts: 32, handspun wool, z, natural white and brown-black, indigo blue, synthetic orange-red. Selvage cords: handspun wool, 2 3z-S, synthetic orange. Corners: augmented tassels.

20.9123 Compound bands, 1870–85. Collected in 1875, presented by John F. Meigs, accessioned 1946. 73½" × 50½" (186.7 × 128.2 cm). Weft-faced plain weave. Warps: 8, handspun wool, z, natural white. Wefts: 56, handspun wool, z, natural white and brown, indigo blue. Selvage cords: warp, handspun wool, 2 3z-Z, indigo (?) blue; weft, handspun wool, 2 2s-S, indigo (?) blue. Corners: augmented tassels.

22.1688 Banded with "diamond stripes," 1865–75. Gen. Nelson A. Miles Collection, presented by Gen. Sherman Miles for himself and in memory of Mrs. Samuel Reber, accessioned 1953. 71⅜" × 51¾" (181.3 × 131.5 cm). Tapestry weave. Warps: 8, handspun wool, z, natural white. Wefts: 40, handspun wool, z, native black, indigo blue, combed pink (natural and cochineal); 52, raveled yarn, z, orange-red (unknown dye), 2s, dull crimson; 80,

commercial yarn, 3s-Z, orange-red (unknown dye). Selvage cords: warp, handspun wool, 2 3z-S, indigo blue; weft, handspun wool, 2 2z-S, indigo blue. Corners: augmented tassels.

23.797 Compound bands with "diamond stripes," 1875–85. Gift of Ellen Thomas, accessioned 1961. 72⅜" × 51⅜" (184 × 130.5 cm). Tapestry weave. Warps: 9, handspun wool, z, natural white. Wefts: 44, handspun wool, z, natural brown-black and tan, indigo dark and medium blue, indigo and native (?) green, synthetic orange-red. Selvage cords: warp, handspun wool, 2 3z-S, indigo blue; weft, handspun wool, 2 2z-S, synthetic orange-red. Corners: traces of augmented tassels.

23.2466 Banded with "beading" and "diamond stripes," 1875–85. Katherine Harvey Collection, bequest of Miss Harvey, accessioned 1963. 69⅞" × 49½" (177.5 × 124.9 cm). Tapestry weave. Warps: 8½, handspun wool, z, natural white. Wefts: 44, handspun wool, z, natural white and brown, indigo blue; commercial yarn, 4z-S, synthetic pink and green. Selvage cords: handspun wool, 2 3z-S, indigo blue. Corners: none intact.

24.7841 Large serrate diamond pattern, 1870–75. Collected by Gen. William Wallace Wotherspoon, purchased by Admr. Alexander Wotherspoon, accessioned 1973. 73⅛" × 52⅞" (187.4 × 134.4 cm). Tapestry weave. Warps: 11, handspun wool, z, natural white. Wefts: 36–40, handspun wool, z, natural white and brown-black, indigo blue; raveled yarn, z, synthetic (?) crimson. Selvage cords: warp, handspun wool, 2 3z-S, indigo blue; weft, commercial 3-ply yarn, 2 3s-Z, synthetic orange-red. Corners: small augmented tassel on two corners.

WEDGE WEAVE BLANKETS

9.9821 Zigzag pattern, about 1885. Collected by Frank Hamilton Cushing, purchase, accessioned 1920. 47" × 36" (119.4 × 91.4 cm). Wedge weave, ends of weft-faced plain weave. Warps: 8, handspun wool, z, natural white and brown. Wefts: 36, handspun wool, z, natural white and brown, indigo blue, native blue-green, blue-black, yellow, and dark yellow-green; commercial yarn, 4z-S, synthetic coral-red. Selvage cords: handspun wool, 2 3z-S, indigo blue. Corners: augmented braided tassels.

11.9324 Fragment of *diyogí*, zigzag pattern, about 1885. Collected by Daniel W. Lord between 1888 and 1889 on the Hemenway Expedition in Arizona and New Mexico, presented by Mary Patterson Lord, accessioned 1923. 46⅞" × 57½" (119 × 146 cm). Alternating bands of wedge weave and weft-faced plain weave. Warps: 5, handspun wool, z, natural white. Wefts: 24, handspun wool, z, natural white, indigo blue, synthetic green and yellow; respun flannel, z, synthetic red. Selvage cords: warp, handspun wool, 2 2z, synthetic red; weft, none present. Corners: none present.

11.9327 Fragment of *diyogí*, zigzag pattern, about 1880. Collected by Daniel W. Lord between 1888 and 1890 on the Hemenway Archeological Expedition in Arizona and New Mexico, presented by Mary Patterson Lord, accessioned 1923. 35" × 59" (89 × 150 cm). Wedge weave, border of weft-faced plain weave. Warps: 7, handspun wool, z, natural white. Wefts: 24, handspun wool, z, natural white and combed gray, indigo blue, synthetic orange and red. Selvage cords: handspun wool, 2 3z-S, synthetic red. Corners: augmented tassels.

19.3023 *Diyogí* with "overstuffed pockets," zigzag pattern, 1880–95. William M. Fitzhugh Collection, accessioned 1936. 73½" × 57½" (186.7 × 146.1 cm). Wedge weave with narrow bands of weft-faced plain weave. Warps: 7, handspun wool, z, natural white. Wefts: 32, handspun wool, z, natural white, indigo blue, native yellow-green, synthetic scarlet, lavender and orange-red. Selvage cords: warp, handspun wool, 2 3z-S, indigo blue; weft, handspun wool, 2 3z-S, synthetic red (faded to orange). Corners: augmented tassels.

25.3708 Zigzag pattern, 1880–90. Presented by Emily Otis Barnes, accessioned 1968. 60" × 56½" (152.4 × 143.5 cm). Wedge weave. Warps: 9, handspun wool, z, natural white. Wefts: 48, handspun wool, z, carded natural grey, indigo blue; commercial yarn, 4z-S, synthetic green (faded to yellow) and orange-scarlet. Selvage cords: handspun wool, 3z-S, indigo blue. Corners: augmented tassels.

"SLAVE" OR "SERVANT" BLANKETS

23.1277 Compound bands and central panel with Chimayo leaf elements, 1875–85. Collected by Frank Applegate before 1900,

gift of Charles and Ruth de Young Elkus, accessioned 1961. 79½" × 53" (202 × 134.6 cm). Tapestry weave. Warps: 6, handspun wool, z, natural white. Wefts: 20, handspun wool, z, natural white, synthetic gold-yellow, pink, mahogany, pale yellow, and red. Selvage cords: handspun wool. No corner information.

PICTORIAL BLANKETS

14.4998 Chief blanket/rug, Fourth Phase, animal and human figures, 1880–90. Joseph Keppler Collection, accessioned 1926. 60" × 82¾" (152.4 × 210.2 cm). Tapestry weave. Warps: 8, handspun wool, z, natural white. Wefts: 48, handspun wool, z, natural white and brown, indigo blue, native black, yellow and yellow-green, synthetic red; raveled yarn, 2z, olive-green (unknown dye); raveled and respun yarn, z, synthetic red. Selvage cords: handspun wool, 2 3z-S, synthetic orange-red. Corners: augmented tassels.

23.2772 Pueblo style woman's shawl with weaving comb and terraced diamonds, 1880–1900. William Randolph Hearst Collection, purchased at Parke-Bernet Auction 2201 (22 May 1963), accessioned 1963. 30¾" × 39" (78 × 99 cm). Tapestry weave. Warps: 6, handspun wool, z, natural white and brown-black. Wefts: 22, handspun wool, z, natural white, synthetic black and red. Selvage cords: handspun wool, 2 2z-S, synthetic red. No corner information.

24.2373 Chief blanket, Third Phase variant with mounted horseman, 1875–80. Collected in 1910, presented by Mrs. Robert E. Montgomery, accessioned 1968. 69¼" × 80⅝" (176 × 204.4 cm). Tapestry weave. Warps: 10, handspun wool, z, native pale yellow. Wefts: 52–56, handspun wool, z, natural white, indigo blue, native brown-black; raveled yarn, 3s, synthetic 50-(?) orange-red. Selvage cords: handspun wool, 2 2z-S, indigo blue. No corner information.

NOTES

INTRODUCTION

1. Franciscan Fathers, *An Ethnologic Dictionary of the Navajo Language* (1910): 243–50, records Navajo names for many nineteenth-century blankets. Two of the names still used are *biil* and *diyogí*, although, today, weavers refer to diyogí as rugs.

2. As of this writing, plans are being discussed to travel the exhibition to Navajo Community College on the Navajo reservation in the spring of 1997.

3. For an account of Wheat's extensive research on Navajo, Pueblo, and Spanish-American textiles and the relationship between the three weaving traditions, see Ann Lane Hedlund, *Beyond the Loom: Keys to Understanding Early Southwestern Weaving* (Boulder: Johnson Books, 1990).

4. See D.Y. Begay, 15 May 1990. Transcript of conference at the Museum of the American Indian–Heye Foundation.

5. The museum's policy regarding conservation treatment of the Navajo textiles in the collection is to leave signs of wear intact. These are considered part of the history of the piece, although some form of stabilization may be undertaken in cases where the textile is at structural risk. Jeanne Brako, a textile conservator specializing in southwestern textiles, writes about textile wear patterns on Navajo blankets and damage resulting from use. See Jeanne Brako, "Recognizing Ethnographic Wear Patterns on Southwestern Textiles," *American Indian Art Magazine* 18, 1(1993): 64–81.

6. See Ann Lane Hedlund (1990): 52. See also Charles Avery Amsden, *Navaho Weaving: Its Technic and History* (Santa Ana, California: Fine Arts Press, 1934); Hedlund, *Reflections of the Weaver's World: The Gloria F. Ross Collection of Contemporary Navajo Weaving* (Denver: Denver Art Museum, 1992); and Kate Peck Kent, *Navajo Weaving: Three Centuries of Change* (Santa Fe, New Mexico: School of American Research Press, 1985). Kent groups Navajo textiles into the Classic period (1650–1865), Transition period (1865–95); and Rug period (1895 to the present).

7. Joe Ben Wheat, personal communication, 15 May 1990.

8. The quotations in this section are taken from transcripts of interviews 27 June–1 July 1995 at Navajo Community College. The transcripts are in the possession of the National Museum of the American Indian.

9. Kate Peck Kent (1985): 116–30.

SHI' SHA' HANE' (MY STORY)

1. When Navajo people meet, we introduce ourselves to each other by clan. We speak of being "born to" our mother's clan

and "born for" our father's clan. In addition to our own clans, it is customary to identify our parents' clans and our grandparents' clans.

SHIŁ YÓÓŁT'OOŁ:
PERSONIFICATION OF NAVAJO WEAVING

1. This paper is a revised version of one prepared for the Navajo weaving session at the Eighth Annual Navajo Studies Conference at San Juan College in Farmington, New Mexico, March 1995.

2. Gary Witherspoon, *Language and Art in the Navajo Universe* (1977): 31–33.

3. James McNeley, *The Holy Wind in Navajo Philosophy* (1981); and Maureen Trudelle Schwarz, *Molded in the Image of Changing Woman: Navajo Views on the Human Body and Personhood* (1997).

4. Gary Witherspoon (1977): 15–17.

5. In English, the term "rug" is a label that indicates function or location. "Rug" came into use about the end of the nineteenth century when many *dah'iistł'ó* were produced to serve as rugs for collectors and others. They were displayed primarily on floors then; they frequently appear on the floors of people's homes and in other locations, such as stores and offices.

6. Rex Lee Jim, ed., *Dancing Voices: Wisdom of the American Indian* (1994): 4.

7. Sue-Ellen Jacobs, et. al. (1997).

8. I am Navajo from Mariano Lake, located southwest of Crownpoint, New Mexico. I am Hashtl'ishnii (Mud Clan) and born for Tabaaha (Edge of Water Clan). This study is based on interviews I conducted with my grandmother whenever I returned to the Navajo Nation.

9. Due to lack of interest in Navajo culture and assimilation into Western culture at a rapid pace, none of the girls and young women in my extended family are interested in learning Navajo weaving.

10. In the past, weavers knew some weaving songs and prayers. Without them, one cannot fully identify oneself as a traditional Navajo weaver. Today many people use "weaver" as an occupational or artistic label; they may not know the full tradition of weaving, but only the techniques of weaving.

11. Elizabeth Yazzie, fieldwork interview tapes, 1995.

12. *The Navajo Times*, 2 March 1995.

13. For further reading, see Gary Witherspoon and Glen Peterson, eds., *Dynamic Symmetry and Holistic Asymmetry in Navajo and Western Art and Cosmology* (New York: Peter Lang Publishing Inc., 1995).

14. Witherspoon (1977).

15. Witherspoon, personal communication, 4 May 1995.

16. Elizabeth Yazzie (1995).

17. Elizabeth Yazzie, fieldwork interview tapes, 1994.

18. Yazzie (1994).

19. Alice Beck Kehoe, *The Ghost Dance: Ethnohistory and Revitalization* (1989); David Humphreys Miller, *Ghost Dance* (1959); and James Mooney, *The Ghost Dance Religion and the Sioux Outbreak of 1890* (1965) [1986].

20. Only pockets of people are still following these procedures; one example is the Ramah Navajo Weaving Project in the extreme southern region of the present Navajo Nation.

21. For further reading, see Schwarz (1997).

22. Aileen O'Bryan briefly mentions this procedure in *Navajo Indian Myths* (1993): 38.

23. Elizabeth Yazzie (1994).

24. The carding tools are of recent invention, and I am not aware of any songs or prayers affiliated with them.

25. *The Navajo Times*, 2 March 1995.

26. Elizabeth Yazzie (1994).

27. Aileen O'Bryan, *Navajo Indian Myths* (1993): 37.

28. Elizabeth Yazzie (1994).

29. A more thorough documentation of what takes place at the separation of a weaver from her or his dah'iistł'ó for money or other exchange will be the subject of my further research on Navajo weaving.

"MORE OF SURVIVAL THAN AN ART"

1. Kezbah Weidner, Navajo creative writer and artist, made this statement during a 1990 interview conducted by Jan Downey, my research assistant at the time. Following in her mother's footsteps, Weidner occasionally weaves rugs on her Navajo-style loom.

2. I would like to thank Eulalie Bonar, Gaye Brown, Joe Ben Wheat, and Cheryl Wilson for their insightful comments on an earlier version of this chapter. I am grateful to the many Navajo weavers, too numerous to name here, who have contributed to my own understanding of this subject, and many of whom are quoted in this chapter: Nanaba "Midge" Aragon, Anna Mae Barber, Bessie Barber, LaVerne Barber, Alice N. Begay, Amy Begay, Della Woody Begay, D.Y. Begay, Gloria Jean Begay, Lena Lee Begay, Mamie P. Begay, Mary Lee Begay, Sandy Begay, Helen Bia, Mary Brown, Irene Clark, Evelyn Curley, Sadie Curtis, Susie Dale, Isabell Myers Deschinny, Majorie Hardy, Isabell John, Annie Kahn, Kalley Keams, Helen Kirk, Bessie Lee, Teresa Martine, Jenny Musial, Sarah Natani, Grace Henderson Nez,

Irene Julia Nez, Barbara J. Teller Ornelas, Irma Spencer Owens, Rose Owens, Ella Rose Perry, Betty B. Roan, Marilou Schultz, Bessie Sellers, Geneva Scott Shabie, Marie Sheppard, Ellen Smith, Brenda Spencer, Marjorie Spencer, Vera Spencer, Pearl Sunrise, Jennie Thomas, Wesley Thomas, Lillie Walker, Laurie Weidner, Audrey Spencer Wilson, Elsie Jim Wilson, Larry Yazzie, Philomena Yazzie, and Ason Yellowhair.

3. The early twentieth century saw establishment of the first Navajo Tribal Council, traumatic stock reduction programs, two World Wars, and the incipient modernization of housing, education, healthcare, employment, politics, and every other aspect of reservation life. All of these, of course, had significant impacts on weavers' lives and work.

4. Washington Matthews reported on one male weaver who was "one of the best of the tribe." Presently, I personally know of more than two dozen men and boys who actively weave. Because they represent an exceptional minority within this predominately female craft, they are not addressed to any extent here. See "Navajo Weavers," in *Third Annual Report of the Bureau of American Ethnology, 1881–1882* (Washington, D.C.: Government Printing Office, 1884): 375–91.

5. See J. Lee Correll's aptly titled series, *Through White Man's Eyes.*

6. See Charlotte Frisbie, "Traditional Navajo Women: Ethnographic and Life History Portrayals." *American Indian Quarterly* 6, 1–2 (1982): 11–33.

7. Peter Iverson, *The Navajo Nation* (Albuquerque: University of New Mexico, 1981): xxvi.

8. See Luci Tapahanso, *Sáanii Dahataał/The Women are Singing: Poems and Stories* (Tucson: University of Arizona Press, 1993).

9. John R. Farella, *The Main Stalk: A Synthesis of Navajo Philosophy.* (Tucson: University of Arizona Press, 1984); and Paul Zolbrod, *Diné bahaane': The Navajo Creation Story* (Albuquerque: University of New Mexico Press, 1984).

10. David Brugge, "Navajo Prehistory and History to 1850," in *Handbook of North American Indians, Volume 10, Southwest,* Alfonso Ortiz, ed. (Washington, D.C.: Smithsonian Institution, 1983): 491.

11. Polygamy has been reported throughout Navajo history. Today there are Navajo people who still remember, earlier in this century, two or more women—often sisters from the same family—who were married to one man. See Brugge, "Navajo Prehistory and History to 1850" (1983): 491; and Brugge, "A History of the Chaco Navajos," *Reports of the Chaco Center 4.* (Albuquerque: Chaco Center, National Park Service, U.S.

Department of the Interior, 1980): 22–23.

12. Joe Ben Wheat, "Early Navajo Weaving," *Plateau* 52, 4 (1981): 3.

13. Wheat, personal communication, 1995.

14. Kate Peck Kent, *Navajo Weaving: Three Centuries of Change* (Santa Fe, New Mexico: School of American Research Press, 1985).

15. I am particularly grateful to Joe Ben Wheat, whose ethnohistoric research into southwestern weaving is reflected throughout this chapter, but especially in this section.

16. Theodore Downs, *The Navajo* (New York: Holt, Rinehart and Winston, Inc., 1972).

17. Evon Z. Vogt, "Navaho," in *Perspectives in American Indian Culture Change,* Edward H. Spicer, ed. (Chicago: University of Chicago Press, 1961): 303–4.

18. Ibid., 278–336.

19. Mary Shepardson, "The Status of Navajo Women," *American Indian Quarterly* 6, 1–2 (1982): 150.

20. Charlotte Frisbie, "Traditional Navajo Women: Ethnographic and Life History Portrayals," *American Indian Quarterly* 6, 1–2 (1982): 13.

21. David Brugge, "A History of the Chaco Navajos" (1980): 22–23.

22. Ibid.

23. Robert A. Griffen, ed. *My Life in the Mountains and on the Plains: The Newly Discovered Autobiography by D.M. Meriwether* (Norman: University of Oklahoma, 1965 [written in 1886]): 209.

24. Evon Z. Vogt, "Navaho" (1961): 306.

25. Jonathan Letterman, cited in Charles Avery Amsden *Navaho Weaving: Its Technic and History* (Santa Ana, California: Fine Arts Press, 1934 [reprinted by the Rio Grande Press, Glorieta, New Mexico, 1972]): 109–110.

26. Marianne L. Stoller notes, "The term Indian 'slaves' is really a misnomer for Anglo minds because the southwest Spanish system never conceived of or treated these people as chattel. The word most commonly used for them in the San Luis Valley, *criado(a),* meaning one who has been reared or educated as a servant, groom, or godchild, should be used in preference to 'slave.'" See Marianne L. Stoller, "Spanish-Americans, Their Servants and Sheep: A Culture History of Weaving in Southern Colorado," in *Spanish Textile Tradition of New Mexico and Colorado,* Museum of International Folk Art, ed. (Santa Fe, New Mexico: Museum of New Mexico Press, 1979): 42; also Lynn R. Bailey, *Indian Slave Trade in the Southwest: A Study of Slave-taking and the*

Traffic of Indian Captives (Los Angeles: Westernlore Press, 1966).

27. Ibid., 42.

28. Joe Ben Wheat, "Rio Grande, Pueblo, and Navajo Weavers: Cross-Cultural Influence," in *Spanish Textile Tradition of New Mexico and Colorado*, Museum of International Folk Art, ed. (Santa Fe: Museum of New Mexico Press, 1983): 33–36.

29. Wheat, personal communication, 1995.

30. Wheat, "Early Trade and Commerce in Southwestern Textiles Before the Curio Shop," *Reflections: Papers on Southwestern Culture History in Honor of Charles H. Lange*, Papers of the Archaeological Society of New Mexico, No. 14, Anne V. Poore, ed. (Santa Fe, New Mexico: Ancient City Press, 1988).

31. Ibid., 60.

32. Frank Mitchell, *Navajo Blessingway Singer: The Autobiography of Frank Mitchell, 1881–1967*, Charlotte J. Frisbie and David P. McAllester, eds. (Tucson: University of Arizona Press, 1978); *The Navajo Nation Overall Economic Development Program* (Window Rock, Arizona: Office of Program Development, 1974): 38.

33. Dana Coolidge and Mary Roberts Coolidge, *The Navajo Indians* (Boston: Houghton, Mifflin, 1930): 248–49.

34. Charlotte Frisbie, "Traditional Navajo Women" (1982): 24.

35. Robert A. Roessel, Jr. "Navajo History, 1850–1923," in *Handbook of North American Indians, Volume 10, Southwest*, Alfonso Ortiz, ed. (Washington, D.C.: Smithsonian Institution, 1983): 518.

36. *Navajo Stories of the Long Walk Period* (Tsaile, Arizona: Navajo Community College Press, 1973).

37. Hosteen Klah's biography by Franc Newcomb (1964); *The Life History of Gregorio the Hand-Trembler* (Leighton and Leighton, 1949); and Gus Bighorse's stories as recounted by his daughter, Tiana Bighorse (1990).

38. Tiana Bighorse (Noel Bennett, ed.), *Bighorse the Warrior* (Tucson: University of Arizona, 1990): 35.

39. Ibid., 51.

40. Joe Ben Wheat, "Early Trade and Commerce in Southwestern Textiles" (1988).

41. Ibid.

42. George Pepper, n.d., cited in Wheat, "Early Trade and Commerce in Southwestern Textiles" (1988).

43. Tiana Bighorse (Noel Bennett, ed.), *Bighorse the Warrior* (1990): 55.

44. Robert A. Roessel, Jr. "Navajo History, 1850–1923," (1983): 522.

45. Lansing B. Bloom, ed., "Bourke on the Southwest," *New Mexico Historical Review* 11 (1936): 227–28; cited in Klara B. Kelley and Peter M. Whiteley (1989): 55–56.

46. Walter Dyk, *Son of Old Man Hat: A Navaho Biography* (Lincoln: University of Nebraska Press, 1966).

47. Ibid., 317.

48. Ibid., 319.

49. Frank McNitt, *The Indian Traders* (Norman: University of Oklahoma Press, 1962): 71.

50. Ibid.

51. Traders frequently married Navajo women, some of whom were weavers. Thomas Keams, licensed to trade with the Hopis and Navajos from 1875 to 1898, and his brother William both married Navajo women. Likewise Daniel DuBois had a Navajo wife and three or four children. Anson Damon traded south of Fort Defiance at Cienega Amarilla during the 1870s and 1880s; he and his Navajo wife Ta-Des-Bah had nine children. See McNitt, *The Indian Traders* (1962): 77, 164, 246.

52. Peter Iverson, *The Navajo Nation* (1981): 12–13.

53. *The Navajo Nation Overall Economic Development Program* (Window Rock, Arizona: Office of Program Development, 1974): 3.

54. *The Navajo Nation Overall Economic Development Plan, 93–94* (Window Rock, Arizona: Support Services Department, Division of Economic Development, 1994b): 1.

55. *The Navajo Nation Overall Economic Development Program* (1974): 9.

56. *Navajo Nation FAX 88: A Statistical Abstract* (Window Rock, Arizona: Technical Support Department, Commission for Accelerating Navajo Development Opportunities, 1988): 2.

57. *The Navajo Nation Overall Economic Development Plan, 93–94* (1994b): 9.

58. Ibid., 7.

59. In 1990, the average Navajo family consisted of 4.5 people (*The Navajo Nation Overall Economic Development Plan 93–94* [1994b]: 11), a decrease from 5.6 persons per family only 16 years earlier (*The Navajo Nation Overall Economic Development Plan* [1974]: 20), despite a steady growth in overall population.

60. Most recently, the "major growth centers" include the communities of Chinle, Crownpoint, Kayenta, Shiprock, Tuba City and Window Rock (*The Navajo Nation Overall Economic Development Program 93–94* [1994a]: 20); the secondary areas include Navajo, Tsaile, Tohatchi, Leupp, Dilcon, Many Farms, Ganado, Pinon, Alamo, Canoncito, Ramah and Chambers/ Sanders (*The Navajo Nation Overall Economic Development Program*

93–94 [1994b]: 17–19). The 1974 roster of areas also included Navajo and Fort Defiance as major centers (*The Navajo Nation Overall Economic Development Program* [1974]: 3).

61. Stephen C. Jett and Virginia E. Spencer, *Navajo Architecture: Forms, History, Distributions* (Tucson: University of Arizona Press, 1981).

62. Luci Tapahanso, *Sáanii Dahataał/The Women are Singing: Poems and Stories* (1993): 90.

63. Ruth Roessel, *Women in Navajo Society* (Rough Rock, Arizona: Navajo Resource Center, Rough Rock Demonstration School, 1981): ix.

64. Although still a distinct minority (probably fewer than a hundred total), male weavers are undoubtedly growing in number and visibility. In addition to the Navajos' flexible gender roles and the money-making possibilities of weaving, this reflects the diminishing opportunities for men in farming and ranching, and the low number of jobs in other economic sectors.

65. In 1990 less than half (41.3%) of Navajos over twenty-five and residing in the Navajo Nation had completed high school (*The Navajo Nation Overall Economic Development Plan 93–94* [1994a]: 13). Although the national average is much higher, these figures represent a major increase for the Navajo Nation: ten years earlier, 34.1% were high school graduates; and twenty years earlier, only 27% of those over eighteen had completed twelve years of schooling (*The Navajo Nation Overall Economic Development Program* [1974]: 21).

66. *The Navajo Nation Overall Economic Development Plan 93–94* (1994a): 17.

67. Joe Ben Wheat, "Navajo Textiles," in *Fred Harvey Fine Arts Collection* (Phoenix: The Heard Museum, 1976); "Spanish-American and Navajo Weaving, 1600 to Now," in *Collected Papers in Honor of Margery Ferguson Lambert*, Papers of the Archaeological Society of New Mexico 3, A. Schroeder, ed. (1976); "The Navajo Chief Blanket," *American Indian Art Magazine* 1, 3 (1976); "Documentary Basis for Material Changes and Design Styles in Navajo Blanket Weaving," in *Ethnographic Textiles of the Western Hemisphere, 1977 Proceedings of the Irene Emery Roundtable on Museum Textiles*, Irene Emery and Patricia Fiske, eds. (Washington, D.C.: The Textile Museum, 1977); and *Navajo Blankets, Australian Exhibition 1978–79* (Netley, South Australia: Art Gallery of South Australia and the Australian Gallery Directors' Council Ltd, 1978).

68. Mary Hunt Kahlenberg and Anthony Berlant, *The Navajo Blanket* (Los Angeles: Praeger Publishers for the Los Angeles County Museum of Art, 1972); and Anthony Berlant and Mary Hunt Kahlenberg, *Walk in Beauty: The Navajo and Their Blankets*

(Boston: New York Graphic Society, 1977).

69. Indeed, in an innovative project begun in 1979, Gloria F. Ross, a New York tapestry *editeur*, has collaborated with Navajo weavers to create a series of wall-hung tapestries that combine indigenous Navajo processes, a classic European medium, and modern American design.

70. Weavers' comments in this section are derived from several sources. During my frequent conversations with weavers in and around the Navajo Nation, I jot notes about what they say and later cross-index them by specific themes and individuals' names. During a 1988 pilot study on the reservation I showed a dozen weavers a series of "flash cards" with photographs of Navajo blankets, dresses and rugs. Their responses were recorded and help to understand the Navajos' sense of aesthetics. See Ann Lane Hedlund, "Designing Among the Navajo: Ethnoaesthetics and Weaving," in *Textiles as Primary Sources, Proceedings of the First Meeting of the Textile Society of America*, John Vollmer, coord. (Minneapolis: Minneapolis Institute of Art, 1989a, 1989b). In 1994–95 the Museum of Northern Arizona hosted an exhibition, *Hanoolchaadí: Historic Textiles Selected by Four Navajo Weavers*, which was co-curated by four Navajo weavers, members of three generations from one family. As coordinating curator for the exhibition, I organized a series of sessions in which the weavers examined the museum's extensive collections and discussed their observations, which were then used in the exhibition's text. In 1994 the Heard Museum held a three-day symposium, "Navajo Weaving Since the Sixties," in which several hundred weavers, scholars, collectors, traders, and the public participated. In 1995, the Navajo Studies Conference included a one-day symposium, "Current Directions in Navajo Weaving and its Study," in which weavers and scholars exchanged views. Both meetings were organized by me. Also in 1995, author Paul Zolbrod, with the Museum of Indian Arts and Culture, invited a group of weavers, principally from the Crownpoint area of New Mexico, to examine dozens of early blankets and rugs in Santa Fe. Most recently, the National Museum of the American Indian sent twenty-four of its superlative nineteenth-century blanket collection to the Ned Hatathli Cultural Center at the Navajo Community College for a temporary exhibition and meeting of weavers. At the latter two venues, I served as a participant observer and made notes on the weavers' comments.

71. Ruth Roessel, *Women in Navajo Society* (1981): 177.

72. John R. Farella, *The Main Stalk: A Synthesis of Navajo Philosophy* (Tucson: University of Arizona Press, 1984): 190.

73. Harry Walters, personal communication, 1995.

74. Maureen E. Schwarz, "Traditional Navajo Female Attire:

Products and Processes of Navajo Aesthetic Artifice," in *Papers from the Third, Fourth, and Sixth Navajo Studies Conferences*, June-el Piper, ed. (Window Rock, Arizona: Navajo Nation Historic Preservation Department, 1993).

75. Ann Lane Hedlund and Louise I. Stiver, "Wedge Weave Textiles of the Navajo," *American Indian Art Magazine* 16, 3 (1991).

76. Joe Ben Wheat, "Early Navajo Weaving," *Plateau* 52, 4 (1981): 4.

77. Considerable influence on the revival of older patterns is exerted by present day traders such as Bill Malone at Hubbell Trading Post, Bruce Burnham at Burnham Trading Post, and a host of other entrepreneurs working in and around the Navajo Nation. However, my focus here is placed upon the weavers' reactions to such influences rather than the specific sources of influence.

78. Kalley Keams, a Navajo weaver who frequently teaches weaving workshops for non-Navajos, illustrates this ironic issue in an anecdote. Some of her students wanted to learn about what they presumed to be "the old way" of Navajo weaving. After providing them with the basic skills for manipulating the tools and yarns, Keams suggested that they weave whatever patterns they would like, just as each young Navajo weaver is taught to think up her own designs. The students initially felt stymied, asking for more guidance. Paradoxically, what these students had hoped for was less "the old way"—being set free to create from one's personal reservoir of ideas—than a copying of old patterns! The tradition, Keams relates, has more to do with using what is at hand and incorporating all manner of ideas and materials. It is, indeed, a process not a product. Personal communication, 1994.

NAVAJO BLANKETS

1. Lansing B. Bloom, "A Trade Invoice of 1638," *New Mexico Historical Review* 10:3 (1935): 242–48.

2. Donald E. Worcester, "The Navaho During the Spanish Regime in New Mexico," *New Mexico Historical Review* 26 (1951): 106.

3. Charles Wilson Hackett, ed., *Historical Documents Relating Nueva Vizcaya, and Approaches Thereto, to 1773* 3 (Washington, D.C., 1926–37): 111, 382. Emphasis mine.

4. W. W. Hill, "Some Navaho Culture Changes During Two Centuries," in *Essays in Historical Anthropology of North America*, Smithsonian Miscellaneous Collections 100 (Washington, D.C., 1940): 395–415.

5. Joe Ben Wheat, "American Indian Weaving, Trade and

Commerce: Before the Curio Shop," *Oriental Rug Review* 8:4 (1988): 35–40; and 5: 11–14.

6. J. Lee Correll, "Letter, Troncoso to Concha, April 12, 1788," in *Navajos Through White Men's Eyes* 1 (Window Rock, Arizona, 1979): 85–86.

A SELECTION OF TEXTILES FROM THE COLLECTION

1. Navajo Community College, *Stories of Traditional Navajo Life and Culture* (Tsaile, Arizona: Navajo Community College, 1977).

CATALOGUE OF THE COLLECTION

1. Kate Peck Kent, *Navajo Weaving: Three Centuries of Change* (Santa Fe, New Mexico: School of American Research Press, 1985); see also Ann Lane Hedlund, *Beyond the Loom: Keys to Understanding Early Southwestern Weaving*. Introduction and observations by Joe Ben Wheat (Boulder: Johnson Books, 1990).

2. Irene Emery, *The Primary Structures of Fabrics* (Washington, D.C.: The Textile Museum, 1966).

NOTES ON SELECTED COLLECTORS

1. The problem of the objectification of objects and the way that museums must change to meet the challenge as well as satisfy their varied constituents is addressed by a number of scholars. See, for example, Michael M. Ames, *Cannibal Tours and Glass Boxes: The Anthropology of Museums* (Vancouver: University of British Columbia Press, 1993). Also, Ivan Karp and Steven D. Lavine, eds., *The Poetics and Politics of Museum Display* (Washington, D.C. and London: Smithsonian Institution Press, 1991).

2. Curtis Hinsley, *Savages and Scientists: The Smithsonian Institution and the Development of American Anthropology, 1846–1910* (Washington, D.C.: Smithsonian Institution Press, 1981); Hinsley, "Collecting Cultures and Cultures of Collecting: The Lure of the American Southwest, 1880–1915," *Museum Anthropology* 16:1 (1992): 12–21. See also Nancy J. Parezo, "The Formation of Ethnographic Collections: The Smithsonian Institution in the American Southwest," in *Advances in Archaeological Method and Theory* 10, Michael Schiffer, ed. (San Diego: Academic, 1987); and Parezo, "Matilda Coxe Stevenson: Pioneer Ethnologist," in *Hidden Scholars: Women Anthropologists and the Native American Southwest*, Nancy J. Parezo, ed. (Albuquerque: University of New Mexico Press, 1993).

3. Parezo, "The Formation of Ethnographic Collection," (1987). See also George W. Stocking, Jr. "Essays on Museums and

Material Culture," and Edwin L. Wade, "The Ethnic Art Market in the American Southwest, 1880–1980," in *Objects and Others: Essays on Museums and Material Culture*, George W. Stocking, Jr., ed. (Madison: University of Wisconsin Press, 1985): 3–15.

4. Emily Barnes, personal communication, 3 March 1996. Also Barnes, *A Walk With Emily* (Santa Fe: privately published, 1990).

5. Barnes, 3 March 1996.

6. George W. Cullum, *Biographical Register of the Officers and Graduates of the U. S. Military Academy at West Point, New York, From Its Establishment, in 1802, to 1890* 2 (Boston and New York: Houghton, Mifflin, and Cambridge: Riverside, 1891). Also Dan L. Thrapp, *Encyclopedia of Frontier Biography*, 3 vols. (Glendale, California: Arthur H. Clark, 1988); and Robert M. Utley, *Frontier Regulars: The United States Army and the Indian, 1866–1891* (Lincoln and London: University of Nebraska Press, 1973).

7. Richard A. Bartlett, *Great Surveys of the American West* (Norman: University of Oklahoma Press, 1962). Also unpublished biographical information provided in a letter to the author 29 February 1996 from the United States Geological Survey.

8. Harold G. Davidson and Edward Borein, *Cowboy Artist: The Life and Works of John Edward Borein 1872–1945* (Garden City, New York: Doubleday, 1974); and Nicholas Woloshuk, Jr., and Edward Borein, *Drawings and Paintings of the Old West* (Flagstaff, Arizona: Northland, 1968).

9. Norman J. Bender, *Missionaries, Outlaws, and Indians: Taylor F. Ealy at Lincoln and Zuni, 1878–1881* (Albuquerque: University of New Mexico Press, 1984); T. J. Ferguson, personal communication, 27 February 1996, citing E. Richard Hart, in *Damage to Zuni Trust Lands*, Expert Testimony (Exhibit 1000), submitted to the United States Claims Court in the case Zuni Indian Tribe v. United States, Docket 327–81L (Ct. Cl., filed 12 May 1981): 100–118, 137, 152; Ferguson, personal communication, 27 February 1996, citing E. Richard Hart, in *The Zuni Mountains: Chronology of an Environmental Disaster*, Expert Testimony commissioned by the Institute of the NorthAmerican West on behalf of the Zuni Indian Tribe, for submission to the United States Claims Court as Plaintiff's Exhibit 13,00 in Docket 327–81L and 224–84L (1988): 90–91; Douglas D. Graham, "Report of School Superintendent in Charge at Zuni Pueblo," in *Annual Reports of the Department of the Interior for the Fiscal Year Ended June 30, 1903: Indian Affairs* (Washington, D.C.: Government Printing Office, 1904); Jesse Green, ed., *Cushing at Zuni: The Correspondence and Journals of Frank Hamilton Cushing, 1879–1884* (Albuquerque: University of New Mexico Press, 1990); Frank

McNitt, *The Indian Traders* (Norman: University of Oklahoma Press, 1962).

10. In 1879, Taylor F. Ealy, the missionary at Zuni Pueblo, noted in his diary that Douglas Graham's hometown was Fishkill on the Hudson, New York. See Norman J. Bender, *Missionaries, Outlaws, and Indians* (1984): 130.

11. T. J. Ferguson, personal communication, 27 February 1996, citing E. Richard Hart, in *Damage to Zuni Trust Lands* (12 May 1981): 100–118, 137, 152.

12. Ferguson, personal communication, 27 February 1996, citing E. Richard Hart, in *The Zuni Mountains: Chronology of an Environmental Disaster* (1988): 90–91.

13. Douglas D. Graham, "Report of School Superintendent in Charge at Zuni Pueblo" (1904): 223.

14. George W. Cullum, *Biographical Register of the Officers and Graduates of the U. S. Military Academy* (1891); Frank McNitt, *Navajo Wars: Military Campaigns, Slave Raids, and Reprisals* (Albuquerque: University of New Mexico Press, 1990); Robert M. Utley, *Frontiersmen in Blue: The United States Army and the Indian, 1848–1865* (Lincoln and London: University of Nebraska Press, 1981).

15. Frank McNitt, *Navajo Wars* (1990): 102–103.

16. Duane H. King, *The Treasures of the National Museum of the American Indian* (unpublished manuscript, 1993); *New York Herald Tribune*, obituary, 13 May 1935; *Letters to Thea and George Heye from their friends at Zuni Pueblo, 1916–1930*, Papers of the Huntington Free Library (Bronx, New York); Kevin Wallace, "Slim-Shin's Monument," *The New Yorker Magazine* (19 November 1960): 104–146.

17. *Letters to Thea and George Heye from their friends at Zuni Pueblo, 1916–1930*.

18. Mary B. Davis, *The Joseph Keppler Iroquois Papers in the Huntington Free Library: A Guide to the Microfilm Edition* (Bronx, New York: The Huntington Free Library, 1994); Davis, *Papers of the Hemenway Southwestern Archaeological Expedition in the Huntington Free Library: A Guide to the Microfilm Edition* (Bronx, New York: Huntington Free Library, 1987); Nicholas Woloshuk, Jr., "A Seneca Adoption," *The Masterkey* 26, 3 (1952): 94–96; Woloshuk, Jr., "A Rare Collection," *The Papoose* 1, 2 (January 1903): 3–9.

19. Lord was probably a resident of Malden, Massachusetts, and may have studied under the popular Professor Norton, who taught art history at Harvard University between 1874 and 1898. Frank Hamilton Cushing, *Letter Books, 1886–1896* (Bronx, New York: Huntington Free Library, 1993); Charles H. Lange,

Carroll L. Riley, and Elizabeth M. Lange, eds., *The Southwestern Journals of Adolph E. Bandelier, 1889–1892* (Albuquerque: University of New Mexico Press, 1984); David Wilcox, personal communication to Mary B. Davis, 5 March 1996.

20. Wilcox, 5 March 1996.

21. Ibid.

22. Frank Hamilton Cushing, letters to Lord, 11 August and 13 August 1888, in Cushing, *Letter Books, 1886–1896* (Bronx, New York: Huntington Free Library, 1993).

23. "Excavations at Kechipauan, New Mexico," *Indian Notes* (1924): 35–36; Brenda Shears, "The Hendricks-Hodge Archaeological Expedition Documentation Project: Preparing a Museum Collection for Research," Master's thesis (Hunter College, City University of New York, 1989).

24. Nicholas Woloshuk, Jr., "The General Nelson A. Miles Collection," *Indian Notes* 3, 1 (1926): 50–53; Dan L. Thrapp, *Encyclopedia of Frontier Biography*, 3 vols. (Glendale, California: Arthur H. Clark, 1988); Robert M. Utley, *Frontier Regulars* (1973); Utley and Wilcomb E. Washburn, *Indian Wars* (Boston: Houghton Mifflin, 1977).

25. Charles Avery Amsden, *Navaho Weaving: Its Technic and History* (Santa Ana, California: The Fine Arts Press, 1934); George G. Heye, "George Hubbard Pepper," *Museum Notes* 1, 3 (1924): 105–110; Frank McNitt, *Richard Wetherill Anasazi* (Albuquerque: University of New Mexico Press, 1978); George Pepper, "The Navajo Indians: An Ethnological Study," *The Papoose* 1, 1 (December 1902): 3–9; and Pepper, "Native Navajo Dyes," *The Papoose* 2 (February 1903): 1–11.

26. Frederick S. Dellenbaugh, *A Canyon Voyage: The Narrative of the Second Powell Expedition down the Green-Colorado River from Wyoming, and the Explorations on Land, in the Years 1871 and 1872* (New York and London: G. P. Putnam's Sons, 1908); Nicholas Woloshuk, Jr., "Notes," *Indian Notes* 5, 2 (1928): 269–70; J. W. Powell, *The Exploration of the Colorado River and Its Canyons* (New York: Dover, 1961).

27. Garrick Bailey and Roberta Glenn Bailey, *A History of the Navajos: The Reservation Years* (Santa Fe: School of American Research, 1986); Robert A. Roessel, Jr., "Navajo History, 1850–1923," in *Handbook of North American Indians, Volume 10, Southwest*, Alfonso Ortiz, ed. (Washington, D.C.: Smithsonian Institution Press, 1983): 506–523; Sherry Smith, *The View from*

Officers' Row: Army Perceptions of Western Indians (Tucson: University of Arizona, 1990); Robert M. Utley, *Frontier Regulars* (1973).

28. Although Sherman accepted a seat on the commission, he believed that the transcontinental railroads, not negotiations, would impose order westward. See Sherry Smith (1990): 161.

29. Doris Ostrander Dawdy, "Smith, DeCost," *Artists of the American West: A Biographical Dictionary* (Chicago: Swallow Press, 1974): 216; Peggy Samuels and Harold Samuels, "Smith, DeCost," *The Illustrated Biographical Encyclopedia of Artists of the American West* (Garden City, New York: Doubleday, 1976): 449.

30. Barbara A. Babcock and Nancy J. Parezo, "Matilda Coxe Stevenson, 1849–1915," in *Daughters of the Desert: Women Anthropologists and the Native American Southwest, 1880–1980, An Illustrated Catalogue* (Albuquerque: University of New Mexico, 1988): 8–13.

31. Babcock and Parezo (1988): 10.

32. George E. Hyde, *Red Cloud's Folk: A History of the Oglala Sioux Indians* (Norman: University of Oklahoma, 1937); Burton S. Hill, "Thomas S. Twiss, Indian Agent," *Great Plains Journal* 6, 2 (1967): 85–96; Dennis Lessard, personal communication, 6 March 1996; Two receipts signed by Daisy Barnett (1918, 1919), NMAI Archives.

33. Hill (1967): 86.

34. Lessard (1996).

35. Daisy Barnett receipts (1918, 1919).

36. Lorenzo Sitgreaves, *Report of an Expedition Down the Zuni and Colorado Rivers, Accompanied by Maps, Sketches, Views, and Illustrations* (Washington, D.C.: Robert Armstrong, Public Printer, 1853); John S. Tomer and Michael J. Brodhead, eds., *A Naturalist in Indian Territory: The Journals of S. W. Woodhouse, 1849–1850* (Norman and Lincoln: University of Oklahoma Press, 1996).

37. Sitgreaves (1953): 4.

38. Constance Wynn Altshuler, "Wotherspoon, William Wallace," in *Cavalry Yellow and Infantry Blue: Army Officers in Arizona between 1851 and 1886* (Tucson: Arizona Historical Society, 1991): 381–82; D. E. Cummings, "William Wotherspoon, Sailor Soldier," *Shipmate* (January 1969): 6–7, 9–11; Letter from Rear Admr. Alexander Wotherspoon to Frederick Dockstader, 30 October 1972, NMAI Archives.

39. Wotherspoon letter to Dockstader, 30 October 1972.

REFERENCES

INTRODUCTION

Amsden, Charles Avery. *Navaho Weaving: Its Technic and History*. Santa Ana, California: The Fine Arts Press, 1934 (reprinted by Rio Grande Press, Chicago, 1964).

Begay, D. Y. Transcript of workshop on 15 May 1990 at the Museum of the American Indian–Heye Foundation. Transcript in possession of the author.

Brako, Jeanne. "Recognizing Ethnographic Wear Patterns on Southwestern Textiles." *American Indian Art Magazine* 18:1 (1983).

Franciscan Fathers. *An Ethnologic Dictionary of the Navajo Language*. St. Michaels, Arizona: St. Michaels Press, 1910 (reprinted 1968).

Hedlund, Ann Lane. *Beyond the Loom: Keys to Understanding Early Southwestern Weaving*. Introduction and observations by Joe Ben Wheat. Boulder: Johnson Books, 1990.

———. *Reflections of the Weaver's World: The Gloria F. Ross Collection of Contemporary Navajo Weaving*. Denver: Denver Art Museum, 1992.

Kent, Kate Peck. *Navajo Weaving: Three Centuries of Change*. Santa Fe, New Mexico: School of American Research Press, 1985.

National Museum of the American Indian. Transcript of interviews on 27 June–1 July 1995 at Navajo Community College, Tsaile, Arizona. Transcript in possession of the National Museum of the American Indian.

Wheat, Joe Ben. Transcript of workshop on 15 May 1990 at the Museum of the American Indian–Heye Foundation. Transcript in possession of the author.

SHIŁ YÓÓŁTʼOOŁ:
PERSONIFICATION OF NAVAJO WEAVING

Jacobs, Sue-Ellen, Wesley Thomas, and Sabine Lang, eds. *Two-Spirit People: Perspectives on Gender, Sexuality and Spirituality in Native American Communities*. Champaign: University of Illinois Press, 1997.

Jim, Rex Lee, ed. *Dancing Voices: Wisdom of the American Indian*. White Plains, New York: Peter Pauper Press, Inc., 1994.

Kehoe, Alice Beck. *The Ghost Dance: Ethnohistory and Revitalization*. Chicago: Holt, Rinehart and Winston, Inc., 1989.

Miller, David Humphreys. *Ghost Dance*. Lincoln: University of Nebraska Press, 1959.

Mooney, James. *The Ghost Dance Religion and the Sioux Outbreak of 1890*. Chicago: University of Chicago Press, 1965 [1986].

McNeley, James. *The Holy Wind In Navajo Philosophy*. Tucson: University of Arizona Press, 1981. *The Navajo Times*, Navajo Nation, Window Rock, Arizona, March 2, 1995.

O'Bryan, Aileen. *Navaho Indian Myths*. New York: Dover Publications, Inc., 1993.

Schwarz, Maureen Trudelle. *Molded in the Image of Changing Woman: Navajo Views on the Human Body and Personhood*. Tucson: University of Arizona Press (1997).

Thomas, Wesley. "Navajo Male Weavers' Perspective: Gender and Economics." Paper presented at "Navajo Weaving Since the Sixties" at the Heard Museum, Phoenix, Arizona. 12 March 1994.

Witherspoon, Gary. *Language and Art in the Navajo Universe*. Ann Arbor: University of Michigan Press, 1977.

———. Personal communication, May 4, 1995.

Yazzie, Elizabeth. Fieldwork interview tapes in the author's possession. Mariano Lake, New Mexico: March 16; August 4–5; September 17; and December 21, 1994. Fieldwork interview tapes in the author's possession; Mariano Lake, New Mexico: June 16–18, 1995.

"MORE OF SURVIVAL THAN AN ART"

Aberle, David. *Matrilineal Kinship*. Edited by David Schneider and Kathleen Gough. Berkeley and Los Angeles: University of California Press, 1961.

Adams, William Y. "Navajo Ecology and Economy: A Problem in Cultural Values." In *Apachean Culture History and Ethnology*. Edited by Keith H. Basso and Morris E. Opler. *Anthropological Papers of the University of Arizona* 21 (1971): 77–81.

Amsden, Charles Avery. *Navaho Weaving: Its Technic and History*. 1934. Reprint, Glorieta, New Mexico: The Rio Grande Press, 1972.

Bailey, Lynn R. *Indian Slave Trade in the Southwest: A Study of Slave-taking and the Traffic of Indian Captives*. Los Angeles, California: Westernlore Press, 1966.

Berlant, Anthony, and Mary Hunt Kahlenberg. *Walk in Beauty: The Navajo and Their Blankets*. Boston: New York Graphic Society, 1977.

Bighorse, Tiana. *Bighorse the Warrior*. Edited by Noel Bennett. Tucson: University of Arizona, 1990.

Bloom, Lansing B., ed. "Bourke on the Southwest." *New Mexico Historical Review* 11 (1936): 77–122, 217–82.

Brako, Jeanne, and Robert Morgan. "The Care of Navajo Textiles in the Home." *Terra* (Los Angeles County Museum of Natural History) 26:5 (1988): 21–24.

Brugge, David. "Navajo Prehistory and History to 1850." In *Handbook of North American Indians, Volume 10, Southwest*. Edited by Alfonso Ortiz, 489–505. Washington, D.C.: Smithsonian Institution, 1983.

———. "A History of the Chaco Navajos." *Reports of the Chaco Center* 4. Albuquerque: Chaco Center, National Park Service, U.S. Department of the Interior, 1980 [cited in Roessel, 1981].

Bunzel, Ruth. "The Pueblo Potter: A Study of Creative Imagination in Primitive Art." *Columbia University Contributions to Anthropology* 8. 1929. Reprint, New York: Dover, 1972.

Coolidge, Dane, and Mary Roberts Coolidge. *The Navajo Indians*. Boston: Houghton, Mifflin, 1930.

Correll, J. Lee. *Navajos Through White Men's Eyes* 1. Window Rock, Arizona, 1979.

Downs, Theodore. *The Navajo*. New York: Holt, Rinehart and Winston, Inc., 1972.

Dyk, Walter. *Son of Old Man Hat: A Navaho Biography*. Lincoln: University of Nebraska Press, 1966.

———. "A Navaho Autobiography." *Viking Fund Publications in Anthropology*, no. 8. New York: Viking Fund Inc., 1947.

Farella, John R. *The Main Stalk: A Synthesis of Navajo Philosophy*. Tucson: University of Arizona Press, 1984.

Frisbie, Charlotte. "Traditional Navajo Women: Ethnographic and Life History Portrayals." *American Indian Quarterly* 6 (1 & 2) (1982):11–33.

———. *Kinaaldá: A Study of the Navaho Girl's Puberty Ceremony*. 1967. Reprint, Salt Lake City: University of Utah Press, 1993.

Griffen, Robert A., ed. *My Life in the Mountains and on the Plains: The Newly Discovered Autobiography by D.M. Meriwether* (written in 1886). Norman: University of Oklahoma, 1965.

Haile, Berard. *Ethnologic Dictionary of the Navajo Language*. St. Michaels, Arizona: Franciscan Fathers, 1910.

Hardin, Margaret. *Gifts of Mother Earth: Ceramics in the Zuni Tradition*. Phoenix: The Heard Museum, 1983.

Hedlund, Ann Lane. "Designing Among the Navajo: Ethnoaesthetics and Weaving." In *Textiles as Primary Sources, Proceedings of the First Meeting of the Textile Society of America*. Coordinated by John Vollmer, 86–93. Minneapolis: Minneapolis Institute of Art, 1989.

———. "In Pursuit of Style: Kate Kent and Navajo Aesthetics." *Museum Anthropology* 12(2–3) (1989): 32–40.

———. "Contemporary Navajo Weaving: An Ethnography of a Native Craft. Ph.D. diss., University of Colorado, Boulder. Ann Arbor, Mich.: University Microfilms, Inc., 1983.

Hedlund, Ann Lane. *Beyond the Loom: Keys to Understanding Early Southwestern Weaving.* Introduction and observations by Joe Ben Wheat. Boulder: Johnson Books, 1990.

———. *Reflections of the Weaver's World: The Gloria F. Ross Collection of Contemporary Navajo Weaving.* Denver: Denver Art Museum, 1992.

Hedlund, Ann Lane, and Louise I. Stiver. "Wedge Weave Textiles of the Navajo." *American Indian Art Magazine* 16(3) (1991): 54–65, 82.

Iverson, Peter. *The Navajo Nation.* Albuquerque: University of New Mexico, 1981.

Jett, Stephen C., and Virginia E. Spencer. *Navajo Architecture: Forms, History, Distributions.* Tucson, Arizona: University of Arizona Press, 1981.

Kahlenberg, Mary Hunt, and Anthony Berlant. *The Navajo Blanket.* Los Angeles, California: Praeger Publishers for the Los Angeles County Museum of Art, 1972.

Kelley, Klara B., and Peter M. Whiteley. *Navajoland: Family Settlement and Land Use.* Tsaile, Arizona: Navajo Community College Press, 1989.

Kelly, Lawrence. *Navajo Roundup.* Boulder, Colorado: Pruett Press, 1970.

Kent, Kate Peck. *Navajo Weaving: Three Centuries of Change* (Santa Fe, New Mexico: School of American Research Press, 1985).

Lamphere, Louise. *To Run After Them: Cultural and Social Bases of Cooperation in a Navajo Community.* Tucson, Arizona: University of Arizona Press, 1977.

Matthews, Washington. "Navajo Weavers." In *Third Annual Report of the Bureau of American Ethnology, 1881–1882.* Washington, D.C.: Government Printing Office, 1884:375–91.

McCarty, T.L., Regina Lynch, Fred Bia, and Gene Johnson. *A Bibliography of Navajo and Native American Teaching Materials: Diné K'eeji Naaltsoos Bee Nida'nitinigii.* Rough Rock, Arizona: Title IV-B Materials Development Project, Rough Rock Demonstration School, 1983.

McNitt, Frank. *The Indian Traders.* Norman: University of Oklahoma Press, 1962.

Mitchell, Frank. *Navajo Blessingway Singer: The Autobiography of Frank Mitchell, 1881–1967.* Charlotte J. Frisbie and David P. McAllester, eds. Tucson, Arizona: University of Arizona Press, 1978.

Navajo Nation FAX 88: A Statistical Abstract. Window Rock, Arizona: Technical Support Department, Commission for Accelerating Navajo Development Opportunities, 1988.

Navajo Nation FAX 93: A Statistical Abstract of the Navajo Nation. Window Rock, Arizona: Support Services Department, Division of Economic Development, Navajo Nation, 1994.

Navajo Nation Overall Economic Development Plan 93–94. Window Rock, Arizona: Support Services Department, Division of Economic Development, 1994.

The Navajo Nation Overall Economic Development Program. Window Rock, Arizona: Office of Program Development, 1974.

Navajo Stories of the Long Walk Period. Tsaile, Arizona: Navajo Community College Press, 1973.

Pepper, George. *Navajo Weaving.* Manuscript. New York: National Museum of the American Indian, Heye Foundation, n.d.

Roessel, Robert A., Jr. "Navajo History, 1850–1923." In *Handbook of North American Indians, Volume 10, Southwest.* Alfonso Ortiz, ed. Washington, D.C.: Smithsonian Institution, 1983: 506–523.

Roessel, Ruth. *Women in Navajo Society.* Rough Rock, Arizona: Navajo Resource Center, Rough Rock Demonstration School, 1981.

Roessel, Ruth, ed. *Navajo Studies at Navajo Community College.* Many Farms, Arizona: Navajo Community College Press, 1971.

Schwarz, Maureen E. "Traditional Navajo Female Attire: Products and Processes of Navajo Aesthetic Artifice." In *Papers from the Third, Fourth, and Sixth Navajo Studies Conferences,* June-el Piper, ed. Window Rock, Arizona: Navajo Nation Historic Preservation Department, 1993:355–78.

Shepardson, Mary. "The Status of Navajo Women." *American Indian Quarterly* 6(1 & 2), 1982:149–69.

Spencer, Katherine. "Reflection of Social Life in the Navaho Origin Myth." *University of New Mexico Publications in Anthropology,* No. 3. Albuquerque, New Mexico: University of New Mexico, 1947.

———. *Mythology and Values: An Analysis of Navaho Chantway Myths.* Philadelphia, Pennsylvania: American Folklore Society, 1957.

Spicer, Edward H., ed. *Perspectives in American Indian Culture Change.* Chicago, Illinois: University of Chicago Press, 1961.

Stoller, Marianne L. "Spanish–Americans, Their Servants and Sheep: A Culture History of Weaving in Southern Colorado." In *Spanish Textile Tradition of New Mexico and Colorado.* Museum of International Folk Art, ed. Santa Fe, New Mexico: Museum of New Mexico Press, 1979:37–52.

Tapahanso, Luci. *Sáanii Dahataał/The Women are Singing: Poems and Stories.* Tucson, Arizona: University of Arizona Press, 1993.

Dine Bina'ach'aah, Bahane', Be'i'ool'iil: Navajo Art, History and Culture. Rough Rock, Arizona: Title IV–B Navajo Materials Development Project, Rough Rock Demonstration School, 1984.

Vogt, Evon Z. "Navaho." In *Perspectives in American Indian Culture Change.* Edward H. Spicer, ed. Chicago, Illinois: University of Chicago Press, 1961:278–336.

Walters, Harry. Introduction in *Navajo Weaving: From Spider Woman to Synthetic Rugs.* Tsaile, Arizona: Ned A. Hatathli Culture Center, Navajo Community College, 1977.

Wheat, Joe Ben. "Navajo Textiles." In *Fred Harvey Fine Arts Collection.* Phoenix, Arizona: The Heard Museum, 1976.

———. "Spanish-American and Navajo Weaving, 1600 to Now." In *Collected Papers in Honor of Margery Ferguson Lambert.* Papers of the Archaeological Society of New Mexico, No. 3., A. Schroeder, ed., 1976:199–226.

———. "The Navajo Chief Blanket." *American Indian Art Magazine* 1(3), 1976:44–53.

———. "Documentary Basis for Material Changes and Design Styles in Navajo Blanket Weaving." In *Ethnographic Textiles of the Western Hemisphere, 1977 Proceedings of the Irene Emery Roundtable on Museum Textiles.* Irene Emery and Patricia Fiske, eds. Washington, D.C.: The Textile Museum, 1977:420–40.

———. *Navajo Blankets, Australian Exhibition 1978–79.* Netley, South Australia: Art Gallery of South Australia and the Australian Gallery Directors' Council Ltd, 1978.

———. "Early Navajo Weaving." *Plateau* 52(4):2–9. Flagstaff, Arizona, 1981.

———. "Rio Grande, Pueblo, and Navajo Weavers: Cross-Cultural Influence." In *Spanish Textile Tradition of New Mexico and Colorado.* Museum of International Folk Art, ed. Santa Fe, New Mexico: Museum of New Mexico Press, 1983:29–36.

———. "Early Trade and Commerce in Southwestern Textiles Before the Curio Shop." *Reflections: Papers on Southwestern Culture History in Honor of Charles H. Lange.* Papers of the Archaeological Society of New Mexico, No. 14. Anne V. Poore, ed. Santa Fe, New Mexico: Ancient City Press, 1988: 57–72.

Zolbrod, Paul. *Diné bahaane': The Navajo Creation Story.* Albuquerque, New Mexico: University of New Mexico Press, 1984.

NAVAJO BLANKETS

Bloom, Lansing B. "A Trade Invoice of 1638." *New Mexico Historical Review* 10:3 (1935): 242–48.

Correll, J. Lee. "Letter, Troncoso to Concha, April 12, 1788." In *Navajos Through White Men's Eyes* 1: 85–86. Window Rock, Arizona, 1979.

Hackett, Charles Wilson, ed. *Historical Documents Relating Nueva Vizcaya, and Approaches Thereto, to 1773* 3: 111, 382. Washington, D.C., 1926–37.

Hill, W. W. "Some Navaho Culture Changes During Two Centuries." *Essays in Historical Anthropology of North America.* Smithsonian Miscellaneous Collections 100: 395–415. Washington, D. C., 1940.

Wheat, Joe Ben. "American Indian Weaving, Trade and Commerce: Before the Curio Shop." *Oriental Rug Review* 8:4 (1988): 35–40; 5: 11–14.

Worcester, Donald E. "The Navaho During the Spanish Regime in New Mexico." *New Mexico Historical Review* 26 (1951): 106.

NOTES ON SELECTED COLLECTORS

Altshuler, Constance Wynn and William Wallace Wotherspoon. *Cavalry Yellow and Infantry Blue: Army Officers in Arizona between 1851 and 1886.* Tucson: Arizona Historical Society, 1991: 381–82.

Ames, Michael M. *Cannibal Tours and Glass Boxes: The Anthropology of Museums.* Vancouver: UBC Press, 1993.

Amsden, Charles Avery. *Navaho Weaving: Its Technic and History.* Santa Ana, California: The Fine Arts Press, 1934.

Babcock, Barbara A., and Nancy J. Parezo. "Matilda Coxe Stevenson, 1849–1915." In *Daughters of the Desert: Women Anthropologists and the Native American Southwest, 1880–1980. An Illustrated Catalogue.* Albuquerque: University of New Mexico Press, 1988: 8–13.

Bailey, Garrick and Roberta Glenn Bailey. *A History of the Navajos: The Reservation Years.* Santa Fe: School of American Research Press, 1986.

Barnes, Emily. *A Walk With Emily.* Santa Fe, New Mexico: Privately published, 1990.

———. Personal communication, March 3, 1996.

Bartlett, Richard A. *Great Surveys of the American West.* Norman: University of Oklahoma Press, 1962.

Bender, Norman J. *Missionaries, Outlaws, and Indians: Taylor F. Ealy at Lincoln and Zuni, 1878–1881.* Albuquerque: University of New Mexico Press, 1984.

Cullum, George W. *Biographical Register of the Officers and Graduates of the U. S. Military Academy at West Point, New York, From Its Establishment, in 1802, to 1890.* Third edition. Vol. 2.

Boston and New York: Houghton, Mifflin and Company, and Cambridge: The Riverside Press, 1891.

Cummings, D. E., "William Wotherspoon, Sailor Soldier." In *Shipmate* (January 1969): 6–7; 9–11.

Cushing, Frank Hamilton. *Letter Books, 1886–1896*, Microfilm Edition. Bronx, New York: Huntington Free Library, 1993.

Davidson, Harold G., *Edward Borein, Cowboy Artist: The Life and Works of John Edward Borein 1872–1945*. Garden City, New York: Doubleday and Company, 1974.

Davis, Mary B. *The Joseph Keppler Iroquois Papers in the Huntington Free Library: A Guide to the Microfilm Edition*. Bronx, New York: The Huntington Free Library, 1994.

———. *Papers of the Hemenway Southwestern Archaeological Expedition in the Huntington Free Library: A Guide to the Microfilm Edition*. Bronx, New York: Huntington Free Library, 1987.

Dawdy, Doris Ostrander, and DeCost Smith. *Artists of the American West: A Biographical Dictionary*. Chicago: The Swallow Press, 1974: 216.

Dellenbaugh, Frederick S. *A Canyon Voyage: The Narrative of the Second Powell Expedition down the Green-Colorado River from Wyoming, and the Explorations on Land, in the Years 1871 and 1872*. New York and London: G. P. Putnam's Sons, 1908.

Ferguson, T. J. Personal communication, 27 February 1996, citing E. Richard Hart, *Damage to Zuni Trust Lands*. Expert Testimony (Exhibit 1000), submitted to the United States Claims Court in the case Zuni Indian Tribe v. United States, Docket 327–81L (Ct. Cl., filed 12 May 1981): 100–118; 137; 152.

———. Personal communication, February 27, 1996, citing E. Richard Hart, 1988, *The Zuni Mountains: Chronology of an Environmental Disaster*. Expert Testimony commissioned by the Institute of the NorthAmerican West, in behalf of the Zuni Indian Tribe, for submission to the United States Claims Court as Plaintiff's Exhibit 13,00 in Docket 327–81L and 224–84L: 90–91.

Graham, Douglas D. "Report of School Superintendent in Charge at Zuni Pueblo." In *Annual Reports of the Department of the Interior for the Fiscal Year Ended June 30, 1903: Indian Affairs*. Washington: Government Printing Office, 1904.

Green, Jesse, ed. *Cushing at Zuni: The Correspondence and Journals of Frank Hamilton Cushing, 1879–1884*. Albuquerque: University of New Mexico Press, 1990.

Heye, George G. "George Hubbard Pepper." In *Museum Notes* 1:3 (105–110). Museum of the American Indian–Heye Foundation, 1924.

Hill, Burton S. "Thomas S. Twiss, Indian Agent." In *Great Plains Journal* 6:2 (1967): 85–96.

Hinsley, Curtis. *Savages and Scientists: The Smithsonian Institution and the Development of American Anthropology, 1846–1910*. Washington, D.C.: Smithsonian Institution Press, 1981.

———. "Collecting Cultures and Cultures of Collecting: The Lure of the American Southwest, 1880–1915." In *Museum Anthropology* 16:1 (1992): 12–21.

Hyde, George E. *Red Cloud's Folk: A History of the Oglala Sioux Indians*. Norman: University of Oklahoma Press, 1937.

Karp, Ivan and Steven D. Lavine, eds. *The Poetics and Politics of Museum Display*. Washington and London: Smithsonian Institution Press, 1991.

King, Duane H. *The Treasures of the National Museum of the American Indian*. Unpublished manuscript, 1993.

Lange, Charles H., Carroll L. Riley, and Elizabeth M. Lange, eds. *The Southwestern Journals of Adolph E. Bandelier, 1889–1892*. Albuquerque: University of New Mexico Press, 1984.

Lessard, Dennis. Personal communication, 6 March 1996.

McNitt, Frank. *The Indian Traders*. Norman: University of Oklahoma Press, 1962.

———. *Richard Wetherill Anasazi*. Revised edition. Albuquerque: University of New Mexico Press, 1978.

———. *Navajo Wars: Military Campaigns, Slave Raids, and Reprisals*. Albuquerque: University of New Mexico Press, 1990.

New York Herald Tribune, 13 May 1935, obituary of Mrs. G. G. Heye. Papers of the Huntington Free Library, Bronx, New York.

Parezo, Nancy J. "The Formation of Ethnographic Collections: The Smithsonian Institution in the American Southwest." In *Advances in Archaeological Method and Theory*. Vol. 10. Edited by Michael Schiffer. San Diego: Academic Press, 1987.

———. "Matilda Coxe Stevenson: Pioneer Ethnologist." In *Hidden Scholars: Women Anthropologists and the Native American Southwest*. Nancy J. Parezo, ed. Albuquerque: University of New Mexico Press, 1993.

Pepper, George. "The Navajo Indians: An Ethnological Study." In *The Papoose* 1:1 (December 1902): 3–9.

———. "Native Navajo Dyes." In *The Papoose*, February 2, 1903: 1–11.

Powell, J. W. *The Exploration of the Colorado River and Its Canyons*. New York: Dover Publications, 1961.

Roessel, Jr., Robert A. "Navajo History, 1850–1923." In *Handbook of North American Indians, Volume 10, Southwest*.

Alfonso Ortiz, ed. Washington, D.C.: Smithsonian Institution, 1983: 506–523.

Samuels, Peggy and Harold, "DeCost, Smith." *The Illustrated Biographical Encyclopedia of Artists of the American West.* Garden City, New York: Doubleday and Company, 1976: 449.

Shears, Brenda. "The Hendricks-Hodge Archaeological Expedition Documentation Project: Preparing a Museum Collection for Research." Master's thesis, Hunter College, City University of New York, 1989.

Sitgreaves, Lorenzo. *Report of an Expedition Down the Zuni and Colorado Rivers, Accompanied by Maps, Sketches, Views, and Illustrations.* Washington, D.C.: Robert Armstrong, Public Printer, 1853.

Smith, Sherry. *The View from Officers' Row: Army Perceptions of Western Indians.* Tucson: University of Arizona Press, 1990.

Stocking, Jr., George W., ed. "Essays on Museums and Material Culture." In *Objects and Others: Essays on Museums and Material Culture.* George W. Stocking, Jr., ed. Madison: University of Wisconsin Press, 1985: 3–15.

Thrapp, Dan L. *Encyclopedia of Frontier Biography.* 3 vols. Glendale, California: The Arthur H. Clark Company, 1988.

Tomer, John S. and Michael J. Brodhead, eds. *A Naturalist in Indian Territory: The Journals of S. W. Woodhouse, 1849–1850.* Norman and Lincoln: University of Oklahoma Press, 1996.

Utley, Robert M. *Frontier Regulars: The United States Army and the Indian, 1866–1891.* Lincoln and London: University of Nebraska Press, 1973.

———. *Frontiersmen in Blue: The United States Army and the Indian, 1848–1865.* Lincoln and London: University of Nebraska Press, 1981.

Utley, Robert M. and Wilcomb E. Washburn. *Indian Wars.* Boston: Houghton Mifflin, 1977.

Wade, Edwin L. "The Ethnic Art Market in the American Southwest, 1880–1980." In *Objects and Others: Essays on Museums and Material Culture.* George W. Stocking, Jr., ed. Madison: University of Wisconsin Press, 1985.

Wallace, Kevin. "Slim-Shin's Monument." In *The New Yorker Magazine*, November 19, 1960: 104–146.

Wilcox, David. Personal communication to Mary B. Davis, March 5, 1996.

Woloshuk, Jr., Nicholas. *Edward Borein: Drawings and Paintings of the Old West.* Flagstaff, Arizona: The Northland Press, 1968.

———. "Excavations at Kechipauan, New Mexico." In *Indian Notes* 1: (35–36). Museum of the American Indian–Heye Foundation, 1924.

———. "The General Nelson A. Miles Collection." In *Indian Notes* 3:1 (50–53). Museum of the American Indian–Heye Foundation, 1926.

———. "Notes." In *Indian Notes* 5:2 (269–70). Museum of the American Indian–Heye Foundation, 1928.

———. "A Seneca Adoption." In *The Masterkey* 26:3 (1952): 94–96.

———. "A Rare Collection." In *The Papoose* 1:2 (January 1903): 3–9.

NMAI Archives

Receipt for $1000 for collection of Indian specimens, signed by Daisy Barnett, 21 December 1918.

Receipt for last payment of $750 for Indian collection, signed by Daisy Barnett, 21 January 1919.

Letters

Letter, United States Geological Survey to the author, February 29, 1896, containing unpublished biographical information about Sumner Homer Bodfish.

Letter, Rear Admiral Alexander Wotherspoon, U.S.N., ret., to Frederick Dockstader, 30 October 1972; Archives of the National Museum of the American Indian, Smithsonian Institution.

Letters to Thea and George Heye from their friends at Zuni Pueblo, 1916–1930, Papers of the Huntington Free Library, Bronx, New York.

PHOTO CREDITS

INDEX

Page numbers in italics refer to illustrations.

Anglo-American influence, 10; after Bosque Redondo, 53–56; classification of blankets, 5; collectors, 174–80; historical documentation, 48
Apache people, 49
art, Navajo concept of, 10, 29–31
Ash-Milby, Kathleen E., 11

Barnes, Emily Otis, 174
batten, 20; cultural significance, 40
bayeta cloth, 71, 72–73, 75, 77, 78
Beaumont, Eugene Beauharnais, 174
Begay, D.Y., 3, 8, 9, 24; ancestry, 13, 14–15; current weaving practice, 19–27; on learning to weave, 16, 17–18; lifeways education, 14, 16; school experiences, 15–16; on women in Navajo culture, 16–17
Begay, Kee Yazzie, 28

Begay, Mary Lee, 18
be'iina, 36, 39
Benally, Byron, 41
Bighorse, Gus, 54–55
biil, 102, 185–86; cultural significance, 64, 168; design evolution, 66, 72–73
Bilone, Alice, 9
black wool, 21–22
bloodroot, 23, 24
Bodfish, Sumner Homer, 174
Bonar, Eulalie H., 7
Borein, Edward, 174
Bosque Redondo, 9, 10, 13, 50, 53, 54, 77–78, 130
brazilwood, 23
Brown, Edsel, 7
Brulé Sioux, 128

carding, 21
chief blankets, 4, 64, 74–77, 112, 116, 142, 162, 186–88

churro wool, 21, 22, 70
Clark, Irene, 6, 7, 24
Classic Period of Navajo weaving, 4–5, 50, 77–80
classification of blankets, 3–5, 11, 64, 181–83; chief blankets, 74–77
Cleveland, Laura, 7
cochineal, 24, 72, 73
colors: biil, 66; during Bosque Redondo period, 77; cultural significance, 29–30; directional, 28, 116; gender-associated, 116; nineteenth-century practice, 66; research descriptions, 183
comb/weaving fork, 20–21, 34, 144; significance, 40
community context: clan organization, 51; nineteenth-century lifeways, 50–51; status of weavers, 18–19, 58–59; of weaving, xi–xii, 36
cotton, 69, 85
cotton string, 22

creation stories, 28, 34, 124, 134
criticism of weaving, 63, 64–65
Curtis, Sadie, *9*
cutch wood, 23, 24

dah'iistł'ó, 10; meaning of, 33–34; weaver's relationship to, 39, 41. *See also* Navajo weaving
Damon, Anson, 55
Deschinny, Isabell, 6
design and decoration: Anglo-American influences, 5; *biil*, 64, 66, 72–73; during Bosque Redondo period, 77–78; chief blankets, 64, 74–77, 142, 162; continuum of Navajo style, 5, 67; cultural significance, 29–31; *diyogí*, 83–85, 192–93; emergence of, in *dah'iistł'ó*, 39; mantas, 73–74; modern era, 61–62, 66–67; modern understanding of historical tradition, 65; Moki, 83–84, 193–94; nineteenth-century, 66, 72, 73, 74; Pueblo weaving, 71; revival weaving, 66–67; rugs, 60; sarape Navajo, 77, 79, 82–83; shoulder blankets, 74–75; slave blankets, 84, 195; sources of, 24–25, 35; Spanish blankets, 71; terraced, 72; use of taboo subjects, 56
diyogí, 64, 83–85, 181, 192–93
Dodge, Chee, 55
door coverings, 154
dresses, Navajo, 72, 102. *See also biil*
dyes, 14, 18; analysis and categorization, 183; commercial, 23; natural sources, 23–24; Spanish, 70, 71; traditional, 22–23; washing wool for dyeing, 23

Esitty, Pauline, 19

family: Anglo-Navajo, 26–27; modern Navajo society, 57; nineteenth-century lifeways, 50, 51, 55; status of weaver in, 18–19; weaving and, xi, 36, 44, 63
Farella, John, 63

First Phase chief blankets, 74–75

Germantown yarn, 5, 77, 79
Graham, Douglas Dher, 4, 174–75
Grier, William Nicholson, 175

Hanley, Andrea R., 11
Hanley, Max, Sr., 156
Hardy, Glennabah, 7, 7
Hardy-Saltclah, Marie, 7, 7
Hatathli Museum, 5, 6, 63
Hedlund, Ann Lane, 3, 8, 9–10, *24*
Hernmarck, Helena, 22
Heye, George Gustav, 2, 173
Heye, Thea Brown, 175
hozho, 30
Hwééldi. See Bosque Redondo

Indian paintbrush root, 23
indigo, 22–23, 70
innovation/experimentation, 9, 19, 67, 94, 170; in design, 25; with dyes, 23; limits of, 39; modern era, 61–62

Jishie, Rita, 7
juniper, 23

Keams, Kalley, 9, 10
Kent, Kate Peck, 11
Keppler, Joseph, 4, 175–76

language and voice: cultural significance, 33; Navajo tradition, 34; in weaving process, 36–37
leaders' blankets, 112. *See also* chief blankets
learning to weave, 16, 17–18, 34–35; current practice, 60–61; language needs, 18; settings for, 25–26; traditional ways, 37–38; weaving songs and, 37–38
Lee, Bessie, *44*
Lee, Neva, *41*
Lewis, Keevin, *24, 41*
logwood, 23, 24

Long Walk, the, 13, 53, 77, 130
loom: design, 20; historical development, 69
Lord, Daniel Walter, 176
Lothrop, Samuel Kirkland, 176

madder root, 23–24
Maher, Peggy, 19
mahogany root, 24
mantas, 71, 72, 73–74, 184–85
marketing of textiles, 18, 26; historical developments, 48; nineteenth-century practice, 52–53, 55–56; recent historical development, 56–57, 61–62; spiritual issues, 40–41
merino wool, 21
Meriwether, David, 51
Mexican pelt design, 82
Miles, Nelson Appleton, 11, 176
mistletoe, 23
mohair, 22
Moki design, 82–83, 193–94
Museum of the American Indian, 2, 173. *See also* National Museum of the American Indian

National Museum of the American Indian, 5; Navajo blanket collection, 1, 2–3, 4–5, 11, 173, 181; Navajo blanket exhibition, 8
Navajo blankets: Anglo-American collectors, 174–80; categorization, 3–5, 64; chief blanket designs, 74–75, 112, 116; *diyogí*, 83–85, 179; historical evolution, 71; Moki-design, 82–83, 193–94; nineteenth-century, 52; protective powers, 108, 114, 132. *See also* Navajo weaving
Navajo Community College (Tsaile, Arizona), 5
Navajo culture and history, 36, 49–50; after Bosque Redondo, 54–55; clan organization, 51; concept of art in, 29; continuity in, 9–10, 44–45, 47–48, 62–63, 67; earliest textile technology, 69; early contact

with Spanish, 69–71; language and voice in, 33, 34; modern era, 56–58, 60–62; modern perceptions of, 65; nineteenth-century lifeways, 50–56; origins of weaving, 27; perpetuation of, 26–27, 45, 59, 67, 100; sacred concepts/conventions, 28, 49; sale of woven goods in, 40–41; significance of *biil*, 168; significant design elements, 29–31; weaving in, 7, 9, 10, 27, 30–31, 34, 40, 45; weaving tools in, 19–20, 40. *See also* women in Navajo culture

Navajo weaving: Anglo-American influence, 5; as art, 10, 29–31; during Bosque Redondo period, 53–54; current practice, 58–59, 67, 85; current understanding, 2; as *dah'iistł'ó*, 33–34; early history, 69–71; eighteenth-century, 71–72; historical continuity, 62–63, 66; historical development, 50; household weavers, 58; introduction of commercial materials, 53–54; mental attitude/preparation for, 34–35, 36; modern perceptions of historical practice, 64–66; nineteenth-century practice, 51–52, 53–54, 55, 56, 72–85; origins of, 27; perpetuation of culture through, 17–18, 45, 47–48, 59, 67, 100; as personification, 33, 36–37, 45, 98; professional weavers, 58–59; Pueblo influence, 9; Spanish influence, 9, 52, 160; spiritual context, 10; status of weavers, 18–19, 58–59; tradition, 5–7, 9–10. *See also* techniques of weaving; tools of weaving

Owens, Rose, 18, *59*

Pepper, George Hubbard, 176–77
perfection, xi, 7, 31, 138
personification, 10; cultural trends, 38–39; in preparation of wool, 38–39; for protection, 38; weaving as, 33, 36–37, 45, 98
Peruvian weavers, 26

pictorial blankets, 195
pine cones, 23
Plains tribes, 52–53, 53
plain weave, 182
plant dyes, 23–24
political context: 1860s versus 1960s, 48; modern Navajo Nation, 57; nineteenth-century Navajo leadership structure, 50–51; recent history, 56
population trends, 57, 60
Powell, John Wesley, 11, 177
prickly pear, 23
process orientation, 9, 166
protective powers of weavings, 108, 114, 132
provenance information, 11
Pueblo people, 9, 27, 49; Spanish interaction, 69, 70; weaving technology, 70, 71

rabbitbrush, 23
Rambouillet wool, 21
replica pieces, 4
research methodology, 2–5, 10–11, 49, 181; analysis and categorization of weavings, 182–83; critical style of Navajo weavers, 63, 64–66; fiber analysis and categorization, 182–83; limitations of historical record, 48–49
restoration of artifacts, 65
revival weaving, 59, 66–67
Roessel, Jr., Robert, 53, 55
Roessel, Ruth, 10, 57–58, 63
Rug Period of Navajo weaving, 50
rugs, 64, 85; historical development, 60; weaving technique, 60

sagebrush, 23, 24
Saltillo design, 5, 78, 79–80, 160
sarapes, Navajo, 77, 188–92; *diyogí*, 83–84; Late Classic/Early Transition, 79, 80–82, 82–83
Schultz, Marilou, 6
Second Phase chief blankets, 75, 76–77

selvage cords, 183
sewing machines, 85
sheep: dye from manure of, 24; introduction of, to Native Americans, 70; in Navajo culture, 14–15, 31; wool characteristics, 21
Sheppard, Marie, *24*, 26
Sherman, William Tecumseh, 11, 79, 177
shirts, 74
shoulder blankets, 74–75, 140. *See also* chief blankets; women's, 183–84
Sioux people, 128
Sitgreaves Expedition, 3, 74, 178
slave blankets, 84, 195
slavery/servitude, 52, 84
Smith, DeCost, 177–78
snakeweed, 23
Spanish/Spanish-American culture, 9, 52; blanket design, 71, 160; early contact with Native Americans, 70–71; influence during Bosque Redondo period, 78–79
Spider Man, 35
Spider Woman, 35, 36, 40, 49, 168
Spider Woman's cross, 74
spindle, 40
spinning, 21
spirit line, xi, 31, 138
spiritual context: copying designs, 66–67; restoration of textiles, 65; of weaving, 10, 36
Stevenson, Matilda Coxe, 178

T'aadezbáh, 34
Ta'chii'nii, 13, 28
tapestry weave, 182
tassels, 183
Teasyatwho, Cherileen, *24*
Teasyatwho, Elnora, *24*
techniques of weaving: batten handling, 20; classification of blankets by, 182; continuum, 44–45, 62–63; modern rugmaking, 60; Navajo critical style, 63, 64–65; nineteenth-century, 72; spinning, 21;

superfine tapestries, 61; warp tension, 20

Third Phase chief blankets, 75–76

Thomas, Wesley, 6, 8, 41

threads and yarns: bayeta, 71, 72–73, 75, 77; commonly used, 182–83

tools of weaving, 10; batten, 20, 40; for carding, 21; comb, 20–21; cultural context, 19–20, 40; evolution of, 20; loom, 20; spindle, 40; for spinning, 21; terminology, 20; traditional prohibitions, 20, 36, 40; weaving fork, 34, 40

Transition Period of Navajo weaving, 4–5, 50, 79–82

twill weave, 182

Twiss, Thomas S., 178

Ute chief blankets, 74, 74

Walters, Harry, 5, 7, 10

wear patterns, 3–4

weavership mark, 118

weaving fork. See comb/weaving fork

weaving songs: application, 37, 38; ending song, 41; number of, 34; origins and growth, 38; transmission of, 37–38, 66; weaving fork rhythms, 34, 144

wedge weave, 84–85, 170, 182, 194–95

weft-faced weaving, 72, 182

Weidner, Kezbah, 47

Wheat, Joe Ben, 2, 3, 8, 9

women: biil and, 102, 168; in modern Navajo society, 57–58, 61; Navajo historical development, 49–50; nineteenth-century lifeways, 51–52, 53

women in Navajo culture, 14, 16–17, 48

Woodhouse, Samuel W., 3, 11, 74, 178-79

wool: assessing quality of, 21; commercially produced, 22, 182; commonly used forms, 182–83; dyeing technique, 23; historical trends, 38; preparation for weaving, 38; pure black, 21–22; selecting, 21

Wotherspoon, William Wallace, 179

Yazzie, Calvin, 41

Yazzie, Esther, 7

Yazzie, Kenneth, 11, 41

Zuni people, 4, 136